GETTYSBURG

GETTYSBURG

★ THE BATTLE FOR LIBERTY, ★
EQUALITY AND BROTHERHOOD

NIGEL CAWTHORNE

CHARTWELL
BOOKS

Four score and seven years ago our fathers brought forth on this continent, a new nation, conceived in Liberty, and dedicated to the proposition that all men are created equal.

Abraham Lincoln

Abraham Lincoln (1809 – 1865).
The 16th President of the United States.

CONTENTS

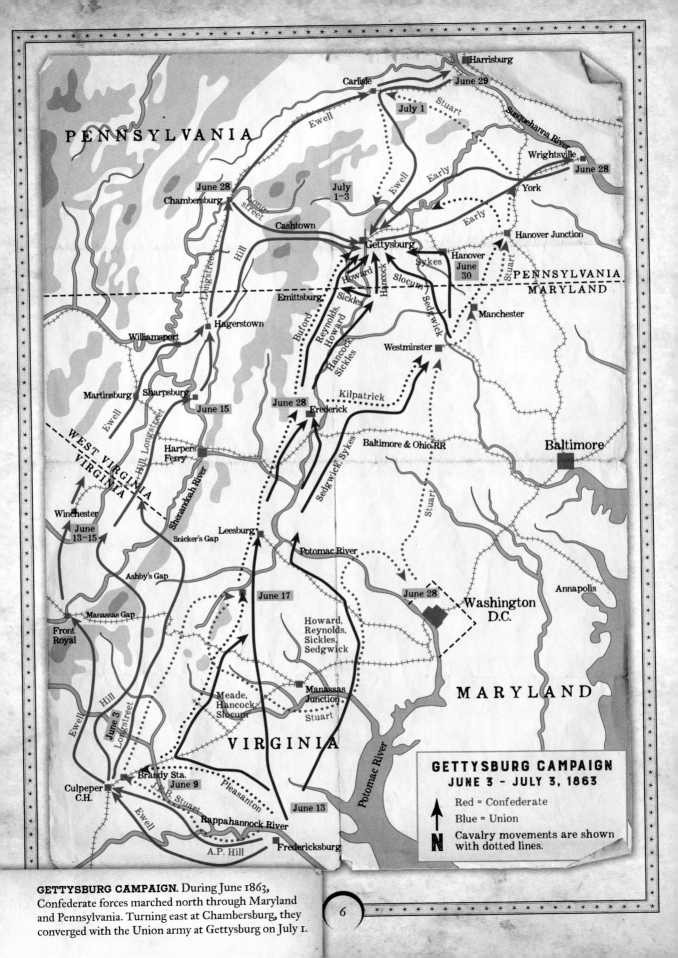

GETTYSBURG CAMPAIGN. JUNE 3 – JULY 3, 1863

Red = Confederate

Blue = Union

Cavalry movements are shown with dotted lines.

GETTYSBURG CAMPAIGN. During June 1863, Confederate forces marched north through Maryland and Pennsylvania. Turning east at Chambersburg, they converged with the Union army at Gettysburg on July 1.

INTRODUCTION

Gettysburg was the most crucial battle of the American Civil War. In 1860, the candidate of the anti-slavery Republican Party, Abraham Lincoln, was elected President of the United States of America. Before Lincoln's inauguration, seven Southern states declared their secession from the Union and later formed the Confederacy. Secessionists from four additional border states joined them when Lincoln's call to restore federal property in the South forced them to take sides, and two states, Kentucky and Missouri, attempted to remain neutral. While Lincoln was not against slavery *per se*, he said famously: 'A house divided against itself cannot stand. I believe the government cannot endure permanently half slave and half free.' He also opposed the extension of slavery to the new territories to the west, which would eventually become states.

The economy of the Southern States depended on large plantations, run with slave labor. They feared that Northerners would try and enforce the complete abolition of slavery and insisted on the rights of individual states to make their own laws in this matter. Consequently South Carolina, Mississippi, Florida, Alabama, Georgia, Louisiana, and Texas seceded and formed the Confederate States of America.

THE FIRST GUN FIRED

Former Army officer and West Point graduate Jefferson Davis quit his seat in the US Senate to return south, where he was commissioned Major General to head Mississippi's armed forces. Within two weeks, the Confederate Convention in Montgomery, Alabama, chose him as provisional president of the Confederacy. His first act in office was to send a peace commission to Washington, DC.

However, Lincoln's incoming administration refused to recognize the Confederacy, fearing that it would cause the entire Union to break up into small squabbling states. Lincoln refused to see Davis's emissaries. In his inaugural address, Lincoln made it clear that he was not going to interfere with the institution of slavery in the South – nor did he think he had the right to do so – but said that secession from the Union was legally void. Negotiating with the Confederate states would be tantamount to recognizing them.

The war began when the Confederacy claimed Fort Sumter, a federal fort in Charleston Bay. On April 12, 1861, Confederate forces began bombarding it, forcing the garrison to lower the American flag and surrender. Lincoln called out the militia to suppress this insurrection, while four more states – Virginia, Arkansas, Tennessee, and North Carolina – joined the Confederacy.

ATTACK AND COUNTERATTACK

At the First Battle of Bull Run, aka First Manassas, on July 21, 1861, the Union troops invading the South were forced to withdraw to Washington, DC. But the Southern victors were too exhausted to pursue them. General George B. McClellan, who had some success in the fighting in western Virginia, was recalled to reorganize the Union forces into what would become the Army of the Potomac.

McClellan led a renewed attack on the Confederate capital, Richmond, Virginia, but was driven back by the Army of Northern Virginia under General Robert E. Lee. A second attack was stopped at the Second Battle of Bull Run, or Second Manassas, on August 29, 1862. Lee then invaded the North, advancing as far as Frederick, Maryland. McClellan counterattacked at the bloody Battle of Antietam on September 17. Lee retreated back into Virginia, but when McClellan did not pursue him, he was replaced by General Ambrose E. Burnside.

Burnside, in turn, was stopped with staggering losses at Fredericksburg, Virginia, on December 13, and replaced by General Joseph 'Fighting Joe' Hooker. The following spring Hooker tried to encircle Lee's forces, but the Confederates counterattacked at Chancellorsville, Virginia, forcing the Union army back once more and losing General Stonewall

Jackson, shot by friendly fire, in the process. The Confederate's strongest general was gone and Lee would miss him badly for the rest of the war.

CRUSADE FOR FREEDOM

President Lincoln altered his position on slavery and clarified the issues of the war with the Emancipation Proclamation on January 1, 1863. This did not free a single slave as its provisions had already largely been enacted by Congress and those still enslaved were in Confederate-held territory where the Union was not in control. However, it did turn the Civil War from a struggle to preserve the Union into a crusade for human freedom, preventing the European powers from intervening on the side of the Confederacy.

Lee invaded the North once more on June 5, 1863. Marching up the Cumberland Valley through Maryland and Pennsylvania, Lee reached Chambersburg, turned east, and menaced Harrisburg.

Hooker wanted to lure Lee back by attacking again at Fredericksburg, but he was ordered to keep his army between Lee and Washington. He resigned and was replaced by General George G. Meade, who moved northward, looking for the enemy.

On June 28, Lee learned to his surprise that the Union army was now north of the Potomac. He set out to concentrate his forces, destroy what he believed to be the demoralized Army of the Potomac, and march on Washington.

The commanding generals never meant to fight at Gettysburg. The armies met there by accident, led together by the twists and turns of the roads. They reached the crossroads near the town at the same time and began to fight, because the tension was so high that the first contact snapped them into action. Once begun, the fight was uncontrollable. What the generals wanted ceased to matter; each man had to cope with what he got – the most momentous battle of the war.

Lincoln presents the first draft of the Emancipation Proclamation to his cabinet. Painting by Francis Bicknell Carpenter (1864).

A reproduction of the Proclamation of Emancipation.

ROLL CALL OF GETTYSBURG COMMANDERS

UNION COMMANDERS

JOHN BUFORD. The commander of a cavalry division in the Army of the Potomac, Buford's troops encountered a Confederate column on June 30 near Gettysburg which set the stage for the battle.

ABNER DOUBLEDAY. He was Commander of the First Corps after the death of General Reynolds. His experienced troops fought on a line west of Seminary Ridge.

OLIVER O. HOWARD. This one-armed general took charge of the Eleventh Corps after the death of Reynolds and secured Cemetery Hill as the final Union position.

JOHN F. REYNOLDS. He was Commander of the First Army Corps of the Army of the Potomac. Reynolds was killed on the first day of the battle. He was badly missed at Gettysburg.

WINFIELD S. HANCOCK. An outstanding battlefield commander, Hancock was sent as Meade's representative to Gettysburg on July 1, where he took command. He was everywhere during the action on July 2 playing a prominent role in directing troops.

HENRY J. HUNT. Chief of Artillery of the Army of the Potomac, Hunt's disciplined use of Union guns at Gettysburg played a major role in defeating the Confederate battle plans.

DANIEL E. SICKLES. Before the war, Sickles had been acquitted of a murder charge, on the grounds of temporary insanity. At Gettysburg, his controversial advance from Cemetery Ridge on July 2, resulted in the bloodiest day of fighting, costing the general a leg.

JOSHUA L. CHAMBERLAIN. Colonel of the 20th Maine Infantry, his troops were involved in a desperate fight with the 15th Alabama Infantry on July 2 and despite overwhelming odds, won the day at Little Round Top.

GEORGE A. CUSTER. At Gettysburg, Custer was only 24 years old but he led dynamic charges that eventually won the cavalry battle east of the battlefield.

GOUVERNEUR K. WARREN. Meade's Chief of Engineers, Warren spied Confederate forces moving towards Little Round Top. Realizing the significance, he rushed troops to the hill's defense, which ultimately saved the Union line on Cemetery Ridge.

ALONZO H. CUSHING. A Lieutenant in the 4th US Artillery, 22-year-old Alonzo Cushing died heroically on Day 3, defending the Union position on Cemetery Ridge. He was awarded the Medal of Honor, in 2013, 150 years after his death.

FRANK A. HASKELL. Haskell was in the center of the Union line on July 2 and 3 and witnessed the climactic events of the battle. He survived Gettysburg, but was killed in battle the following year.

George G. Meade

The son of a US naval agent in Spain, George G. Meade was born in Cádiz in 1815. His father was ruined financially during the Napoleonic Wars. The family returned to the United States, where he enrolled at West Point, graduating in 1835, nineteenth in a class of fifty-six. Commissioned in the 3rd US Artillery, he fought against the Seminole Indians in Florida for a year, before resigning to become a surveyor and marry Margaretta Sergeant, the daughter of John Sergeant, once a candidate for Vice President on the National Republican ticket.

Meade rejoined the Army as a second lieutenant in 1842 and fought in the Mexican-American war. Assigned to the staff of General Zachary Taylor, he was brevetted lieutenant for 'performing a daring reconnaissance' at the Battle of Monterrey.

When the Civil War broke out, the governor general of Pennsylvania appointed Meade a Brigadier General in command of the 2nd Pennsylvania Reserves. In June 1862, he was promoted to major in the regular Army and fought in the battles of Mechanicsville, Gaines's Mill, and Glendale, where he was wounded several times. A ball went above his hip, pierced his liver, and passed out near his spine. Another ball went through his arm. But he stayed on his horse until forced to quit the field due to loss of blood. He was never wounded in battle again, although his hat was riddled with balls and several mounts were shot out from under him.

After returning from the hospital, Meade fought in the Second Battle of Bull Run, the South Mountain campaign, and took command of the 1st Corps at Antietam, after General Hooker was wounded. After Fredericksburg, he was placed in command of the Fifth Corps which he led in the Battle of Chancellorsville. While leading the corps northward, paralleling Lee, on June 25, 1863 Meade received a letter from Lincoln, giving him command of the Army of the Potomac, just five days before the Battle of Gettysburg.

Robert E. Lee

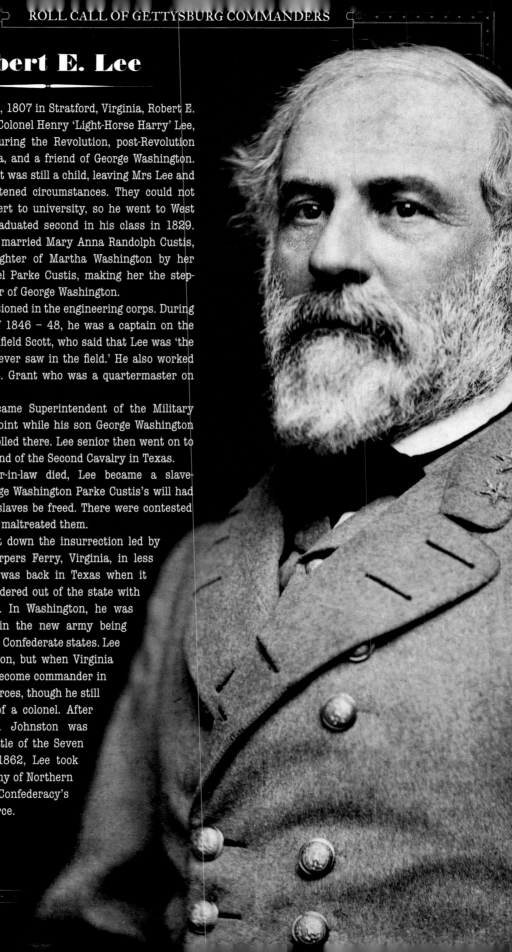

Born in January 19, 1807 in Stratford, Virginia, Robert E. Lee was the son of Colonel Henry 'Light-Horse Harry' Lee, a cavalry leader during the Revolution, post-Revolution governor of Virginia, and a friend of George Washington. He died while Robert was still a child, leaving Mrs Lee and the family in straitened circumstances. They could not afford to send Robert to university, so he went to West Point, where he graduated second in his class in 1829. Two years later he married Mary Anna Randolph Custis, the great-granddaughter of Martha Washington by her first husband Daniel Parke Custis, making her the step-great granddaughter of George Washington.

Lee was commissioned in the engineering corps. During the Mexican War of 1846 – 48, he was a captain on the staff of General Winfield Scott, who said that Lee was 'the very best soldier I ever saw in the field.' He also worked alongside Ulysses S. Grant who was a quartermaster on the campaign.

In 1852, he became Superintendent of the Military Academy at West Point while his son George Washington Custis Lee was enrolled there. Lee senior then went on to be second-in-command of the Second Cavalry in Texas.

When his father-in-law died, Lee became a slave-owner, though George Washington Parke Custis's will had stipulated that his slaves be freed. There were contested allegations that Lee maltreated them.

In 1859, Lee put down the insurrection led by John Brown at Harpers Ferry, Virginia, in less than an hour. Lee was back in Texas when it seceded and was ordered out of the state with other Union forces. In Washington, he was given a command in the new army being formed to invade the Confederate states. Lee was against secession, but when Virginia seceded he quit to become commander in chief of Virginia's forces, though he still wore the insignia of a colonel. After General Joseph E. Johnston was wounded at the Battle of the Seven Pines on June 1, 1862, Lee took command of the Army of Northern Virginia, the Confederacy's principal fighting force.

CONFEDERATE COMMANDERS

JAMES LONGSTREET. He was the most trusted of Lee's corps commanders, Longstreet was in charge of the main Southern attack on the last day of the battle. Much of the Confederate controversy about Gettysburg centers around Longstreet's decisions.

AMBROSE POWELL HILL. Commander of the Third Corps, A.P. Hill's troops fought every day of the battle contributing two divisions to 'Pickett's Charge'. Hill was killed in Virginia a week before the final Confederate surrender in 1865.

JOHN BELL HOOD. A brave and aggressive commander from Texas, Hood's troops marched 18 miles on July 2 and then attacked Union troops on Little Round Top and at Devil's Den.

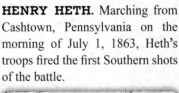

RICHARD S. EWELL. The Commander of the Second Corps, Richard Ewell's troops were first on the scene at Gettysburg, stampeding Union soldiers through the town and capturing hundreds.

HENRY HETH. Marching from Cashtown, Pennsylvania on the morning of July 1, 1863, Heth's troops fired the first Southern shots of the battle.

GEORGE E. PICKETT. Pickett constantly worried that his division of Virginians wouldn't be used at Gettysburg. As it turned out, his name is forever associated with the final climactic Confederate attack known as 'Pickett's Charge'.

J.E.B. STUART. Commander of the Confederate cavalry, Stuart was raiding through Maryland and Pennsylvania which delayed his arrival at Gettysburg until long after the battle had begun.

JOHN B. GORDON. Commander of a Georgia brigade in Ewell's corps, Gordon's troops put many of the Union troops to flight on July 1 after which he occupied the town of Gettysburg. He survived the conflict to serve several terms as the Governor of Georgia.

EDWARD P. ALEXANDER. In command of a reserve artillery battalion, it was Alexander who sent the message to General Pickett begging him to advance while his depleted artillery could still support the charge.

LEWIS ARMISTEAD. Bravely, Armistead led his troops on foot across nearly a mile of open field and into the Union line where he was wounded and captured. He died in a Union field hospital the following day.

WILLIAM C. OATES. As colonel of the 15th Alabama Infantry, Oates and his regiment fought in the bitter contest with the 20th Maine Infantry on the boulder-strewn slope of Little Round Top. He lost almost half of his regiment, including his brother.

JUBAL A. EARLY. Commander of a division in Ewell's corps, Early's troops defeated the Union Eleventh Corps on July 1 but could not break the Union defenses on East Cemetery Hill the next day.

J. JOHNSTON PETTIGREW. In charge of a North Carolina brigade on July 1 and a division in Pickett's Charge on July 3, Pettigrew survived the battle, but was mortally wounded eleven days later at Williamsport.

GETTYSBURG

Topographic map of Gettysburg battlefield, showing positions of Union and Confederate armies. Facsimile signatures of generals verify the accuracy of troop positions as shown on the map. Created around 1863 by John B. Bachelder.

MINE EYES HAVE
SEEN THE GLORY
OF THE COMING
OF THE LORD.

PART 1

THE
FIRST
DAY

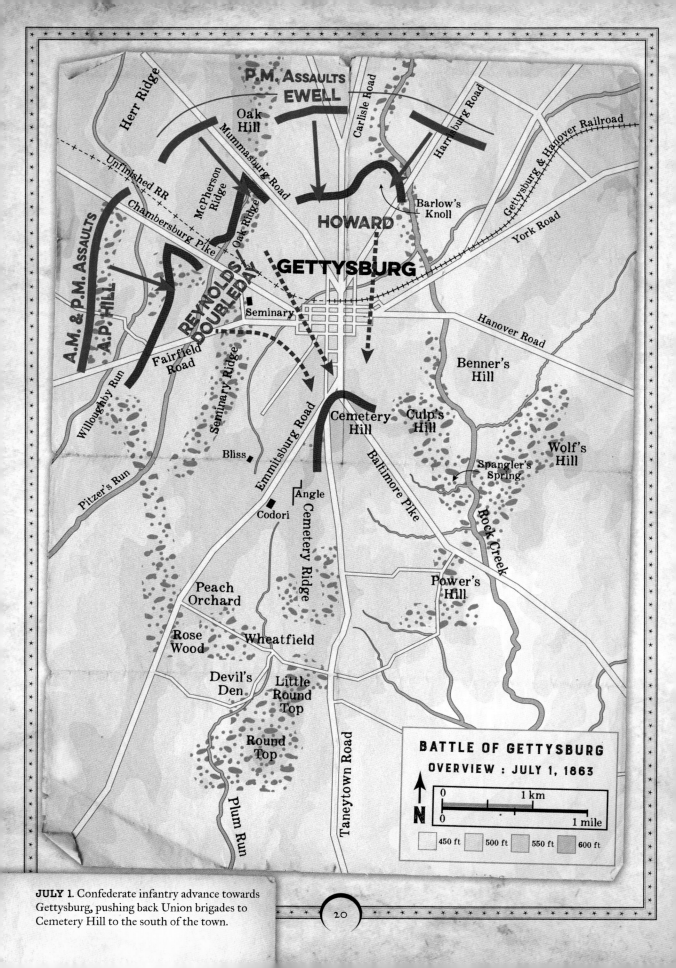

P.M. ASSAULTS
EWELL

Herr Ridge

Oak
Hill

Carlisle Road

Harrisburg Road

Gettysburg & Hanover Railroad

Unfinished RR

Mummasburg Road

HOWARD

Barlow's
Knoll

York Road

A.M. & P.M. ASSAULTS

A.P. HILL

Chambersburg Pike

McPherson Ridge

Oak Ridge

REYNOLDS

DOUBLEDAY

GETTYSBURG

Hanover Road

Willoughby Run

Fairfield Road

Seminary

Seminary Ridge

Benner's
Hill

Pitzer's Run

Bliss

Cemetery
Hill

Culp's
Hill

Spangler's
Spring

Wolf's
Hill

Emmitsburg Road

Codori

Angle

Cemetery Ridge

Baltimore Pike

Rock Creek

Peach
Orchard

Power's
Hill

Rose
Wood

Wheatfield

Devil's
Den

Little
Round
Top

Round
Top

Plum Run

Taneytown Road

BATTLE OF GETTYSBURG

OVERVIEW : JULY 1, 1863

N

0   1 km

0   1 mile

450 ft   500 ft   550 ft   600 ft

JULY 1. Confederate infantry advance towards
Gettysburg, pushing back Union brigades to
Cemetery Hill to the south of the town.

CHAPTER 1

THE ENEMY IS ON OUR SOIL

At dawn on Wednesday, July 1, 1863, the Pennsylvania countryside around Gettysburg was shrouded in mist and rain. It was to be a hot, humid day with a gentle breeze blowing from the south. But as the clouds cleared, the sun rose blood-red.

General Robert E. Lee was riding eastward along the Chambersburg Pike toward Cashtown, some six miles north-west of Gettysburg. He was accompanied by his trusted lieutenant, General James Longstreet, who reported that Lee was composed and in good spirits. Although the Union Army they faced was larger and better equipped, the Confederates had a string of victories behind them.

Lee may have seemed outwardly calm but deep down he was worried. He had issued orders that the army would unite near Gettysburg, but something had gone badly wrong. Somehow his cavalry general J.E.B. Stuart had been blocked from meeting up with the rest of the army. Lee relied on Stuart more than he dared admit. Stuart and his cavalry would join the battle at Gettysburg in twenty-four hours – but it would be twenty-four hours too late.

> The world will little note, nor long remember what we say here, but it can never forget what they did here.
>
> ABRAHAM LINCOLN

MOUNTED INFANTRY

Meanwhile the Union commander, General George G. Meade, at his headquarters in Taneytown, twelve miles to the south of Gettysburg, was also less than confident. His plans, like Lee's, were sketchy, subject to change and relied on a strong element of wait-and-see. While the Army of the Potomac had come to the relief of Harrisburg and thwarted Lee's attempt to invade Philadelphia, Meade did not know where the enemy was and was considering falling back to a defensive line behind a stream called Pipe Creek in Maryland. However, his orders did not reach General John F. Reynolds, commander of his left wing, who was making his way to Gettysburg.

Brigadier General John Buford's Union cavalry had already occupied the town. Hearing from the people there that a Confederate column was north-west of the town, up Chambersburg Pike, he had sent out a reconnaissance party. They had seen rebels at a distance and set up defensive positions.

On the morning of July 1, two Union brigades were strung out among the clover and wildflowers along McPherson's Ridge and Oak Ridge. These were 'dismounted cavalry' – more accurately 'mounted infantry'. They fought on foot, only using their horses to get swiftly from one engagement to the next. Every fourth man was designated to hold the horses some way to the rear, while the other three went into action. This reduced the effective fighting force by a quarter – from 3,000 to 2,250. They were supported by six three-inch cannon.

THE CONFEDERATE ADVANCE

As four brigades of Confederate infantry – Major General Henry Heth's Second Division of A.P. Hill's corps – advanced down the Chambersburg Pike towards Gettysburg, one of their number came across an advertisement in a Charleston, South Carolina newspaper. It read: 'Good news to soldiers! Air-tight coffins!' This was not a comforting message.

Realizing that Buford's forward parties were greatly outnumbered, Reynolds told Major General Abner Doubleday, then commanding the US First Corps, that he was going to the aid of Buford. He would take with him his nearest division – Brigadier General James A. Wadsworth's First. Meanwhile Doubleday was to bring the rest of the First Corps up to Gettysburg as quickly as possible. To save time, the chaplains blessed the troops while the cartridges and a breakfast of hardtack, pork, and coffee were issued.

At 8:00 am, while Wadsworth's men were leaving their overnight bivouacs, Major General Oliver O. Howard received orders from Reynolds to move his Eleventh Corps toward Gettysburg. An-hour-and-a-half later Brigadier General Thomas Rowley's Third Division left Marsh Creek following Wadsworth. As they marched, the columns kicked up stifling clouds of yellow dust that settled on the ranks like a blanket.

Marching Rations

At the beginning of a march, men were issued with three days' rations. These were supposed to be supplemented by supply trains along the way, though this seldom happened. A Union soldier got one pound of hardtack (hard bread or cracker), three-quarters of a pound of salt pork, $1\frac{1}{2}$ pounds of fresh meat, sugar, coffee, and salt. This was stowed in the haversack. The hardtack was supposed to be soaked to make it soft enough to be edible. It tasted good when it was fresh, but usually it had been stored so long it was as hard as rock. It was known as 'sheet-iron crackers,' 'worm castles,' or 'tooth dullers.' This was a problem as soldiers with muskets need good front teeth to bite the top off a paper cartridge. To make it more palatable, soldiers would toast hardtack over a fire, crumble it into soup, or crumble and fry it with bacon or pork fat to make 'skillygallee,' a favorite dish.

A Confederate soldier's ration was less than his Union counterpart, but included cornmeal, bacon, molasses, peas, vegetables, rice, a coffee substitute, and tobacco. One of the reasons Lee had come north was so that his men could forage in the rich farmlands of Maryland and Pennsylvania, as the breadbasket of Virginia then lay empty due to the predations of the Union army earlier in the war.

Army food and rations at a Union camp, Company D, 93rd New York Infantry.

CARBINE VERSUS MUSKET

Buford's men were already taking potshots at the oncoming Confederates. They concealed themselves in the tall grass and fired from behind trees, bushes, and fences. The Union cavalry had the advantage, soon keeping up incessant fire with their breech-loading carbines. The Confederate infantrymen could only answer with their single-shot, muzzle-loading muskets. Each shot had to be pushed home with a ramrod. However, though slower, muskets could shoot further and were generally more accurate.

Not knowing how many men they were facing, the Southern officers were wary and held back. Then Buford heard a second Confederate column was approaching from the north. This was Lieutenant General Richard S. Ewell's Second Corps. Their pickets had been met by Captain Hanley's 9th New York cavalry.

FIRST CASUALTIES

The Confederates took cover behind a farmhouse. Hanley's men dismounted and drove them out. Numerically superior, the Confederates advanced again, this time crawling on their hands and knees through a cornfield, but a sudden cheer from the Union troops caused them to turn tail, perhaps fearing that they were about to be charged by an overwhelming force.

During this encounter, the first Union soldier, Cyrus W. James of Company G, 9th New York, was killed; while Henry Raison of the 7th Tennessee became the first Confederate killed. Perry Nichols of Company F, 9th New York, also took the first prisoner when he found a Johnny Reb hiding behind a tree.

THIN BLUE LINE

Back at Chambersburg Pike, General Henry Heth was watching the main action through his field glasses. His men pushed forward, but he could see no Union battle line until he reached Herr's Ridge. Then, looking across Willoughby Run, he saw a thin blue line of Buford's dismounted troops along McPherson's Ridge.

He ordered the Third Brigade under Brigadier General James J. Archer and the Fourth Division under Brigadier General Joseph R. Davis to move

forward. They met Buford's men at the stream and forced them back up the slope of McPherson's Ridge. The Union troops fought every inch of the way, outnumbered but out-firing the Confederates with their carbines. When the first Confederate prisoners came in, one said: 'What do y'all do – load on Sundays and fire all week?'

ARTILLERY DUEL

Nine Confederate artillery batteries were brought up, massively outgunning the Union with twelve-pounders, ten-pounders, and twelve-pound howitzers to give high-angle fire. Thinking that Union troops might have sought shelter in McPherson's Grove, they pounded the woods for thirty minutes. The Union artillery answered them as best they could, but by 10:00 am Heth's men were safely across Willoughby Run.

The Confederate First Division under Major General Jubal A. Early, the Third Division under Major General Robert E. Rodes, and the Third Corps under Lieutenant General A.P. Hill were now on their way to Gettysburg – and Buford knew it. He fired off a dispatch saying:

> *The enemy's forces are advancing on me at this point, and driving my pickets and skirmishers very rapidly. There is also a large force at Heidlersburg that is driving my pickets at that point from that direction. General Reynolds is advancing; and is within three miles of this point with his leading division. I am positive that the whole of A.P. Hill's force is advancing.*

Nevertheless, Buford's orders from Taneytown told him: 'The cavalry will dispute every inch of ground.'

And that is what his men did. It was only after two hours fighting, when they were just about to be relieved by Reynolds, that they pulled back a few hundred yards to a position that was more secure and sheltered. But they had held the advancing Confederates in check long enough for Reynolds and the First Division to take the vital Cemetery Ridge to the south of Gettysburg.

SOUND OF DISTANT CANNON

Lee and Longstreet had reached the top of the South Mountain range when they heard the cannon in the

BREECH-LOADING CARBINES

The Union cavalry carried breech-loading carbines, along with a revolver and a saber. These could fire three times as fast as any muzzle-loader and were easier to handle on horseback. A Sharps carbine in the hands of Captain Marcellus E. Jones was supposed to have fired the first shot of the battle. It was .52 caliber with a breechblock that was lowered by pushing forward a lever that doubled as a trigger guard. When it closed the sharp end cut off the end of the paper or linen cartridge, allowing the powder to ignite when the manually clocked hammer hit the percussion cap. Sometimes powder leaked, burning the shooter and disabling the carbine. The government bought over 80,000 of them and twenty-eight of the three-thirty Union cavalry regiments at Gettysburg carried them.

The Union cavalry also carried the .54 caliber Burnside carbine. It had been patented in 1856 by Ambrose E. Burnside, who as General Burnside was commander of the Army of the Potomac defeated by Lee at Fredericksburg. The breechblock rotated when the two trigger guards were squeezed together. Its advantage was that it used brass cartridges, which Confederate manufacturers found hard to copy, so captured Burnsides were no use to the Rebels.

There were some Gallagher and Merrill .54 caliber carbines. They were sporting weapons, not rugged enough for army use. They used paper cartridges and a large consignment was captured by the Rebels.

Two Union cavalry regiments – the 5th and 6th Michigan, under Brigadier General Custer – carried the new .52-caliber Spencer breech-loading repeater rifle that became the most sought-after weapon of the war. A tubular magazine was loaded through the stock. A spring pushed the copper-rimmed cartridge toward the breech. Pulling down the trigger guard dropped the breechblock and expelled the spent shell. Pulling the guard up again pushed another round into the chamber which was fired by a hammer cocked up by the thumb. It could fire seven rounds as fast as the soldier could pull the trigger.

(Top) .52 Spencer repeater; (middle) .54 Burnside; (bottom) cross-section of a 7-shot Spencer repeating rifle.

HEADQUARTERS, ARMY OF NORTHERN VIRGINIA

Chambersburg, June 28, 1863 – 7:30 am
Lieut. Gen R.S. Ewell
Commanding Corps:
General: ... if you have no good reason against it, I desire you to move in the direction of Gettysburg, via Heidlersburg, where you will have turnpike most of the way, and you can thus join your other divisions to Early's which is east of the mountains. I think it preferable to keep on the east side of the mountains. When you come to Heidlersburg, you can either move directly on Gettysburg or turn down to Cashtown. Your trains and heavy artillery you can send, if you think proper, on the road to Chambersburg. But if the roads which your troops take are good, they had better follow you.
R.E. Lee
General

HEADQUARTERS OF THE ARMY OF THE POTOMAC

June 30, 1863

Circular

The commanding general requests that, previous to the engagement soon expected with the enemy, corps and all other commanding officers address their troops, explaining to them briefly the immense issues involved in this struggle. The enemy are on our soil; the whole country now looks anxiously to this army to deliver it from the presence of the foe. Our failure to do so will leave us no such welcome as the swelling millions of hearts with pride and joy at our success would give every soldier of this army. Homes, firesides, and domestic altars are involved. The army has fought well heretofore; it is believed that it will fight more desperately and bravely than ever if it is addressed in fitting terms.

Corps and other commanders are authorized to order the instant death of any soldier who fails in his duty at this hour.
By order of General Meade:
S. Williams
Assistant Adjutant General

(Top) Lee's headquarters on the Chambersburg Pike. (Bottom) Meade's headquarters, the Leister Farm.

distance. Lee was more than a little annoyed that battle had been joined without him knowing about it. Without Stuart and his cavalry scouting ahead as his advance 'eyes' he was very much in the dark as to what was happening.

Bidding Longstreet goodbye, Lee rode on to Cashtown to see Hill. But Hill knew little more than he did. From there, they could hear muskets firing. Plainly a full-scale battle was already underway.

THE SEMINARY

When General Reynolds arrived in Gettysburg, Union scout Peter Culp at the Eagle Hotel directed him to Buford's headquarters at the Seminary. Reynolds asked him if he could hold out until Doubleday's infantry arrived. 'I reckon I can,' Buford replied.

Reynolds then sent a message to General Meade, which said:

The enemy is advancing in strong force, and I fear he will get to the heights beyond the town before I can. I will fight him every inch of the way. I will fight him inch by inch, and if driven into the town I will barricade the streets, and hold him back as long as possible.

When General Meade received the note at around 11:20 am, he exclaimed: 'Good! That's just like Reynolds, he will hold out to the bitter end.'

Reynolds then rode south, back down the Emmitsburg Road, meeting the infantry around a mile from the town. He directed them to double-quick across the fields to the west and make directly for the Seminary. The 76th New York regiment in advance of the column passed through a cherry orchard. They had been given orders against pilfering fruit. Their commanding officer Major Andrew J. Grover reminded them: 'Boys, the General charges you to be very particular to keep strictly within the rules, and not meddle with those cherry trees. Be sure you don't break the trees down.'

The officers then turned their backs. The trees were quickly denuded, but the men were careful, as ordered, not to break the trees down.

The main column was led by pioneers, foot soldiers armed with axes and other implements to clear the way for the infantry. They leveled the fences. The infantry rushed across the fields to the Seminary, then moved on up the Chambersburg Pike.

THE IRON BRIGADE

By the time Reynold's men reached McPherson's Ridge, Buford's men had pulled back to the rear of the ridge. Between them, Brigadier General Lysander Cutler leading the Second Brigade of Wadsworth's

CHERRY PICKING

The food that was most abundant during the march toward Gettysburg was cherries. One veteran from South Carolina was so impressed that he sent back samples, with a note saying: 'I send you some cherry seed which you must plant. The fruit is the large white cherry, as large, if not larger, than a partridge egg.'

Local farmers begged the troops not to rob them of their cherries, but one officer said: 'It is impossible to keep men from breaking the small limbs and picking the cherries as they marched.'

Some simply gave way, giving the appropriate orders: 'Halt, stack arms, cherry trees, charge!' No one hung back from that assault.

Although the Confederate army were warned against looting, it seemed to some that in Pennsylvania there was 'enough wheat to supply the whole world.' The local 'Dutch' seemed to hand over food willingly enough as they 'know how their soldiers have behaved in Virginia and they fear that ours will retaliate.' Private William Daniel of the 2nd South Carolina said: 'Our men feasted themselves on cherries of which the country affords the greatest abundance, mutton, chickens, turkeys, etc.'

However, Rachel Cormany, a resident of Chambersburg, was not happy. She said: 'While I am writing thousands are passing – such a rough dirty ragged rowdyist set one does not often see ... Many have chickens as they pass. There a number are going with honey – robbed some man of it no doubt – they are even carrying buckets ... they are poorly clad – many have no shoes on. As they pass along they take the hats off our citizens heads and throw their old ones in exchange.'

First Division, Captain James A. Hall's Second Maine battery, and the First Brigade – aka the 'Iron Brigade' – under Brigadier General Solomon Meredith brought with them 3,600 men. They faced roughly the same number of Confederates.

As they were relieved and fell back, Buford's men shouted to the infantry: 'Go in and give them hell.'

Reynolds sent Doubleday to hold the Hagerstown road to the south-west, though no Confederate troops arrived from that direction that day. Key to the engagement was McPherson's Grove that lay between the two roads. Reynolds led the 2nd Wisconsin into the grove.

'Forward men, forward,' he shouted. 'For God's sake, drive those fellows out of the woods.'

At the corner of the Grove, he stopped and looked back to see how many regiments were following. As he turned in his saddle, a Minié ball from a muzzle-loader, possibly a stray shot, hit him in the back of the head. It came out under his right eye. His body was carried from the field. Few saw him fall and Doubleday took command. Captured Confederate soldiers later expressed their respect for General Reynolds who they had faced at Mechanicsville (Beaver Creek Dam), Gaines's Mill, the Second Battle of Bull Run, Fredericksburg, and Chancellorsville.

RAILROAD GRADING

Two hundred yards to the north of the Chambersburg Pike was the railroad grading for a new line that was to be put in. There was no time for reconnaissance. Wadsworth sent the remaining three regiments of Cutler's brigade into battle on McPherson's Ridge to the north of it. Awaiting them there were Davis's Fourth Division. Both had around two thousand men.

Davis's men were concealed in tall grass just over the ridge. When Cutler's men appeared over the crest, they were greeted with murderous fire. This was so unexpected that Major Grover with the 76th New York to the right thought it was friendly fire coming from Union troops. They took several volleys to the right flank before returning fire. By then, Grover was dead. He was succeeded by Captain John E. Cook. In the next half-hour of vicious fighting, the 76th lost 234 officers and men out of the 370 engaged.

To the left, the 147th New York were advancing through wheat fields toward the withering fire of the 2nd and 42nd Mississippi regiments. Hall's 2nd Maine battery on the other side of the railroad grading tried to halt the Confederates, but after a moment's pause they renewed their attack.

ENFILADING FIRE

Enfilade and defilade are concepts in military tactics used to describe a military formation's exposure to enemy fire. A formation or position is 'in enfilade' if weapons fire can be directed along its longest axis. For instance, a trench is enfiladed if the opponent can fire down the length of the trench. A column of marching troops is enfiladed if fired on from the front or rear such that the projectiles travel the length of the column. A rank or line of advancing troops is enfiladed if fired on from the side (from the flank). The benefit of enfilading an enemy formation is that, by firing along the long axis, it becomes easier to hit targets within that formation.

Enfilade fire, a gunfire directed against an enfiladed formation or position, is also commonly known as 'flanking fire'. Raking fire is the equivalent term in naval warfare. Strafing, firing on targets from a flying platform, is often done with enfilade fire.

Enfilading fire – the cannon at the top are firing on a rank of soldiers from a flanking position.

Meanwhile the 55th North Carolina had found its way around the 76th New York's flank and was threatening its rear. To counter deadly enfilading fire, the right flank of the 76th tried to maneuver their front to the north, a difficult task under a lethal fusillade.

Seeing the three regiments were in difficulty, Wadsworth recalled them to Seminary Ridge. The orders did not get through to the 147th New York, so when the 76th New York and 56th Pennsylvania retreated as ordered, their right flank came under attack, as did the 14th Brooklyn and 95th New York on the other side of the railroad grading.

CANISTER SHOT

Half-an-hour later, Davis's men were charging Hall's 2nd Maine battery, which had to turn its front to the north and fire canister shot – cans of metal balls that break apart and cut through advancing troops. Hall lost twenty-two men and thirty-four horses, and was forced to withdraw. But rather than abandon his gun, one artilleryman hitched a team of horses to it. The Rebels were upon him and a Confederate lieutenant put his hand on the piece and demanded he surrender it. When the artilleryman refused, the Southern lieutenant put a gun to his head, but the blue-coat lashed the reins. As the team raced off with the gun, the Rebel officer shot him in the back. The artilleryman died, but the gun reached the Union lines.

As the 6th Wisconsin moved to halt Davis at the railroad cut, the commanding officer Lieutenant Colonel Rufus R. Dawes was approached by a young soldier who came to attention and saluted. Dawes thought he had brought a message, but the young man said: 'Tell my friends at home that I died like a man and a soldier.' He then tore open his tunic to reveal a terrible chest wound and fell dead.

There were also instances of cowardice. Captain Pierce commanding Company A of the 76th New York who had retired to Seminary Ridge found a man behind a stone wall, wrapped up in a blanket with his head covered. He claimed to be wounded in the side. When Pierce examined him and found no wound, he claimed it was somewhere else. 'Get up you coward,' ordered Pierce. 'And fall in.'

The terrified man sprang to his feet and sprinted to the frontline where his comrades in Company A kept him for the rest of the day.

HIT IN THE THROAT

Under attack on the right flank by the 2nd and 42nd Mississippi, the 147th New York fought on. Their commander Lieutenant Colonel Miller who had finally received the order to withdraw was hit in the throat. But he was replaced by Major Harney, who knew nothing of the order. He managed to turn the front to the north, though at times they were less than forty yards from the enemy. They now had the cover of the rail fence, while the 2nd Mississippi were exposed in the field. But they were soon joined by the 55th North Carolina who, again, tried to outflank the 147th New York. A Confederate officer who corrected their alignment as coolly as if he were on a dress parade drew the admiration of the Union officers.

A Union officer was seen waving his cap and, finally, the order to withdraw reached Major Harney. It was brought by Wadsworth's adjutant general, Captain T.E. Ellsworth who fearlessly galloped into the maelstrom.

As the left wing of the 147th New York withdrew toward Seminary Ridge down Chambersburg Pike, the color-bearer Sergeant William A. Wyburn was hit by a bullet and fell as if dead. Captain Volney J. Pierce tried to wrest the colors from him, but Wyburn clung on. When the captain ordered him to let go, Wyburn said: 'Hold on, I will be up in a minute.' Then he staggered to his feet and marched on, carrying the colors for the rest of the battle. He was later commissioned for his devotion.

In that engagement, the 147th lost 220 men out of 380, losing 301 in all that day.

RAILROAD CUT

As Davis's men pursued the retreating men, the 14th Brooklyn and 95th New York, who had been relieved by Meredith's Iron Brigade, were paralleling them, but then they turned their front to the north and attacked Davis's flank, forcing the Confederates to take cover in the railroad cut.

The 6th Wisconsin joined the 14th Brooklyn and 95th New York attacking them there. It was only some 175 paces from the pike to the cut but the 6th Wisconsin lost some 180 men out of 420, including the entire color guard. There was then hand-to-hand fighting along the edge of the cut as the Confederates were driven back.

The 6th Wisconsin finally got two companies under Adjutant Brooks into the eastern end of the cut, who began to pour in enfilading fire. Corporal Eggleston of Company H leapt forward to seize the colors of the 2nd Mississippi, but was shot dead as his hand touched the flag. Furious Private Anderson clubbed the gray-coat who had killed Eggleston with his musket, splitting his skull and Corporal Francis A. Waller of the 6th Wisconsin seized the 2nd Mississippi's colors.

Colonel Dawes then demanded that the Confederates surrender. Major John A. Blair of the 2nd Mississippi and about 250 Rebels did so and Dawes collected a bundle of swords from their officers. The 14th Brooklyn and 95th New York also took prisoners, but those at the west end of the cut managed to escape – though, according to Dawes, at least a thousand Confederates abandoned their muskets in the cut. Davis's brigade had also lost all but two of its field officers.

One of Hall's officers then brought up an artillery piece to the eastern end of the cut. This would prevent the Confederates using it as cover or an infiltration route again. Meanwhile, the remnants of the 76th New York, 56th Pennsylvania, and 147th New York regrouped behind Seminary Ridge. Swift action by Hall's men meant they also recaptured a gun that they had abandoned during their withdrawal. Davis's men fell back towards Herr's Ridge. They had discovered that it was harder to fight in the open countryside of Pennsylvania than the woods of Virginia.

The Iron Brigade

The First Brigade of Wadsworth's First Division comprise five western regiments – the 2nd, 6th, and 7th Wisconsin, 19th Indiana, and 24th Michigan, who had joined them at Fredericksburg. When they were mustered into Union service, the Army had run out of the regular blue kepis worn by other units and were issued with black felt hats with a wide brim. At the Second Battle of Bull Run, they held off the onslaught of a superior force under Major General Thomas J. 'Stonewall' Jackson and became known to the Confederates as 'The Black Hats.' At the Battle of South Mountain on September 14, 1862, they made an uphill charge, causing General Hooker to exclaim that the men 'fought like iron.' General McClellan is also thought to have remarked that they were 'made of iron' at the Battle of Antietam three days later. From then on, they were known as the Iron Brigade. In both actions, they were commanded by Brigadier General John Gibbon. After that at Antietam, he was promoted to command the 2nd Division and replaced by Brigade General Solomon 'Long Sol' Meredith.

The charge of the Iron Brigade at the Battle of Antietam, 1862. Painting by Thure de Thulstrup (1887).

OUR BANNER IN THE SKY
BY FREDERIC EDWIN CHURCH

In 1861 artist Frederic Edwin Church painted a vividly colored American flag in the sky as a patriotic response to the Confederate attack on Fort Sumter. A tree stands like a flagpole with an American eagle soaring alongside the flag in the heavens, as if the Union was guided by a higher purpose.

CHAPTER 2

THE REBEL YELL

MCPHERSON'S GROVE

The Iron Brigade had relieved Colonel William Gamble's cavalry brigade, fixing their bayonets as they rushed into the woods. Facing them were the men of Brigadier General James J. Archer's Third Brigade who, issuing their famous high-pitched, staccato rebel yell, plunged across Willoughby Run, up the western slope of McPherson's Ridge and into the grove, meeting the Iron Brigade head on.

Archer's men loosed off the first volley when the lines were less than fifty yards apart. Meredith was wounded by fragments of a shell which exploded in front of his horse. Command was passed to Colonel William W. Robinson of the 7th Wisconsin.

The blue line faltered, but then surged on. Suddenly, the Confederates realized who they were up against. The cry went up: 'There are those black-hatted fellows again! 'Taint no militia' – as they had been told – 'It's the Army of the Potomac!'

Meredith's left overlapped Archer's right, so 1st Tennessee found themselves outflanked by the 24th Michigan. But the Confederates fought tenaciously. The 24th Michigan's colors were downed fourteen times as nine men of the color-guard were killed or wounded. The original color-bearer, Sergeant Abel Peck, was killed almost as soon as contact was made.

> ## Like the rumbling of a distant train, it came rushing down the lines like the surging waves upon the ocean.
>
> CONFEDERATE SOLDIER
> ABOUT THE REBEL YELL

A GENERAL CAPTURED

Nevertheless, Archer's line was pushed back and he was forced to withdraw across Willoughby Run, leaving several hundred men prisoner. Among them was General Archer himself, found exhausted by the extreme heat behind a clump of willows. He was taken by Private Patrick Maloney of the 2nd Wisconsin, but offered his sword to Captain Charles Dow nearby.

THE REBEL YELL

First raised at the First Battle of Manassas on July 21, 1861, the Rebel yell was heard above the roar of battle for the three days of the Battle of Gettysburg. A high-pitched shout, it was thought to have derived from the Southern foxhunter's cry, while J. Harvie Drew of the 9th Virginia Cavalry said that the origin was: 'Hollering, screaming, yelling from one person or another to their dog, or at some of the cattle on the plantation, with accompanying reverberations from hilltops, over valleys and plains, [that] were familiar sounds throughout the farming districts of the South in days gone by.' His version went: 'Who – who – ey! Who – ey! Who – ey! Woo – who-ey! Who – ey!'

To Yankee ears, it was a series of 'yelp, staccato, and shrill,' according to a Northern surgeon, while the *New York Herald* called it 'shrill, exultant, savage.' Nevertheless the effect on the battlefield was electrifying. Colonel O.M. Roberts of the 11th Texas Infantry said:

When the command was given 'Forward, charge!' it, too, would be rapidly passed, and then simultaneously the Texas 'rebel yell' burst out from the whole line, as all together they dashed at double quick toward the enemy. The effect of the yell was marvelous ... Such yells exploded in the air in one combined sound have been heard distinctly three miles off across the prairie, above the din of musketry and artillery.

'Keep your sword, General, and go to the rear,' said Dow. 'One sword is all I need on this line.'

Archer was the first Confederate general to be captured since Lee had taken over the Army of Northern Virginia. At the rear, he was greeted by Doubleday, who had been a classmate at West Point.

'Good morning, Archer,' said Doubleday. 'How are you? I'm glad to see you.'

'Well, I'm not glad to see you, by a damned sight, Doubleday,' said Archer, refusing to shake his classmate's hand.

STRENGTHEN THE LINE

The Iron Brigade pursued the Confederates across the run and up the slope a hundred yards beyond. Fearing that they were becoming too exposed, Doubleday ordered them back to McPherson's Grove to strengthen the line there. There was a lull while both sides awaited reinforcements. Meanwhile Heth regrouped his four brigades for a new onslaught and the Confederate artillery kept up a sporadic bombardment from Herr Ridge where the artillerymen had dug themselves in for protection from counter-battery fire.

After around fifteen minutes the rest of Doubleday's Corps arrived. The Second Division under Brigadier General John C. Robinson and the Third Division under Brigadier General Thomas A. Rowley comprised some six thousand infantrymen. They were accompanied by the four batteries of Colonel Charles S. Wainwright's First Corp artillery brigade. They brought with them twelve twelve-pounder bronze Napoleons and four three-inch rifles.

FORWARD!

The Second Division was held in reserve at the Seminary, while the two brigades of the Third were sent to aid Wadsworth. When Colonel Langhorne Wister commanding the 150th Pennsylvania gave the order 'Forward!' he was greeted with a chorus reminding him that he had forgotten to give the order to load muskets.

The division was split with the Second Brigade under Colonel Roy Stone going to Meredith's right, with its own right on the Chambersburg Pike. The First Brigade under Colonel Chapman Biddle went to the left, down Hagerstown Road. Passing

NAPOLEON

The most popular field piece of the Civil War, the Napoleon was named for Napoleon III of France, who in 1850 ordered his ordnance department to produce a standardized cannon. His uncle, Napoleon I, had been an artilleryman by training and called his heavy twelve-pounders with his Imperial Guard at Waterloo his 'Beautiful Daughters.' They impressed the US Military Mission who toured Europe in 1855 – 56 and began arriving in the US in 1857.

The 1857 Napoleon was a muzzle-loading, smoothbore cannon. It was strong and reliable, fired a variety of ammunition, and was light enough to be hauled by men over short distances, though they were normally moved by a six-horse team. Its bronze barrel was less likely to burst on firing than an iron one. The range was 1,680 yards with a solid iron cannonball. At a thousand yards, a solid shot would penetrate a foot of oak. With canister its range was 350 yards.

Napoleons made in the North had a bulge at the muzzle, strengthening it; Southern Napoleons were straight. At Gettysburg, Lee had a hundred Napoleons, including one out-dated six pounder; Meade had 142.

An African-American soldier guarding a line of twelve-pounder Napoleons, City Point, Virginia.

THREE-INCH ORDNANCE RIFLE

Adding rifling to the barrel spins the shot, increasing range and accuracy, but it made the gun more difficult to manufacture. The three-inch ordnance rifle – originally called the Griffen Gun, after its designer John Griffen – was the most widely used rifled cannon of the Civil War. The barrel was made of wrought iron, which is also resistant to rupturing. When Griffen was demonstrating it to the US Ordnance department in 1856, he challenged them to burst one. They only succeeded after five hundred shots, when they packed the barrel with a charge of seven pounds and thirteen cannon balls, completely filling it. Only one burst in action during the war.

Griffen Guns were cheap to make. The North produced over a thousand during the war at a cost of around $350 each. The South made theirs in the Tredegar Iron Works in Richmond, Virginia, and in Rome, Georgia.

They were light making them suitable for fast-moving horse artillery. The range was over four thousand yards – some 2.5 miles. They fired explosive shells, rather than solid shot.

'The Yankee three-inch rifle was a dead shot at any distance under a mile,' said one Confederate soldier. 'They could hit the end of a flour barrel more often than miss, unless the gunner got rattled.'

The disadvantages were that the high-velocity of the projectile meant a shell would bury itself in the ground before exploding, reducing its effectiveness. Its small, three-inch caliber also meant that it was not as effective with canister as a smoothbore. The Army of the Potomac had too high a ratio of rifles to smoothbores – 214 out of 358 – for the best tactical mix. General McClellan had tried unsuccessfully to reduce the ratio to 1:2. At Gettysburg, Lee had 77 three-inch ordnance rifles; Meade had 144.

Three-Inch Ordnance Rifle.

over Willoughby Run to the ridge beyond, it turned northwards. After about three hundred yards, it found a large Confederate force of infantry and artillery.

The brigade crossed back over Willoughby Run, moving to the crest of McPherson's Ridge, between the grove and the Hagerstown Road. It was joined by Gamble's cavalry brigade and a battery of four three-inch rifles under Captain James H. Cooper.

Ordered forward, they moved down the ravine of Willoughby Run, coming under heavy fire from the Confederates under cover on the other side. Unable to return fire effectively, they returned to their position on top of McPherson's Ridge. This did not reflect well on Biddle, but it seems to have been the fault of his commanding officer Brigadier General Rowley, who may have been drunk and was later court-martialed.

SPLIT BRIGADE

Colonel Biddle split his brigade, retaining command of the 142nd and the soon-to-arrive 151st Pennsylvania to the north of Cooper's battery, handing command of 80th New York and 121st Pennsylvania to Colonel Theodore B. Gates of the 80th to the south. Their left was supposed to be protected by the remnants of Gamble's cavalry, Brigadier General James H. Lane's Second Brigade neutralized them, swung round and began to roll up Gates' left. The 121st were told to lie down in the grass behind the crest to escape attention and protect them from the Confederate artillery fire from Herr Ridge to the west.

The Confederates had ten batteries there, while the Union had five along McPherson's Ridge. One was commanded by Captain Reynolds. Going into action he had been wounded on the left side, losing his left eye. While his command devolved to Lieutenant George Breck, Reynolds stayed on the field, though in great pain, to encourage his men. This was vital as Doubleday could muster only thirty-six guns against sixty Confederate pieces.

THE BUCKTAILS

When Stone's 'Bucktail' brigade – so-called because of the insignia that looked like a buck's tail on the left side of their kepis – arrived in position, they chanted: 'We have come to stay.' It was true. Many of them stayed forever at Gettysburg.

One company from each regiment was deployed forward in a skirmish line, watching for the enemy coming across Willoughby Run. As they moved forward, they came across a skirmish line of Confederates formed up along a fence and drove them back across the run.

The Rebel infantry attacked further north when Confederate artillery arrived on Oak Hill to the north and began delivering enfilading fire, forcing Cutler's brigade to Stone's right to withdraw to the Seminary. Stone then turned his right wing, deploying it along the Chambersburg Pike so it faced north. This had to be done under fire from both Oak Hill and Herr Ridge.

As no attack seemed imminent, the 150th Pennsylvania were given permission to shelter in McPherson's stone barn when they saw a man in a dark swallow-tail coat with shiny buttons walking cross the battlefield with a gun in his hand. This was seventy-year-old John Burns.

LEG CLEAN OFF

While Robinson's Second Division were held in reserve at the Seminary, the First Brigade under Brigadier General Gabriel R. Paul were put to work constructing temporary breastworks fortifications in the grove to the west.

A number of spent, solid-shot cannon balls fired from the Confederate batteries on Herr Ridge were seen rolling slowly along the ground toward the Seminary. A soldier from a Wisconsin regiment put out his foot to stop one and it took his leg clean off. Crying in agony, he sobbed that he would always be ashamed to say how he lost it.

Paul's First Brigade would be involved in heavy fighting after that, during which five successive commanders were wounded.

CONFEDERATE REINFORCEMENTS

Around midday, the Third Division of Ewell's Second Corps arrived at Oak Hill, under the command of Major General Robert Emmett Rodes. He ordered Major Blackfords's battalion of Alabama sharpshooters and General Doles' crack Georgia brigade to go to the Carlisle Road to watch for the arrival of Early's First Division. They were also to engage Colonel Thomas C. Devin's Second Brigade which Buford had deployed there to guard the northern approaches.

John Burns

Born in 1793, John Burns was a veteran of the War of 1812, fighting alongside Winfield Scott at the Battle of Lundy's Lane, also known as the Battle of Niagara Falls. He fought again in the Mexican-American War, but when he volunteered in the Civil War, he was rejected because of his age.

After serving as a teamster supporting the Union Army, he was sent home to Gettysburg, where he became constable. When the Confederates briefly occupied on June 26, 1863, Burns was jailed. When released, he managed to arrest some of the Confederate stragglers.

When Buford arrived in Gettysburg on July 1 and the fighting began, Burns picked up his flintlock and headed for the sound of gunfire. On the way, a wounded Union soldier offered him a more modern rifle. Arriving on McPherson's Ridge he asked permission to fight alongside the 150th Pennsylvania, where he demonstrated his skill as a sharpshooter. But it was a hot day, so he went into the grove to help the men of the Iron Brigade, who said he was cool and deliberate under fire.

He was wounded three times in the arm, leg, and chest. When they withdrew, the Union soldiers had to leave him behind on the battlefield. He managed to bury his ammunition and crawl away from his rifle. Then he managed to persuade the Confederates that he was a non-combatant, an old man out looking for his invalid wife. A Confederate surgeon dressed his wounds.

Fearing that he might be unmasked as a non-uniformed combatant and, under rules of war, shot, he crawled into the cellar of a nearby house. He received high praise in Doubleday's report on the battle.

When Abraham Lincoln came to Gettysburg, he asked to meet him and Burns became a national hero. He died in 1872 and a statue of him, gun in hand, stands on McPherson's Ridge, where he saw his last action.

The Bucktails

Without a doubt, the Bucktails are Pennsylvania's most famous Civil War unit. The regiment first formed in April 1861, when Thomas L. Kane sought permission to raise a company of riflemen from among the hardy woodsmen of McKean County. Each man who came to the regiment's rendezvous point wore civilian clothes and a buck's tail in his hat – a symbol of his marksmanship. Indeed, the marksman test for joining the unit was unique at this early stage of the war. Most volunteers who joined the Union army did not have much proficiency with a weapon, let alone the newfangled rifled-muskets first introduced in the 1850s.

The Bucktails – Company D, 149th Pennsylvania Infantry, Petersburg, Virginia, 1864.

Rodes' arrival had not been spotted by Doubleday because of the heavy woods on Oak Hill. His men were almost immediately under threat. However, Howard's Eleventh Corps of some 9,500 then arrived on the plain north of the town.

Howard outranked Doubleday and took command, leaving Major General Carl Schurz in command of the Eleventh Corps. He set up his headquarters on East Cemetery Hill to the south of the town, then climbed to the top of the Fahnestock Brothers Store at Baltimore and Middle where he saw several regiments of Cutler's brigade making a temporary withdrawal and reported to Meade erroneously that the First Corps was crumbling. This led to Doubleday eventually being replaced by Major General John Newton, despite Doubleday's skilful handling of the situation up to that point.

For the moment though, Howard sent a message to Doubleday, telling him to fight on the left while Howard and the Eleventh fought on the right. Doubleday was also given instructions to hold Seminary Ridge, if forced off McPherson's. Whatever Howard's deficiencies as a commander he, too, had identified the Cemetery Heights to the south of the town as the key to the ensuing battle.

OUT OF BREATH

Every regiment of the Eleventh Corps was deployed as soon as it arrived. When the 45th New York infantry regiment reached Gettysburg 'panting and out of breath', its four right companies were sent up the Mummasburg Road to the north-west of the town to take McLean's large red barn at the foot of the eastern slope of Oak Ridge. Skirmishers were sent out to the Carlisle Road. More companies were to follow when they had caught their breath.

The skirmishers passed successfully through the wheat fields to the north, but the four companies came under fire from the four Napoleons of the Confederate battery under Captain R.C.M. Page near the McLean barn and Blackford's sharpshooters stretched along the lane at the bottom of Oak Hill and in the wheat fields. While under Confederate fire and taking casualties, the Union forces were augmented by the six remaining companies of the regiment and the six Napoleons of Battery I of the 1st Ohio Light Artillery under Captain Hubert Dilger.

Dilger himself sighted and fired a gun,

temporarily knocking out an enemy piece. Five Confederate gun carriages were reported destroyed. However, the Southern guns were soon reinforced, while Dilger was joined by the 13th New York Light Battery under Lieutenant William Wheeler with four three-inch rifles.

OAK HILL

While the four leading companies of the 45th New York continued their advance, skirmishers from Rodes' Fifth Brigade under Colonel Edward O'Neal slipped down the lane at the bottom of Oak Hill in an attempt to cut them off from Robinson's Division who had been sent by Doubleday to a position on Oak Ridge just west of the Mummasburg Road, facing westwards. However, they were slowed by the fire the 45th New York poured into their flank.

The six companies of the 45th following then moved obliquely to the left to fill the gap between the First and Eleventh Corps. Fire from them and Robinson's men forced O'Neal's brigade to retreat to the eastern slopes of Oak Hill, near McLean's barn. Meanwhile the 61st Ohio and the 74th Pennsylvania reinforced the 45th New York to the right where they were soon involved in a desperate fight with Doles' Georgia brigade.

Page's Confederate battery then retreated further up the hill. The 45th charged the stragglers, capturing the barn and some three hundred gray-coats chiefly from the 5th and 6th Alabama regiments.

ALONG THE RIDGE

The prisoners were being sent to the rear when Rodes' Second Brigade under Brigadier General Alfred Iverson was seen moving along the ridge from the north-west. The 45th New York opened up on their flank. Then they charged, capturing another three hundred Confederates.

Howard's Second Division under Brigadier General Adolp von Steinwehr was held in reserve on Cemetery Hill. The First Brigade under Colonel Charles R. Coster were posted on the summit, while three regiments of Colonel Orland Smith's Second Brigade were posted at the base to the north where they occupied some of the houses at the edge of town. When Battery I of the 1st New York Light Artillery under Captain Wiedrich arrived on East Cemetery Hill to support them,

THE PARROTT RIFLE

The Parrott was another type of muzzle-loading rifled cannon that varied in size from the ten-pounder to the rare 300-pounder. Only ten- and twenty-pounders were used at Gettysburg, mainly the former. They were designed by Captain Robert P. Parrott who resigned from the Army to become superintendent at the West Point Foundry in Cold Spring, New York.

Parrott cannon had a distinctive reinforcing wrought-iron band around the breech where the pressure was greatest when the gun was fired. In the case of the ten-pounder this was thirteen inches wide. However, it did not entirely solve the problem. The rest of the barrel was cast iron, which cracked in hard use, causing the barrel to burst at the muzzle without warning.

Private Augustus Buell of Battery B, 4th US Artillery (a Napoleon battery) said: 'So long as the Parrott gun held together it was as good as any muzzle-loading rifle.' However, 'if anything could justify desertion by a cannoneer, it would be assignment to a Parrott battery.'

The 1863 model had its bore increased from 2.9 to three inches, so it could take the same explosive shells as the three-inch ordnance rifle. The muzzle-swell found on the 1861 was also eliminated.

A ten-pounder could be produced quickly for just $187, so it was the workhorse of the artillery at the beginning of the war. By the end it had been superseded entirely by the three-inch ordnance. The range of the ten-pounder was 2,400 yards; the twenty-pounder 3,000 yards, though with an extremely high elevation it could reach over three miles.

Like other rifled guns, it was not as effective as a smoothbore when firing canister, though bolt fired at four hundred yards could penetrate wood almost six feet thick. At Gettysburg it did not fire solid shot. Lee had forty-three ten-pounders and eleven twenty-pounders; Meade had sixty ten-pounders and six twenty-pounders.

Twenty-pounder Parrott rifles of the 1st New York Battery, Richmond, Virginia, 1862.

Howard said: 'Boys, I want you to hold this position at all hazards.'

When the First Division under Brigadier General Francis Channing Barlow and the Third Division under Brigadier General Alexander Schimmelfennig – six thousand men in all – arrived, Howard sent them to connect with Doubleday's right flank and guard against the arrival of Early's Confederate division from Heidlersburg. Howard rode with Barlow as he deployed, then inspected the lines of the Eleventh and First Corps.

ARTILLERY BATTLE

In the artillery battle between Page and Dilger and Wheeler, Page lost four men killed, twenty-six wounded, and seventeen horses before he was reinforced by The Jeff Davis Artillery battery under Captain W.J. Reese with four three-inch rifles and The King William Artillery battery under Captain W.P. Carter with two twelve-pounder Napoleons and two ten-pounder Parrotts.

Battery G of the 4th United States (Regular Army) Artillery with six Napoleons under Lieutenant Bayard Wilkeson had also arrived at Gettysburg. The left section was detached and sent to the Almshouse on the western side of the Harrisburg pike, while the other two sections under Wilkeson himself went further down the pike and deployed on Barlow's Knoll, near the bridge over Rock Creek where the First Brigade under Colonel Leopold von Gilsa was posted at the extreme right of Barlow's First Division.

To the left of the lines was Schimmelfennig's First Brigade under Colonel George von Amsberg. Devin's cavalry brigade, which had been in position since early morning were relieved and moved to the rear. There they were mistaken for Confederates by the Union gunners on East Cemetery Hill, who opened fire. Firing was halted before anyone was killed.

BARLOW'S KNOLL

As Barlow moved forward from the Almshouse to the knoll, he met some of Doles' Confederate skirmishers who were easily brushed aside. The Third Division moved in behind him. On the knoll, Barlow was supported by Wilkeson's battery, but by moving on from the Almshouse, he had extended and weakened the line.

By 2:00 pm the deployment of the Eleventh Corps was complete. They were not in a good position. Apart from Barlow's Knoll, they were stretched out across a flat plain with no high ground and fields of golden grain that would provide the Confederates with cover until the Rebels were almost on top of them. They had no shelter from the shelling from the batteries on Oak Hill. And the gap between the Eleventh and the First was still a quarter of a mile. They were outnumbered almost two to one and Early's division was on its way.

The Eleventh Corps had already come in for criticism in the press. At Chancellorsville, they had been overwhelmed by a sudden flank attack and were blamed for the Union defeat. Morale was not high.

Howard inspected the line. He was not brimming with confidence and told Doubleday, in case of defeat, to fall back on Cemetery Hill. Meanwhile, he could not attack the enemy on Oak Hill in case Early turned up.

Barlow watched as Doles' brigade advanced, figuring Gilsa's brigade could turn his flank. Amsberg's brigade was thrown at Doles' right. But the Union troops came under bombardment from Oak Hill, while the Union artillery were concentrating on counter-battery fire.

While Doles' brigade was coming to grips with Schimmelfennig's division, Doles' horse suddenly bolted, but the general fell off before he reached the Union lines.

OLD JUBE ENTERS THE FRAY

Around 3:00 pm, Early's First Division arrived with 6,300 men. 'Old Jube' (most of General Jubal Early's soldiers referred to him as 'Old Jube' or 'Old Jubilee' with enthusiasm and affection) deployed his brigades facing south-west across the Harrisburg Road, north of the bridge over Rock Creek. The Third Brigade under Brigadier General William 'Extra Billy' Smith was held in reserve.

Along with the infantry, there was the divisional artillery battery under Lieutenant Colonel H.P. Jones with eight Napoleons, six three-inch rifles, and two ten-pounder Parrotts. They went into position on the eastern side of the Harrisburg Road, about one-half mile north of the bridge over Rock Creek. From there, they would pour enfilading fire on Barlow's right flank.

Wilkeson's battery engaged them as best it could, but were also under attack by Carter's battery on Oak Hill. Wilkeson 'had a leg nearly severed from his body by a shell'. He pulled out a penknife, amputated what was left of his leg, then dragged himself to the Almshouse, where he died. He was just nineteen.

One officer and one man were killed, eleven men wounded, four men missing, and thirty-one horses killed. Meanwhile Carter lost four men killed and seven wounded, while expending 572 rounds.

Jones' battery lost two men killed and six wounded. One Napoleon was knocked out when a shot hit its muzzle, but it was later replaced by a captured cannon. One of the Parrotts and two other pieces were disabled when a shot that was too large got stuck in the barrel.

Old Jube

Jubal Anderson Early (1816 – 94) was a lawyer and Confederate general in the American Civil War. He served under Stonewall Jackson and then Robert E. Lee for almost the entire war, rising from regimental command to Lieutenant General and the command of an infantry corps in the Army of Northern Virginia. He was the Confederate commander in key battles of the Valley Campaigns of 1864, including a daring raid to the outskirts of Washington, DC. The articles written by him for the Southern Historical Society in the 1870s established the Lost Cause point of view as a long-lasting literary and cultural phenomenon.

Jubal Anderson Early.

When a Union shell burst among the guns, it damaged a wheel of one of the field pieces. An officer marched up and told the battery commander to change the wheel. The artilleryman replied that his men were too busy or had been killed or wounded, and pointed to a mangle mass of flesh that had once been a man. The officer took a look and noted: 'There lay our noble comrade, each several limb [sic] thrice broken, the body gashed with wounds, the top of the skull blown off and the brain actually fallen out upon the ground in two bloody, palpitating lobes.'

FORAGING

While Old Jube Early rode around with an ostrich feather in his hat, his men indulged in a little foraging. One young pioneer corpsman was seen 'carrying under each arm a great round Dutch loaf of bread about the size of a cart-wheel, giving him, in side view, the appearance of rolling in on wheels.'

After half-an-hour, Early ordered an attack on Gilsa's brigade at Barlow's Knoll. The Fourth Brigade to the west of the road under Brigadier General John B. Gordon moved forward to connect with Doles' left. To Gordon's left, the First Brigade under Brigadier General Harry T. Hays and Brigadier General Robert F. Hoke's Second Brigade, under the command of Colonel Isaac E. Avery, also advanced, squeezing Barlow in a vice.

Gordon's 1,500 Georgians charged Barlow's front line with 'swinging lines of bright muskets gleaming among the trembling wheat.' Colonel Arthur Fremantle, an English officer who had taken a leave of absence from the Coldstream Guards to come to America as an observer said:

> Like the sickles of a great line of reapers the sharp bayonets came nearer through the ruddy gold of ripening wheat to emerge unbroken and unhesitating from the willows which lined the little stream of Rock Creek.

CANISTER AND GRAPE

Meanwhile Barlow's Union guns belched canister and grapeshot – where the metal shot was carried in a canvas bag – but they could not stem the Confederates. By the time the lines were fifty paces apart, the musket volleys were continuous. Then fighting was hand-to-hand. Confederate artilleryman saw General Gordon mounted on his magnificent black steed 'standing in his stirrups, bare-headed, hat in hand, arms extended ... voice like a trumpet, exhorting his men.'

The 82nd supporting Dilger's battery moved forward 125 yards to threaten Gordon's right, but were met with frontal fire from Doles and had to retreat. Barlow was wounded and taken prisoner. He was replaced by Brigadier General Adelbert Ames.

Gordon's assault drove Gilsa's regiment back into the ranks of Ames' brigade, creating confusion. The 45th New York were then withdrawn from their advanced position near McLean's barn to support the 157th New York, who had moved to the right against Gordon. It did no good. Gordon now attacked Ames' right and was on the verge of routing Barlow's entire First Division.

THE ALMSHOUSE

The Union men fell back five hundred yards to a defensive position around the masonry-built Almshouse. This left Schimmelfennig's right exposed. Jones sent The Charlottesville Artillery battery under Captain James M. Carrington forward with its four Napoleons to support Gordon's advancing line. Hays and Avery attacked Ames's right, forcing him to withdraw further. Gordon then halted at the Almshouse, while Hays and Avery were held up on the Harrisburg Road by Devin's cavalry.

The Union soldiers were forced to withdraw, but they had delayed the Confederate advance enough for Coster's First Brigade to race from Cemetery Hill to a point near the railway depot on the northeast outskirts of the town. The 73rd Pennsylvania under Captain Daniel F. Kelly brought up the rear, while Battery K of the 1st Ohio Light Artillery under Captain Lewis Heckman with four Napoleons moved into position on the Carlisle Road near the grounds of Pennsylvania College.

Coster deployed the 27th Pennsylvania under Lieutenant Colonel Lorenz Cantador to the left, but a stout fence prevented them reaching the high ground there, allowing them only to fire obliquely to the right.

Almost immediately Hays attack Coster's front and Avery his right flank. They suffered terrible casualties, but this took pressure off Ames, who pulled his brigade back. In the centre was the 154th New York under Lieutenant Colonel Daniel B. Allen. One of their number was 'found on the field after the battle was over, and in his hand was an ambrotype picture of three children upon whose faces his last look had been fixed, and on which his sightless eyes were still directed.' On the right, in a wheat field, was the 134th New York under Lieutenant Colonel Allen H. Jackson.

The pressure on Coster's brigade was intense. Each regiment only had time to fire between six and nine musket volleys before having to fall back.

Union soldier disemboweled by a shell at Gettysburg with his arm blown off.

MUSKETS

- The US Model 1861 Springfield Rifle Musket was the most common Union infantry weapon. It cost $15 and around a million were made during the war. It weighed 9.25 pounds and was 58.5 inches long. Firing a .58 conical Minié bullet it had a maximum range of a thousand yards and an effective range of five hundred. It had a two-leaf rear sight and the front fight doubled as a lug for its 21-inch bayonet.

- The Enfield Rifle Musket was a British musket originally used in the Crimean War. Some 800,000 were used and they were imported by both sides. Its .577 caliber bullet was normally interchangeable with the standard American .58 caliber rifle ammunition. It weighed 9.20 pounds and was 55.25 inches long. Maximum range was 1,100 yards, effective range eight hundred.

- The Austrian Model 1854 Lorenz Rifle Musket came in the earlier .54 caliber, later rebored to .58 caliber. They were carried by twenty-one Union regiments and an unknown number of Confederate regiments at Gettysburg. The Union imported over 226,000 while the Confederacy bought at least 100,000. The earlier version had a fixed rear sight calibrated for targets up to three hundred paces. Later models had a leaf rear sight adjustable up to eight hundred paces. The 37.5-inch barrel took a quadrangular socket bayonet.

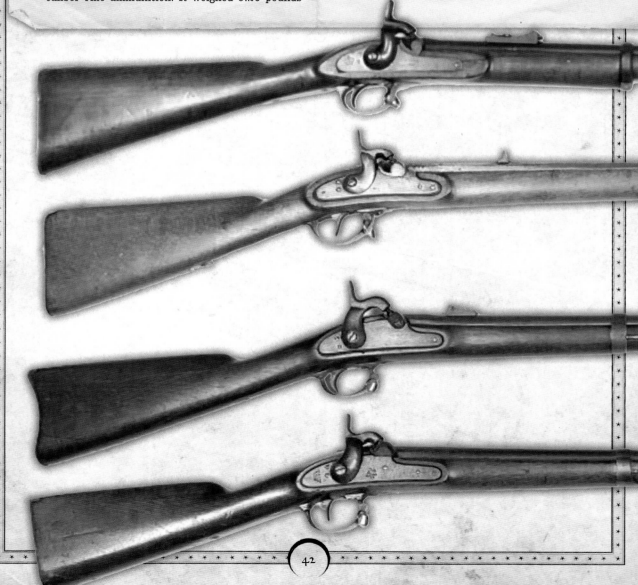

- The Mississippi Model 1841 US Percussion Rifle Musket was used by a handful of regiments on both sides during the war. It got its nickname because it was favored by the Mississippi Volunteer regiment under Jefferson Davis in the Mexican-American War. It was a .54 caliber weapon whose ammunition was also used in the .54 Lorenz, though after 1855 it was rifled to take .58 bullets, fitted with a lug to fit a sword bayonet, and leaf-sight for longer ranges. Copied by Southern manufacturers, it was carried by a large number of Confederate infantrymen at Gettysburg.

- The Richmond Percussion Rifle Musket was manufactured at the Richmond Armory, using equipment captured at the US arsenal at Harpers Ferry, which changed hands eight times during the Civil War. It closely resembled the 1855 Springfield, but with a different two-leaf rear sight. Weighing nine pounds, it had a thirty-inch barrel and fired a .58 Minié bullet and effective range of five hundred yards.

- The Springfield Model 1842 US Smoothbore Musket, though obsolete, were still popular with some regiments and several thousand were carried at Gettysburg. Of the 172,000 made, some 10,000 were rebored and converted to rifles before the war. A .69 caliber weapon, it fired a single ball, or a single ball with three smaller balls in a 'buck and ball' cartridge. Effective range was just a hundred yards.

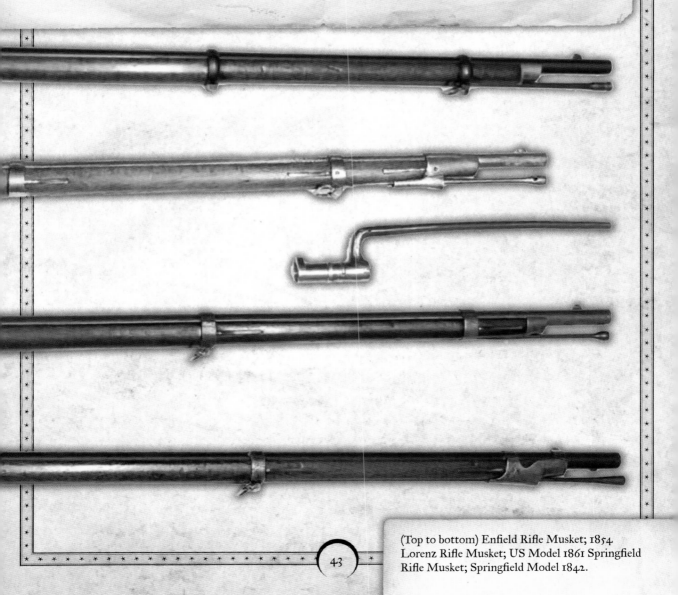

(Top to bottom) Enfield Rifle Musket; 1854 Lorenz Rifle Musket; US Model 1861 Springfield Rifle Musket; Springfield Model 1842.

CHAPTER 3

NONE BUT COWARDS RUN

In an attempt to support hard-pressed infantrymen of Coster's brigade, Heckman's battery fired 113 rounds of canister. He lost two men killed, eleven wounded, and two missing. After thirty minutes he was forced to withdraw, leaving two of his guns in the hands of 6th North Carolina with Avery's brigade.

Coster was already suffering enfilading fire from the right. Then his left was also threatened. A rapid retreat was his only option. The national and state colors of the 134th New York were retrieved by Captain M.B. Cheney of the 154th New York. A soldier of the 134th returned the compliment, rescuing the national flag of the 154th.

A Union officer on horseback tried to prevent a rout – 'Don't run, men,' he shouted. 'None but cowards run.'

Some Confederates cheered his gallantry. 'Don't shoot that man,' cried one. Nevertheless a fusillade of muskets dropped him.

The Confederates had won victory at comparatively little cost. Some of Hays' and Avery's men made it into the town but, fearing confusion in the narrow streets, Jubal Early ordered them back.

> ## Lay down your arms! Don't let one escape!

CONFEDERATE PINCERS CLOSING

It was now the turn of the Third Division to withdraw. Schimmelfennig fell back to the crossroads five hundred yards to the rear, where he tried to reform the line. But the situation was hopeless. His Second Brigade under Colonel Wlodzimierz Krzyzanowski lost every one of its regimental commanders.

As the Confederate pincers closed, Wheeler withdrew his four three-inch rifles. He set up his guns again outside the town, but a Confederate shell knocked one off its mount. He tried slinging it under a gun carriage with rope, but after some way had to abandon it.

Lieutenant Gates of the 157th New York lay severely wounded. As the Confederate line swept by, Captain J.H. Connolly of Company E, 44th Georgia stopped and gave him a canteen of water.

The Eleventh Corps retired in fairly good order until they reached the streets of Gettysburg. Many were captured there, but some Confederates cried: 'Shoot the Yankees! Lay down your arms! Don't let one escape!'

OAK RIDGE

To the west of Gettysburg, the Union First Corps still held out. When news came that Rodes had arrived on Oak Hill with some 8,125 men, the Second Brigade of Robinson's Second Division under Brigadier General Henry Baxter was sent along Oak Ridge, the extension of Seminary Ridge north of the railroad cut, to defend the right flank of Doubleday's line on McPherson's Ridge. Baxter had with him 1,200 men, while the 1,800 men of Paul's First Brigade remained behind at the Seminary.

Baxter's brigade took up position on the eastern slope of Oak Ridge, just south of the Mummasburg Road. There, they came under fire from Rodes' divisional artillery battalion under Lieutenant Colonel Thomas H. Carter massed there.

While Page and Reese, and later Captain W.P. Carter's King William Artillery battery, bombarded the Eleventh Corps, The Orange Artillery under Captain C.W. Fry with two ten-pounder Parrotts and two twelve-pounder Napoleons enfiladed the First Corps' right flank, firing 882 rounds. Cooper's Union battery, then moved south-east into a meadow between McPherson Ridge and Seminary Ridge to provide counter-battery fire.

HEAT EXHAUSTION

Rodes was now in position to attack but, in the soaring summer heat, moving across the wooded and rocky terrain to the north of Oak Hill had left his men with heat exhaustion. Heth now wanted to reverse the defeats he had suffered that morning. When General Lee arrived, he asked Lee whether he could renew his attack on Doubleday.

'No,' said Lee. 'I am not prepared to bring on a general engagement today. Longstreet is not up.'

When he saw Robinson's men moving up to face Rodes, he asked Lee again for permission to attack. This time Lee gave his assent and Heth moved up his First Brigade under Brigadier General James J. Pettigrew and his Second Brigade under Colonel John M. Brockenbrough.

Unable to withstand the fire from Oak Hill in open ground, Cutler withdrew his brigade from McPherson Ridge to the woods on Oak Ridge just north of the railroad cut. But the trees there offered

little protection and he was still under fire from Heth's batteries who were pounding Doubleday's battered line.

Baxter's men took cover behind a stone wall. Immediately across the Mummasburg Road were Page's artillery battery and O'Neal's Confederate brigade of 1,794 men. However, when O'Neal attacked, he was deprived of the 5th Alabama, who had been told to stay where they were to cover the gap between O'Neal's left and Doles' right, and the 3rd Alabama, who had been pulled back to join Daniel's brigade.

O'Neal's advance was confused. He did not follow the line that Rodes had given him and his left came under fire from Dilger's battery and the muskets of the 45th New York. He expected to be supported on the right by Iverson's brigade, but they halted their advance while the Union positions were shelled. As a result, O'Neal's men were repelled by Baxter's with heavy loss.

O'Neal himself had remained behind with the 5th Alabama. Only at the last minute were they ordered into the action as well, but it was too late.

Bodies of Union soldiers, killed on July 1, near McPherson Ridge. Photograph by Timothy H. O'Sullivan.

NEW LINE

Rodes then ordered Iverson to attack Baxter's left flank. Knowing they were coming, Baxter hurried his men up Oak Ridge under cover of the stone wall and formed a new line along the crest facing westward, with the 90th Pennsylvania at the apex guarding the road against any further attack by O'Neal.

As Iverson advanced, he moved northward to close the gap between him and O'Neal, forcing Daniel to his left to do likewise. Daniel's right also suffered enfilading fire from Stone's Bucktail regiment along the Chambersburg Pike.

When Iverson's line neared Oak Ridge, Cutler wheeled right so his brigade faced Iverson's exposed right flank, raking them with fire. But the Confederates pressed on. Plainly Iverson had not seen Baxter's men who were crouched down behind a stone wall along the crest of Oak Ridge with hooded colors.

Iverson's brigade were within seventy-five paces of the wall, when Baxter's men rose up and delivered a volley full in their faces. It was one of the most effective fusillades of the battle. Five hundred fell dead and maimed in a straight line across the slope. According to an eyewitness:

> *Iverson's line was indicated by the ghastly row of dead and wounded men, whose blood trailed the course of their line with a crimson stain clearly discernible for several days after the battle, until the rain washed the gory record away.*

WHITE FLAG

Iverson later told Rodes that 'one of his regiments had raised the white flag and gone over to the enemy.' It was not true. Some of the injured troops had waved handkerchiefs to halt the horrible slaughter. The rest gamely regrouped and tried a second assault. This again was repulsed by murderous musket volleys. The survivors withdrew to a gully a hundred yards to the rear. From there, they kept up fire on Baxter's men behind the stone wall.

Oak Ridge, Gettysburg.

This was not entirely ineffective. Sergeant Evans of Company B and Private John Witmoyer of Company H, both with the 88th Pennsylvania, crouched side-by-side behind the stone wall, taking potshots at the Confederates in the gully. When Evans saw a Southern color-bearer waving his flag, he said to his comrade: 'John, I will give those colors a whack.'

As Evans snapped his musket to his shoulder, Witmoyer heard a dull thud. He turned and asked the sergeant if he had been hit. Evans kept his eyes straight ahead as he lowered the musket from his shoulder and, without a word, he fell dead at Witmoyer's feet. A Rebel bullet had gone straight through his heart.

Almost immediately Baxter staged a counterstroke. By then his men were short of ammunition and they finished their work with the bayonet. A thousand men of Iverson's brigade were captured, along with the colors of the 23rd North Carolina and 26th Alabama. The colors of the 20th North Carolina were also taken, but were recaptured by Daniel's brigade later in the day.

The 12th North Carolina escaped but raising the white flag, which halted the Union fire long enough for them to make off. Even so, this was one of the most crushing defeats any brigade had suffered during the Civil War. Iverson himself was so shattered that his assistant adjutant-general Captain D.P. Halsey had to take command and rally the men. Iverson later exonerated his men, saying that none had gone over to the enemy under the white flag.

Baxter's brigade were not without their casualties. The 11th Pennsylvania had lost three successive commanders.

SHOT IN THE FACE

O'Neal tried again and managed to seize the north end of the stone wall. Meanwhile Rodes' Fourth Brigade under the experienced Brigadier General Stephen D. Ramseur with over a thousand men was sent to relieve Iverson. Robinson then ordered up General Paul's First Brigade from the Seminary to reinforce the position on Oak Ridge. They formed up a little to the rear of Baxter's original position along the crest. As they did so, they came under fire from Confederates behind the stone wall and in the grove to the north of the Mummasburg Road. While still

in the rear with the 104th New York General Paul was shot in the face, losing both his eyes. Command was handed to Colonel Samuel H. Leonard of the 13th Massachusetts.

Leonard himself was wounded and Colonel Adrian Root of the 94th New York took over. Root, in turn, was wounded and captured, and Colonel Richard Coulter of the 11th Pennsylvania took charge.

Under heavy fire from across the road and the ridge that faced them, seven color-bearers of the 104th New York were lost. Ordering them forward, Colonel Gilbert G. Prey told his men that they would all soon be dead if they did not silence the Confederate volleys. When they hesitated, Prey leapt in front of the line and shouted: 'I'll lead you, boys!'

They surged forward, took the wall – along with sixty prisoners – and held it for some time.

Paul's brigade made several attacks across the fields to the west, but they were repulsed by Ramseur. However, they did succeed in delaying any Confederate assault from that quarter.

Ramseur positioned the 14th North Carolina under Colonel R. Tyler Bennett and the 30th North Carolina under Colonel Francis M. Parker in Iverson's position to the west, while the 2nd North Carolina under Major D.W. Hurtt and the 4th North Carolina under Colonel Bryan Grimes replaced O'Neal to the north. The remnants of Iverson's and O'Neal's brigades joined them. Meanwhile Baxter's brigade had left the field.

Ramseur's first assault was repulsed and the Union soldiers countercharged. The next day, eighty-one Confederate bodies were counted in front of the 94th New York's position alone. The 13th Massachusetts took 132 prisoners in a bayonet counterattack, only to find themselves surrounded. They extricated themselves at the cost of three-quarters of their men.

Paul's brigade were running short of ammunition and even General Robinson helped out collecting charges from the cartridge-boxes of the dead. Meanwhile a heavy column of Confederates were seen massing in McLean's woods. Before they could attack, the 97th New York made a swift counterattack taking eighty of Ramseur's men prisoner.

A STRANGER IN THE RANKS

John Burns was not the only civilian to join in. Lieutenant Thompson of the 16th Maine spotted a stranger standing about fifteen paces to the rear of the line, loading and firing independently. According to the regimental history:

> *Thinking the man might do mischief to his comrades, Thompson went to him, said something in his low peculiar tone, and receiving a reply, immediately knocked him down, and then raising him from the ground by the collar, kicked him rapidly to the rear, much to the merriment and satisfaction of the men, who didn't care to be shot in the back.*

The regimental history records another bizarre incident from the fray:

> *Lieutenant G.A. Deering of Company G, 16 Maine, sheathed his sword, and seized a musket from a fallen man, and went into the ranks. He was evidently excited, and every once in a while would forget to return his rammer after loading, hence would send it over to the enemy. The peculiar swishing noise made by the rammer, as it hurtled through the wood was laughable to the boys, and must have been a holy terror to the rebels.*

ATTACK EN MASSE

Ramseur then launched an attack en masse. The 14th and 30th North Carolina regiments to the west were joined by O'Neal's 3rd Alabama, while he was assisted on the right by two of Daniel's regiments – the 43rd North Carolina under Colonel T.S. Kenan and the 45th North Carolina under Lieutenant Colonel S.H. Boyd. Daniel's other two regiments moved southward to attack along the railroad cut and Stone's brigade on McPherson Ridge.

The First Brigade came under an overwhelming attack from both the north and the west. At 4:15 pm, Robinson ordered it to withdraw. But the only way for this to be done was for the 16th Maine to make a suicidal stand at the apex where the ridge met the road. They were ordered to hold this position 'at any cost.'

The 16th Maine lost 232 men killed, wounded, and missing out of the 298 who were there. The retreating survivors tore their colors into small pieces and distributed them, so they would not fall into Confederate hands. Nevertheless, their brave stand had allowed most of the brigade to escape.

Among the prisoners taken by Ramseur were Colonel Wheelock and Lieutenant Colonel Spofford of the 97th New York, but their flag was saved by Corporal James McLaren, though he was wounded. Color-Corporal Bonnin returned the flag of the 88th Pennsylvania to the regiment in the town, though he had almost collapsed from loss of blood. Although Sergeant David E. Curtis was wounded, he also carried the state flag of the 104th New York to safety, while the regiment's national flag was torn from the staff by Sergeant Moses Wallace of Company E to prevent it falling into the enemy's hands.

AWAITING THE ONSLAUGHT

While Robinson was withdrawing from Oak Ridge, Cutler moved his brigade to the railroad cut in Seminary Ridge, facing northward, ready to check Rodes' advance. Sending to the Seminary for help, he was soon joined by the 76th New York, 14th Brooklyn, and 147th New York. Awaiting the onslaught, Cutler had one horse shot from under him and another wounded.

Early in the fighting on Oak Ridge, Rodes spotted the opportunity to make an attack on Doubleday's exposed right flank on McPherson's Ridge. Daniel moved south with the 2nd and 45th North Carolina. Cutler's brigade, which had been firing on Iverson's flank, wheeled backward on Oak Ridge facing west to fire on Daniel's left.

Meanwhile enfilading fire from Hill's artillery on Herr's Ridge to the west was causing casualties among Stone's 143rd and 149th Pennsylvania, spread out along Chambersburg Pike, facing northward, with the 150th Pennsylvania along the ridge facing west. They opened fire on Daniel as soon as he came in range. He also came under fire from Cooper's battery near the Hagerstown Road, between Seminary Ridge and McPherson's Ridge.

TOO DAMAGED TO HELP

As Daniel neared the railroad cut, he saw some of Hill's men and requested their support, but they were too shattered to help. The remnants of Davis's Mississippi brigade were also too damaged to help.

So the 2nd and 45th North Carolina alone made the first charge down the railroad cut.

The 149th Pennsylvania rushed forward to the line of the cut. The Bucktails then fired a volley and charged across the cut, forcing Daniel's men over the fence to the rear. The 2nd and 45th North Carolina retreated some forty paces to the crest of the hill to regroup. Daniel then called up the 32nd, 43rd and 53rd North Carolina that had been supporting Iverson.

The 149th Pennsylvania hid in the long grass to the north of the cut with their colors twenty paces to the left of their left flank. This proved too tempting a target. Daniel's reinforced line swept forward and at a range of a little over twenty paces, the 149th delivered a volley full in the face.

THE COLORS

The Confederates were baffled. The 149th's colors had made them think that the Union regiment was more to their right. But Daniel attacked again. The 149th were also coming under heavy fire from the 32nd North Carolina and the artillery on Herr Ridge to the west and were forced to retreat. The right managed to get back across the railroad grading to the pike because the cut there was shallow. But when the left had to cross it, the sides were steep. Many were shot as they slipped down the north side, or tried to scale the cliff to the south. Others were captured in the cut itself, while the colors remained stranded to the north.

Back at the pike Colonel Roy Stone was wounded in the arm and the hip. He had to hand command of the Second Brigade to Colonel Langhorne Wister of the 150th Pennsylvania, which had joined the 143rd and what remained of the 149th on the pike.

Daniel pushed forward again in an attempt to take the 149th's colors into the face of what he said was the most destructive infantry volley he had ever seen. Despite their superior numbers, Daniel's brigade was thrown back.

In the confusion, the Confederates crept up on the 149th color guard. Sergeant Price seized the 149th's national flag and made off to the Confederate line. The color guard recovered quickly and shot down every one of the retreating Confederates except Price.

Seeing Price, covered in dust, running forward with the Union flag, a Confederate officer dismounted, grabbed up a musket from a dying man, and shot at him. Luckily for Price, he missed.

DISCOLORING THE SKIN

At the pike, the 150th Pennsylvania were coming under heavy fire from the Confederate batteries. A shell grazed the chest of Sergeant Major Lyon which, according to the regimental history, 'tore away his clothing, discoloring the skin and causing intense pain, but without lacerating the flesh in the slightest.'

Colonel Wister was shot in the face. The ball passed through his mouth which, while not completely disabling him, made it impossible for him to give verbal orders, so command was passed to Colonel Edmund L. Dana of the 143rd Pennsylvania. When Stone's Bucktails withdrew, Wister was captured, but he managed to escape later.

The commander of the 149th, Lieutenant Colonel Walton Dwight was wounded, while the commander of the 150th, Lieutenant Colonel Henry S. Huidekoper, was hit in both the arm and the leg. He went to the stone-basement barn to have his wounds tended, but when he came back to the regiment he was too weak from loss of blood to continue in command and retired from the field. Major Thomas Chamberlain took over, but he too was wounded, as was his successor Adjutant R.L. Ashhurst, though he stayed on the field. He was standing beside First Sergeant Weidensaul of Company D when he suddenly doubled over, clutching his body as if in agony.

'Are you wounded?' asked Ashhurst.

'No, killed,' the sergeant replied.

ALL-OUT ASSAULT

Though he had been repulsed several times now, Daniel ordered another all-out assault. He was reinforced by the 12th North Carolina that had escaped Baxter's onslaught under a white flag, along with Davis's remnants. They pushed forward across the cut under the steady, but waning, fire of the 143rd and 149th Pennsylvania along the pike.

The 150th were being attacked from the west by a fresh brigade of Major General Dorsey Pender's Third Division that had followed Heth's Second Division from Cashtown. Another brigade of the newly arrived division was outflanking it.

Seeing the Union reinforcements arrive, Daniel's men let out 'a chorus of yelps.' Nevertheless, the 150th's flag-bearer Sergeant Phifer 'fell bleeding from a mortal wound, while proudly flaunting the colors in the face of the foe.' What remained of Stone's brigade were now forced to withdraw to Seminary Ridge, firing as they went. After an initial repulse, the 32nd North Carolina moved in and cleared the area around McPherson's stone-basement barn.

SWEARING ETERNAL VENGEANCE

When Ashhurst received the order to fall back, Lieutenant Bell came up to him and accused him of 'damned cowardice.' However they had no choice but to fall back or be annihilated.

As the 150th Pennsylvania fell back, they fought as they went. At one position in the field, the pursuing Confederates found fifty dead in a straight line. The 142nd Pennsylvania's beloved commander Colonel Robert P. Cummins was killed. An eyewitness said:

Three or four of the remnant of the column ... faithful to their old commander, endeavored to carry his lifeless body along; but the enemy was too close. Several of the boys were shot dead while trying to perform this solemn duty. One was left, and seeing the impossibility to accomplish this purpose himself, he unbuckled the colonel's belt and came off the field, swinging the colonel's sword, not, however, escaping being wounded; for, as he passed by me the blood was streaming out of his mouth, and the tears down his cheeks. But with the courage of an infuriated lion, he was swearing eternal vengeance on our enemies.

As Color-Sergeant Ben Crippen of the 143rd Pennsylvania retreated to Seminary Hill, he turned around several times and shook his fist at the Confederates, before he fell mortally wounded. Seeing the flag fall, Major Conyngham shouted: '143rd rally your colors!' They were seized and raised. Watching this Confederate General A.P. Hill said he was sorry to see such a gallant man as Crippen meet his doom.

FULFILLED THEIR PURPOSE

At 3:15 pm, Major General Daniel E. Sickles informed Meade and Howard that his Third Corps were now moving towards Gettysburg. A quarter of an hour later, Howard ordered the First and Eleventh Corps to Cemetery Hill. They had fulfilled their purpose, which was to hold the Confederates back until the bulk of the Union Army could occupy the heights to the south of the town. However, the order did not get through to Doubleday who fought on to the west of the town in the vain hope of reinforcements.

Five minutes after issuing the order to withdraw, Howard got more good news. A dispatch from Major General Henry W. Slocum arrived, telling him: 'I am moving the Twelfth Corps so as to come in about one mile to the right of Gettysburg.'

Cemetery Hill was at the junction of the road these two corps were coming up. Until then, the Union forces had been outnumbered. The numerical balance was now about to tip in their favor.

AUDACIOUS MOVE

While Doubleday continued to hold on to the west of the town, a company of the 80th New York from Biddle's brigade under Captain Ambrose N. Baldwin, crossed Willoughby Run and advanced 165 yards to clear a small force of Confederates out from Harman's farm buildings. They were quickly reinforced by a second Union company under Captain William H. Cunningham.

This audacious move led the Confederates to overestimate the number of Union troops that were defending McPherson's Ridge. Union troops continued to occupy the Harman Farm for the rest of the afternoon.

Meanwhile the Confederate artillery built a considerable superiority over the Union's, forcing Battery A of the 2nd United States Artillery under Lieutenant John H. Calef to pull back his six three-inch rifles from their position straddling the pike on the western crest of McPherson's Ridge. Cooper's battery, which had been supporting Biddle's brigade, from the eastern crest of the ridge, south of the grove, to the professor's house near the Seminary, became involved in an artillery duel with Fry's battery on Oak Hill. Then they engaged with The Letcher Artillery under Captain T.A. Brander, whose two Napoleons and two ten-pounder Parrotts were now on a hill to the north of the railway cut, on the east side of Willoughby Run. As a result Doubleday's men were robbed of artillery support. On foot, they also faced superior numbers.

WITHIN RANGE

After a heavy bombardment, Heth ordered Pettigrew and Brockenbrough across Willoughby Run. While Brockenbrough joined the attack on Stone's Bucktails, Pettigrew went after the Iron Brigade in the woods and Biddle's brigade in the woods toward the Hagerstown Road. As his men crossed the run and moved up the slope, they came within range of Union muskets.

Near the top of the ridge, Pettigrew found Meredith's Iron Brigade in the grove. He attacked the southernmost regiment, the 19th Indiana, pushing them back to expose the left flank of the 24th Michigan. It was their 'maiden battle.' They waited until the enemy was within eight paces before opening fire. Under a murderous response, they managed to turn their front to the left.

They were so close, the soldiers could hear the shouted orders of their opponent's officers.

'Give 'em hell boy!' yelled a Confederate colonel mounted on a mule. A Union bullet knocked off his hat. He caught the hat before it hit the ground and returned to urging on his men.

Despite their bravery, the previous unblooded 24th Michigan lost 363 out of the 496 men engaged.

Meade (center) and his staff at Culpeper, Virginia, 1863. Photograph by Timothy H. O'Sullivan.

THE MINIÉ BALL

The Minié ball is not a ball, but a short, cylindrical, soft-lead bullet with a conical point. It was designed by Captain Claude-Étienne Minié of the French Army and later improved in the US. Previously, due to the rifling groove in the barrel it was hard to force a snug-fitting bullet home. Often a wooden mallet had to be used, making reloading slow. Burnt powder would also build up in the barrel and cleaning it out would cause further delays.

However, the diameter of the Minié was smaller than that of the barrel, so loading was quick and easy. It came in a paper cartridge with the gunpowder, which was poured down the barrel first. The Minié was then pushed passed the rifling and any detritus from previous shots.

The secret of the Minié ball was that it had a conical cavity in its base. When it was rammed home, this filled with gunpowder. Then, when the gun was fired, the gunpowder exploded, distorting the bullet and pushing the edges of the cavity outward to make it fit tightly against the walls of the barrel.

The expanding gases from the gunpowder would force the bullet, sealed against the walls, up the barrel, cleaning out the detritus as it went. The seal gave the bullet a higher muzzle velocity, hence a longer range. The deformation of the bullet also helped it engage with the rifling groove, spinning the bullet for greater accuracy. This gave it a characteristic whizzing sound which you heard if it missed you.

Minié balls were more deadly than round balls from smoothbore muskets, due to their higher muzzle velocity and greater weight. Round balls tended to lodge in the flesh, or deflect. Minié rounds went straight through, hitting vital organs or shattering bones, resulting in the amputation of an arm or leg.

.58 Caliber Minié ball lead bullets with a flask of gunpowder.

SCHOOLTEACHER'S REGIMENT

As Pettigrew's 26th North Carolina approached Biddle's line, it suffered a flanking attack from the 19th Indiana, as well a few salvoes from Cooper's battery. The Tarheelers were within twenty paces of the 151st Pennsylvania line when both sides opened fire. According to the Pennsylvanian's regimental history, this produced 'losses the most remarkable in the annals of war!'

The 151st Pennsylvania lost 337 out of the 467 engaged. This was the so-called 'Schoolteacher's Regiment,' comprising teachers and schoolboys from Juniata County. Its commander, Lieutenant George I. MacFarland, was the superintendent of the local academy. He lost one leg and was hopelessly maimed in the other.

On other side, the 26th North Carolina lost 588 out of 800 – Southern regiments tended to be bigger than Northern ones. This was the heaviest loss in the Army of Northern Virginia during the entire campaign. In Company F, thirty-nine of the eight officers and thirty-one men were dead, and every man in the company had been hit by a bullet, except one who had been knocked out by the explosion of a shell while they were crossing the run. Eleven men were shot down while holding the colors. There were three sets of twins in the regiment. By the end of the action, five of the six were dead.

When the Confederates eventually occupied the 151st position Heth said: 'The dead of the enemy marked its line with the accuracy of a dress parade.' But, for the moment, though heavily outnumbered, the Union line held, though the Confederates, who were out of ammunition, managed to replenish their supplies from the Pennsylvanian dead.

ORDERED TO RETIRE

Brockenbrough's advance was hindered by a small quarry. His brigade swung south towards Meredith's Iron Brigade in the woods. The Confederate's first charge was repulsed. But the Iron Brigade pulled back two hundred yards to get in line with Biddle's brigade.

Despite stubborn Union resistance, renewed Confederate attacks forced them back. The Rebel soldiers were fresh, while the Union troops had been in the fray all day. When ordered to retire to Seminary Ridge, the 7th Wisconsin did so slowly and deliberately, reloading and firing step by step.

During the 24th Michigan's retreat, they stopped and formed three lines of battle within the grove, two more on the fields between the grove and the ridge, and a sixth on Seminary Ridge itself.

As they crossed the five-hundred yards of open field between McPherson Ridge and Seminary Ridge, the last member of the color-guard was killed and their commander Colonel Henry A. Morrow seized the flag. It was immediately grabbed from his hand by Private William Kelly of Company E, who said: 'The colonel of the 24th Michigan shall not carry the colors while I am alive.'

An instant later, Private Kelly fell dead. Colonel Morrow took them again, only relinquishing them when they reached the comparative safety of Seminary Ridge, where he himself was wounded in the head.

The 19th Indiana also lost their eighth color-bearer. Lieutenant Colonel W.W. Dudley picked up the flag. Waving it with a cheer, he fell, shot in the right leg.

ENFILADING FIRE

Pettigrew's rightmost regiment, the 52nd North Carolina, outflanked Biddle's left and laid down devastating enfilading fire. The 121st Pennsylvania managed to turn to the left to face them. It did little good as they now had the 47th North Carolina, to the 52nd's left, to their right.

Colonel Biddle's horse was shot out from under him, while Biddle himself received a slight scalp wound from a Minié ball. Colonel Gates of the 80th New York was the only officer who remained on horseback. He carried the colors as he led his men back to Seminary Ridge.

During this action, Pettigrew's men suffered further losses. One company of the 11th North Carolina lost two officers and the thirty-one men out of three officers and thirty-five men. When they went into action again on the third day of the battle, they lost a further three men, leaving just two out of the entire company.

THE FIRST DAY AT GETTYSBURG
BY JAMES ALEXANDER WALKER

A troop of North Carolinians attack the Union line during the first day of the battle. More significant than simply a prelude to the bloody second and third days – about one quarter of Meade's army (22,000 men) and one third of Lee's army (27,000) were engaged. Union casualties were almost 9,000, Confederate slightly more than 6,000.

CHAPTER 4
COUNTING THE TERRIBLE COST

The entire Union First Corp had now been forced back to Seminary Ridge, but at a terrible cost to the Confederates. Heth had been hit in the head, but his life had been saved by a wad of paper tucked inside the sweatband to keep his oversized hat in place. Pender has been mortally wounded and replaced on the field by Brigadier General James H. Lane.

Still not having received orders to withdraw, Doubleday again sent for reinforcements. This time he dispatched his adjutant general, Major E.P. Halstead. But when Halstead told Howard that Pender's lines were approaching, he was told he must have 'mistaken rail fences for troops at a distance' and sent him to find Buford to ask for cavalry support.

With Pender's division in the field, Doubleday was now seriously outnumbered. At around 4:00 pm, he reformed his lines in relatively strong defensive positions along the ridge. They were joined by Buford's dismounted cavalrymen on the left. Their carbine fire held off the Confederate right. Though they inflicted few casualties Lane was forced to form his men into squares in case there was a cavalry charge.

At Seminary Ridge there is about six hundred yards between the Chambersburg Pike and Hagerstown Road, with the Seminary midway between them. There were twenty artillery pieces ready to open up on the advancing Confederates.

15 MINUTES TO PREPARE

Doubleday's men only had 15 minutes to prepare themselves before Pender's four fresh brigades were upon them.

When Pender's brigades, now under the command of Brigadier General Alfred M. Scales, were around eighty yards away, the six Napoleons of Battery B of the 4th US Artillery under Lieutenant James Stewart, either side of the railroad cut to the north, fired canister into the lines of gray-coats. The guns were far enough to the right to give enfilading fire as the Confederates climbed the slope. The effect was murderous. Even General Scales was wounded in the leg and handed command to Lieutenant Colonel George T. Gordon of the 34th North Carolina. Only one field officer was left standing, and of the 1,250 that had gone into battle only five hundred answered roll call that evening.

An aide, giving orders for the 14th Brooklyn who were supporting Stewart's battery, raised his hand to point to their new position. As he did so, it was shot off by a shell zeroed in on the Union position.

> # The muskets grew hot in our hands, and the darkness ... settled upon us.

Doubleday threw his own headquarters' guard into the fray. The firing was so furious that one soldier said the muskets 'grew hot in our hands, and the darkness [from the clouds of smoke], as of night, had settled upon us.'

CRIPPLING LOSSES

Despite their crippling losses, the Confederates reformed and attacked again. Although his arm had practically been ripped from the socket by a shell, the color-bearer of the 13th North Carolina, W.F. Faucette of Big Falls, held high the flag with his left hand, while the tatters of his right hand hung by his side, and shouted: 'Forward! Forward!'

At the Seminary, Colonel Gates of the 80th New York fell, the horse under him hit five times. Colonel McFarland of the 151st Pennsylvania was shot through both legs as his horse was shot from under him. Captain Owens assumed command of the 151st, while McFarland was taken to the Seminary that served as a field hospital for both sides.

The hastily constructed breastwork fortification on the Union's left came under attack by the First Brigade under Colonel Abner M. Perrin. Only one soldier – a color-bearer – reached the Union entrenchment. They were under fire from Cooper's battery. Though reduced in number, Biddle's men fired volleys which Perrin described as 'the most destructive fire I have ever been exposed to.'

DISMOUNTED CAVALRY

To Perrin's right, the Second Battalion, attacking through the woods to the south of Hagerstown Road, were still held up by Gamble's dismounted cavalry who had taken cover behind a stone wall.

Despite having no support to the right or the left, two of Perrin's regiments – the 1st and 14th South Carolina – managed to breach the Union line just south of the Seminary. They broke through and poured heavy enfilading fire down the Union lines, despite flanking fired from Gamble's cavalry.

CARE OF THE WOUNDED

The fate of the Union wounded left behind on Seminary Ridge was not a happy one. After all, the Confederates were still busy fighting and had their own wounded to attend to. The regimental history of the 88th Pennsylvania records the words of an eyewitness:

Many received an additional wound lying on the field, and relief did not come for several days and nights, nor until the maggots began to crawl and fatten in their festering wounds ... Last night the Colonel visited the scene of the conflict and brought in some of the wounded who had lain there three days with no care except what the rebels bestowed, who gave them water and treated them well. They, however, stripped and robbed the bodies of the dead who still lie there so bloated as to be unrecognizable.

Orderly Sergeant Henry Cliff of Company F, 76th New York, formerly of the British Army and discharged for being under age, fell early in the action. Unable to move, he asked a Confederate soldier to move him out of the blazing sun into the shade of a nearby tree. The embittered Rebel said: 'I shan't do it. Get some of your damned Yankee horde to help you. If you had been at home, where you belonged, instead of fighting for the damned nigger, you would not have needed any help!'

The seventeen-year-old sergeant remained on that spot, unable to stir, with nothing to eat or drink, for fifty-two hours, until the rebels retreated, when he was removed to a hospital and his limb amputated. His commanding officer, now Lieutenant Colonel Cook, recommended him for promotion to First Lieutenant. President Lincoln approved the commission, but it was not taken up as Cliff had already been discharged.

Tending and treating wounded Union soldiers.

Biddle's position was now untenable and, after an initial check, the 12th and 13th South Carolina managed to drive Gamble's cavalry men out from behind their stone wall. Now Doubleday had no choice but to withdraw.

HIT IN THE HEAD

Colonel Morrow of the 24th Michigan was waving the regimental flag aloft in a last effort to rally his men, when he was hit in the head. He was captured, but managed to escape by donning the green scarf of the Medical Corps and pretending to be a surgeon.

On the Union right, Cutler's brigade with the 6th Wisconsin of the Iron Brigade and the right section of Stewart's battery were holding back Daniel, Ramseur, and O'Neal long enough to extricate themselves and escape up the railroad fill.

Stewart's horses had been killed and several of his guns were hauled over the ridge with ropes by the 14th Brooklyn. All the guns were retrieved, except for one in Lieutenant Wilber's section of Reynold's battery which had to be abandoned when they had no time to cut the four dead horses from their harnesses.

A number of Union prisoners were taken before the order to pull back got through and the wounded had to be left to the hands of the Confederates. The rest scurried down the eastern slope of Seminary Ridge in a near rout, though some retired in good order, marching at a steady pace making for Cemetery Hill and stopping to shoot at their pursuers on the way. The 6th Wisconsin found time to turn and give 'three cheers for the Old Flag and the 6th Wisconsin.'

Chaplain Horatio S. Howell

On the steps of the Christ Lutheran Church at 44 Chambersburg Street there is a monument to Chaplain Horatio S. Howell of the 90th Pennsylvania who was 'cruelly shot' on that spot, it is said. Sergeant Archibald B. Snow of the 97th New York, who had been shot in the jaw and attended at the field hospital there, believed that Howell was shot because he was in a dress uniform very similar to that of a Union officer. He retold the story:

I had just had my wound dressed and was leaving through the front door just behind Chaplain Howell, at the same time when the advance skirmishers of the Confederates were coming up the street on a run. Howell, in addition to his shoulder straps and uniform, wore the straight dress sword prescribed in Army Regulations for chaplains, but which was very seldom worn by them. The first skirmisher arrived at the foot of the church steps just as the chaplain and I came out. Placing one foot on the first step the soldier called on the chaplain to surrender; but Howell, instead of throwing up his hands promptly and uttering the usual 'I surrender,' attempted some dignified explanation to the effect that he was a noncombatant and as such was exempt from capture, when a shot from the skirmisher's rifle ended the controversy. A Confederate lieutenant, who came up at this time, placed a guard at the church door, and, to the protests of the surgeons against shooting the chaplain, replied that the dead officer was armed, in proof of which he pointed to the chaplain's sash, and light, rapier-like sword belted around the chaplain's body.

The man who fired the shot stood on the exact spot where the memorial tablet has since been erected. Chaplain Howell fell upon the landing at the top of the steps. The man who had killed him was then left on sentry duty there.

THE FLAG OF THE 150TH PENNSYLVANIA

After the entire color-guard of the 150th Pennsylvania had been killed or wounded, Corporal Joseph Gutelius of Company D seized the flag and fled with it. In the town, he stopped for a rest on a doorstep at South Washington and West High streets, where he was shot by pursuing Confederates. The flag was taken by Lieutenant F.M. Harvey of the 14th North Carolina Infantry Regiment who was shot and mortally wounded shortly afterwards.

His dying request was for the captured flag to be given to Confederate President Jefferson Davis.

This was arranged by North Carolina's Governor Zebulon Vance. When Union cavalry captured Jefferson Davis near Milledgeville, Georgia in May 1865, the flag of the 150th Pennsylvania Infantry Regiment was found carefully packed in his baggage. The flag was taken back to Washington, DC, and placed in the War Department collection where it remained until it was released to the Commonwealth of Pennsylvania in 1869 and placed in that state's collection of Civil War flags.

Belle Plain, Virginia. Camp of the 150th Pennsylvania Infantry, 1863.

UP ON CEMETERY HILL

The Eleventh Corps knew where Cemetery Hill was because they had come in that way earlier in the day, but the First Corps had cut across the fields from the Emmitsburg Road and by-passed it.

The men on the southern part of Seminary Ridge retreated down the Hagerstown Road into the southern outskirts of the town. The rest came down the Chambersburg Pike into the center of town, where the Confederates pursuing the Eleventh Corps awaited them.

In the town there was a scene of terrible confusion. Canister swept the streets. Union soldiers would be running down one street to find Confederates rushing from a side street, piercing the air with their rebel yells. They set up an ambush and shouted: 'Come in here, you Yankee sons of bitches!'

On the whole, the town was not badly damaged, although there were some injuries from falling masonry. Only one of the townsfolk was killed and that was on the third day of the battle. Pretty twenty-year-old Jennie Wade was cooking bread in the kitchen of her sister's house on Baltimore Street when she was shot though the heart by a Minié ball that had passed through two doors. It was also recorded by a Union soldier that when they pulled back to Cemetery Hill 'one pale and frightened woman came out and offered us coffee and food, and implored us to not abandon them.'

Some three thousand Union soldiers were taken prisoner in the town. The remnants of the 45th New York were trapped in a blind alley. Fourteen officers and 164 men were captured. Elsewhere trapped soldiers threw their muskets down a well to prevent them falling into the hands of the enemy. A 'chubby boy of sixteen' with a Georgia regiment named George Greer rounded up fifty demoralized Union prisoners. But others managed to escape, climbing fences and crossing backyards, or storming through shops and homes.

General Schimmelfennig dived under a woodpile and pulled the logs over him. He lay there in a cramped position for two days and nights until the enemy left.

FIELD HOSPITALS

Many of the houses and all of the churches in Gettysburg were turned into temporary field hospitals. Terribly wounded Private Little of the 88th Pennsylvania was told he was going to die. According to the regimental history:

General Hospital, Gettysburg.

Colonel Wheelock's Sword

Colonel Charles Wheelock of the 97th New York took refuge in the Sheads' house, a seminary for girls on Buford Avenue and Chambersburg Pike. According to a Washington newspaper:

Standing in a vortex of fire, from front, rear, and both flanks, encouraging his men to fight with the naked bayonet, hoping to force a passage through the walls of steel which surrounded him. Finding all his efforts in vain, he ascended the steps of the seminary, and waved a white pocket handkerchief in token of surrender. The rebels, not seeing it, or taking no notice of it, continued to pour their murderous volleys into the helpless ranks. The colonel then opened the door, and called for a large white cloth. Carrie Sheads stood there, and readily supplied him with one.

When the rebels saw his token of surrender they ceased firing, and the colonel went into the basement to rest himself, for he was thoroughly exhausted. Soon a rebel officer came in, with a detail of men, and, on entering, declared, with an oath, that he would show them 'southern grit.' He then began taking the officers' side arms.

Seeing Colonel Wheelock vainly endeavoring to break his sword, which was of trusty metal, and resisted all his efforts, the rebel demanded the weapon; but the colonel was of the same temper as his sword, and turning to the rebel soldier, declared he would never surrender his sword to a traitor while he lived.

The rebel then drew a revolver, and told him if he did not surrender his sword he would shoot him. But the colonel was a veteran, and had been in close places before. Drawing himself up proudly, he tore open his uniform, and still grasping his well-tried blade, bared his bosom, and bade the rebel 'shoot,' but he would guard his sword with his life. At this moment, Elias Sheads, Carrie's father, stepped between the two, and begged them not to be rash; but he was soon pushed aside, and the rebel repeated his threat. Seeing the danger to which the colonel was exposed, Miss Sheads, true to the instincts of her sex, rushed between them, and besought the rebel not to kill a man so completely in his power, there was already enough blood shed, and why add another defenseless victim to the list? Then turning to the colonel, she pleaded with him not to be so rash, but to surrender his sword, and save his life; that by refusing he would lose both, and the government would lose a valuable officer. But the colonel still refused, saying, 'This sword was given me by my friends for meritorious conduct, and I promised to guard it sacredly, and never surrender or disgrace it; and I never will while I live.'

Fortunately, at this moment the attention of the rebel officer was drawn away for the time by the entrance of other prisoners, and while he was thus occupied Miss Sheads, seizing the favorable opportunity, with admirable presence of mind unclasped the colonel's sword from his belt, and hid it in the folds of her dress. When the rebel officer returned, the colonel told him he was willing to surrender, and that one of his men had taken his sword and passed out. This artifice succeeded, and the colonel 'fell in' with the other prisoners, who were drawn up in line to march to the rear, and thence to some one of the loathsome southern prison pens, many of them to meet a terrible death, and fill an unknown grave.

When the prisoners had all been collected, and were about starting, Miss Sheads, remembering the wounded men in the house, turned to the rebel officer, and told him that there were seventy-two wounded men in the building, and asked him if he would not leave some of the prisoners to help take care of them. The officer replied that he had already left three. 'But,' said Miss Sheads, 'three are not sufficient.' 'Then keep five, and select those you want, except commissioned officers,' was the rebel's unexpected reply.

On the fifth day after the battle, Colonel Wheelock unexpectedly made his appearance, and received his sword from the hands of its noble guardian, with those profound emotions which only the soldier can feel and understand, and, with the sacred blade again in his possession, started at once to the front, where he won for himself new laurels, and was promoted to the rank of a Brigadier General. He had managed to effect his escape from the rebels while crossing South Mountain, and, after considerable difficulty and suffering, succeeded in reaching Gettysburg in safety.

General Wheelock finally died of camp fever, in Washington City, in January 1865.

When the surgeon examined Little's wound he pronounced it mortal, saying that he would not live two hours. On hearing this the wounded man flared up in unrighteous indignation, and swore by many strange oaths that he would not die just yet, but would outlive the surgeon, which prediction, notwithstanding his horrible wound, he lived to verify.

Many of the wounded, especially those of the Union, received scant treatment. A Union lieutenant said they were simply left 'lying uncared for on the field, suffering untold agony from their festering wounds.' He then went over to the McPherson barn on the Chambersburg Pike, which had been used as a hospital by both sides. There, according to regimental history of the 88th Pennsylvania:

The most distressing cases of suffering met his sight, the barn being filled with helpless soldiers, torn and mangled, who in the heat of the fight had been carried there by their comrades and had lain since without care or attention of any kind ... Their lacerated limbs were frightfully swollen and, turning black, had begun to decompose. The blood flowing from gaping wounds had glued some of the sufferers to the floor.

The officer tore up his own underclothes to bandage some of the men.

PRIVATE BATTLES

Brigadier General John B. Gordon's Georgia brigade suffered remarkably light casualties. When they marched into town, a young Southern officer shouted out: 'General, where are your dead?'

From the back of his magnificent steed, the general replied: 'I haven't any, sir. The Almighty has covered my men with his shield and buckler.'

Private battles ensued. When a Union prisoner of Irish descent was brought in, a Confederate gunner who was also an Irishman mocked him for his ill-fortune. One was an Orangemen, the other sported the green. The result was a bout of fisticuffs. A Confederate onlooker noted that the Union prisoner's right hand had two bloody stumps where the fingers had been blown off during the day's fighting. When this was pointed out to the Confederate combatant, he dropped his fists and shook hands with his adversary.

The Union had taken prisoners too. One Confederate captive named Schwarz was greeted by his brother, who wore blue. They embraced each other there and then.

Despite the large number of prisoners taken and the heavy casualties, most of the First and Eleventh Corps made it to Cemetery Hill. After witnessing the Union retreat, Lee sent word to Ewell to take Cemetery Hill and Culp's Hill next to it, 'if practicable.' But Lee did not ride with any great dispatch towards the battlefield and Hill complained that his troops were exhausted.

A VERY WELCOME SIGHT

When the Union stragglers reached Cemetery Hill, they were greeted by a very welcome sight – a reserve brigade under Colonel Orland Smith and Captain Michael Wiedrich's New York battery of six three-inch rifles. They were in place around 5:00 pm. The First Division were assembled on the left in the Citizens' Evergreen Cemetery, with the Eleventh Division on East Cemetery Hill, the highest part of the elevation, to the east of the Baltimore Pike. The remains of Buford's division formed up near the Emmitsburg Road, awaiting a Confederate attack.

'The splendid spectacle of that gallant cavalry as it stood there, unshaken and undaunted, was one of the most inspiring sights of my military experience,' said General Winfield S. Hancock.

Traversing the town had left the Confederate units confused too. They had suffered unexpectedly high casualties particularly due to the tenacity of Doubleday. It had been a hot and humid day. Even Lee conceded that his troopers were too weakened and exhausted to attack 'the strong position that the enemy had assumed.' He set up his headquarters in the apple orchard between the Seminary building and Chambersburg Pike.

Meade had still been expecting to fall back to Pipe Creek in Maryland when he sent General Hancock forward to Gettysburg after he heard of the death of Reynolds. Meade's chief of staff, Major General Daniel Butterfield told Hancock: 'If you think the ground and position there are a better one to fight a battle under existing circumstances, you will so advise the general, and he will order all the troops up.'

SABERS IN THE CIVIL WAR

UNION SABERS

Every Union mounted soldier had a saber. The most common was the 1840 model, a heavy saber known as the 'wrist breaker.' A lighter version was introduced in 1860. Both followed a French design with a gently curved blade and a brass hand guard. The handle has a leather grip bound to it with twisted wire. A leather strap, or sword knot, attached to the hand guard was wrapped around the wrist so the sword would not be dropped in action. Scabbards were made of iron and often covered in leather or fabric.

At the start of the war, most sabers were blunt and were used to bludgeon the enemy rather than cut them. By the Gettysburg campaign, they were sharpened. But as cavalry charges were rare, most cavalry attached their sabers to their saddles, so they would hamper them when dismounted.

CONFEDERATE SABERS

The Confederate saber was a crude copy of the Union 'wrist-breaker.' Jeb Stuart was a fan of the saber and the old-fashioned cavalry charge. One of his officers said: 'Dismounted fighting was never popular with the Southern trooper, who felt he was only half a man when separated from his horse.'

Others were not so keen. Stuart's friend and his scout during the Gettysburg campaign Major John S. Mosby said: 'We had been furnished with sabers before we left Abingdon but the only real use I ever heard of their being put to was to hold a piece of meat over the fire for frying. I dragged one through the first year, but when I became a commander I discarded it ... the saber is of no use against gunpowder.'

Riding with Longstreet's Corps, British observer Lieutenant Colonel Arthur Fremantle said: 'They wear swords, but seem to have little idea of using them – they constantly ride with their sword between their left leg and the saddle which has a very funny appearance; but their horses are generally good, and they ride well.'

(Left) An unidentified Union soldier with saber and scabbard. (Right) A young soldier in Confederate uniform with saber.

GENERAL HANCOCK TAKES COMMAND

Hancock traveled in an ambulance so he could study maps of the area. He arrived on the field at 4:30 pm, just as the last of the retreating First and Eleventh Corps were getting there.

He and Howard then discussed who was in charge. Hancock said that Meade had instructed him to take command of all forces in the field, which Howard maintained that he was the senior of the two. They decided to work side-by-side.

The appearance of Hancock did a lot to raise morale. He saw to it that the men were well dug in, in good defensive positions. With the arrival of the Army of the Potomac's chief engineer, Major General Gouverneur K. Warren, Culp's Hill was also occupied by Wadsworth's men to guard the Union's right flank.

At 5:25 pm Hancock sent a communiqué to Meade, saying:

When I arrived here an hour since, I found that our troops had given up the front of Gettysburg and the town. We have now taken up a position in the cemetery, and cannot well be taken. It is a position, however, easily turned. Slocum is now coming on the ground, and is taking position on the right, which will protect the right. But we have, as yet, no troops on the left, the Third Corps not having yet reported; but I suppose that it is marching up. If so, its flank march will in a degree protect our left flank. In the meantime Gibbon had better march on so as to take position on our right or left, to our rear, as may be necessary, in some commanding position ... The battle is quiet now. I think we will be all right until night. I have sent all the trains back. When night comes, it can be told better what had best be done. I think we can retire; if not, we can fight here, as the ground appears not unfavorable with good troops. I will communicate in a few moments with General Slocum, and transfer the command to him.

PICKET LINE

The 7th Indiana of Cutler's brigade, who had been on wagon train duty during the day and were still fresh, provided a picket line for Wadsworth's division.

Skirmishers from the Eleventh Corps occupied the second floors of the houses on the southern outskirts of the town to discourage Confederate reconnaissance parties. It is thought that one of them put a Minié ball in Ewell's wooden leg.

General 'Extra Billy' Smith reported to Jubal Early that Union reinforcements were approaching down the York Pike. By 5:00 pm, Brigadier General John W. Geary's Second Division of the Twelfth Corps and units of Brigadier General Thomas H. Ruger's First Division, including the 5th and 20th Connecticut, were one and a half miles east of Gettysburg. This immediately tied down a large Confederate force, making any attack on Cemetery Hill that night impossible.

Brigadier General Alpheus S. Williams assumed command of the Twelfth Corps. When Slocum arrived at 6:30 pm, he assumed overall command as he outranked both Howard and Hancock, until Meade arrived hours later.

PAPER COLLAR BRIGADE

Sickles' Third Corps arrived on the field at around the same time as the Twelfth. At dusk Brigadier General George J. Stannard's Third Brigade of the Third Division, First Corps arrived – this was the so-called 'Paper Collar Brigade' because they had only enlisted for nine months and their uniforms looked nice and clean. Hancock's own Second Division arrived at nightfall at the Round Tops to the rear.

The weary and bloodied soldiers of the First and Eleventh Corps were delighted to see what appeared to be the whole Army of the Potomac riding to their rescue.

'We made hideous by our yells of joy because of their opportune arrival,' said one of the 142nd New York regiment which had started the day with sixteen officers and 320 men and could, by then, only muster three officers and seventy-five men.

MEADE'S CHOICE

Even before the arrival of Hancock's note, Meade's choice had been made for him.

'It seems to me,' he said, 'that we have so concentrated that a battle at Gettysburg is now forced on us, and that if we can get up our people and attack with our whole force tomorrow we ought to defeat the force the enemy has.'

TELEGRAPHY AND SAMUEL MORSE

Messages from General Meade to Henry W. Halleck, General-in-Chief of all the Union armies, in Washington, DC, were taken by courier to the nearest telegraph station, then sent by wire to the capital.

The idea of sending messages this way had started with the discovery of electricity, but the first commercial system was developed in 1837 in England by Sir William Fothergill Cooke and Sir Charles Wheatstone for use on the new railroad between London and Birmingham. It used six wires and five needles that pointed to letters. However, Samuel F.B.

Morse, professor of painting and sculpture at the University of the City of New York (later New York University), had already developed a system of dots and dashes that represented letters and numbers. It became known as Morse code.

In 1837, Morse was granted a patent for the telegraphic system using his code, which he developed with the engineer Alfred Vail. The advantage of this system was that only one wire was needed. The message was keyed in using a simple switch that would make and break the contact between a battery and the transmitting wire. At first, at the receiver, the dots and dashes were embossed on a strip of paper that passed under a stylus. Later sound was used, with trained operators writing out the message in longhand.

In 1843, the US government gave Morse the money to build a telegraph line along the railroad from Washington to Baltimore. It was completed the following year and the first message sent on it was: 'What hath God wrought!'

The telegraph system spread with the railroad and, by 1851, there were more than fifty telegraph companies in the US. A number merged to form the Western Union Telegraph Company in 1856. Five years later, the first transcontinental telegraph line was completed, putting an end to the Pony Express.

During the Battle of Gettysburg, President Lincoln spent many hours in the military telegraph office in Washington, monitoring the news from the front.

The telegraph was also needed by reporters, but Jeb Stuart's cavalry had torn down the wires east of Hanover. Homer Byington of the *New York Tribune* bribed a telegrapher and hired some workmen to replace the five-miles of wire that had been cut down. Plied with money from the paper, the crew agreed that repaired section would be reserved exclusively by the *Tribune* and the *Philadelphia Press*. Byington then rode to the battlefield, returned that evening, and sent his story through to New York.

Samuel Morse with his invention the telegraph.

He sent a telegram to Henry W. Halleck, General-in-Chief of all the Union armies, in Washington, saying: 'A.P. Hill and Ewell are certainly concentrating; Longstreet's whereabouts I do not know. If he is not up tomorrow, I hope with the force I have concentrated to defeat Hill and Ewell. At any rate, I see no other course than to hazard a general battle.'

Halleck responded at 9:15 pm, saying:

Your tactical arrangements for battle seem good, so far as I can judge from my knowledge of the character of the country; but in a strategic view are you not too far east, and may not Lee attempt to turn your left and cut you off from Frederick? Please give your full attention to this suggestion …

The combatants were now assembled. The next day, they knew, there would be a great battle. Men sang hymns. Others tried to snatch some sleep, maybe for the last time on this earth.

To the north and west of the town the lanterns of the Confederate ambulances could be seen and the surgeons scoured the heaps of dead and wounded to find men they could help.

MOONLIGHT AND TOMBSTONES

Hancock had left Gettysburg at dusk, returning to Taneytown to discuss the situation with Meade. The commander of the Union army, then mounted his horse and rode toward Gettysburg. Along the way, around 11:00 pm, he stopped at the headquarters of Brigadier General John Gibbon, commanding the Second Corps. Meade told Gibbon that, if the Confederates attacked, the entire Army of the Potomac would be thrown into battle at Gettysburg. Then Meade rode on for his meeting with destiny.

When he arrived at Cemetery Hill at around 1:00 am on the morning of July 2, 1863, the moonlight was reflecting off the tombstones. Under the tall pines that surrounded the cemetery he had a meeting with Slocum, Sickles, Howard, Warren, and other officers. He asked each of them if Cemetery Ridge was a suitable place for a major battle. Each said it was.

'I am glad to hear you say so, gentlemen,' he said. 'I have already ordered the other corps to concentrate here and it is too late to change.'

He then inspected the lines, confident that he had chosen the battlefield and Lee would have to fight on his terms.

The Confederates could claim a victory on the first day. But the Union had exacted a heavy price on key units. They had also denied them the heights at the key junction between the roads where further Union reinforcements would be arriving. Now there was nothing further to be done, but sleep. General Abner Doubleday said:

We lay on our arms that night among the tombs of the Cemetery, so suggestive of the shortness of life and the nothingness of fame. But the men were little disposed to moralize on themes like these and were much too exhausted to think of anything but much needed rest.

View of Gettysburg from Cemetery Hill, 1863. The road on the left is the Baltimore Pike.

Winfield S. Hancock

Born in Montgomery County, Pennsylvania in 1824, Winfield Scott Hancock was named after the prominent general from the War of 1812. In 1844, he graduated eighteenth in his class of twenty-five at West Point.

He was commissioned as a brevet second lieutenant in the 6th US Infantry Regiment and served in Indian Territory in the Red River Valley. With the outbreak of the Mexican-American War in 1846, he was a successful recruiter in Kentucky. The following year, he joined his regiment in Mexico, serving under his namesake General Winfield Scott.

For gallantry in battle, he was promoted brevet first lieutenant, but he was wounded in the knee and fever prevented him joining the final breakthrough to Mexico City, the source of lifelong regret.

Promoted to captain, he served in the Third Seminole War as a quartermaster. In the political turmoil over the issue of extending slavery into the territories to the west, he served in 'Bleeding Kansas' – where violent political battles broke out – and the confrontation with Mormon settlers known as the Utah War. Then he was stationed in California until the Civil War broke out when he returned east to serve as a quartermaster in the rapidly growing Union Army.

Promoted to Brigadier General in September 1861, he was given command of an infantry brigade in the Army of the Potomac. 'Hancock was superb today,' McClellan telegraphed after Hancock had led a counterattack at the Battle of Williamsburg. The epithet stuck and he became known as 'Hancock the Superb.'

In the Battle of Antietam, Hancock assumed command of the 1st Division Second Corps, following the mortal wounding of Major General Israel B. Richardson in the horrific fighting at 'Bloody Lane.' Hancock and his staff made a dramatic entrance to the battlefield, galloping between his troops and the enemy, parallel to the Sunken Road.

Promoted to Major General of volunteers in November 1862, he led his division in the disastrous attack on Marye's Heights in the Battle of Fredericksburg and was wounded in the abdomen. He was wounded again at the Battle of Chancellorsville, but assumed command of the Second Corps.

Wounded once more at Gettysburg, he underwent a long period of recuperation before returning to action the following year. After seeing the war to its conclusion, he was put in charge of the execution of the conspirators in the assassination of Abraham Lincoln.

After a brief return to the west, he supervised Reconstruction in Louisiana and Texas, where he won favor. He was the Democratic candidate for president in 1880. Narrowly losing to James A. Garfield, he returned to military life, and died in 1886.

HANCOCK AT GETTYSBURG
BY THURE DE THULSTRUP (1887)

Thure de Thulstrup (1848→1930), was a Swedish-born artist who, after emigrating to America in 1873, became one of the leading illustrators there, with contributions for numerous magazines, including three decades of work for *Harper's Weekly*. His pictures include a series of paintings depicting the American Civil War. Thulstrup was praised by one of his publishers, Louis Prang, as 'the foremost military artist in America', a sentiment echoed by many other contemporary critics.

HE HATH LOOSED THE FATEFUL LIGHTNING OF HIS TERRIBLE SWIFT SWORD.

PART 2

THE
SECOND
DAY

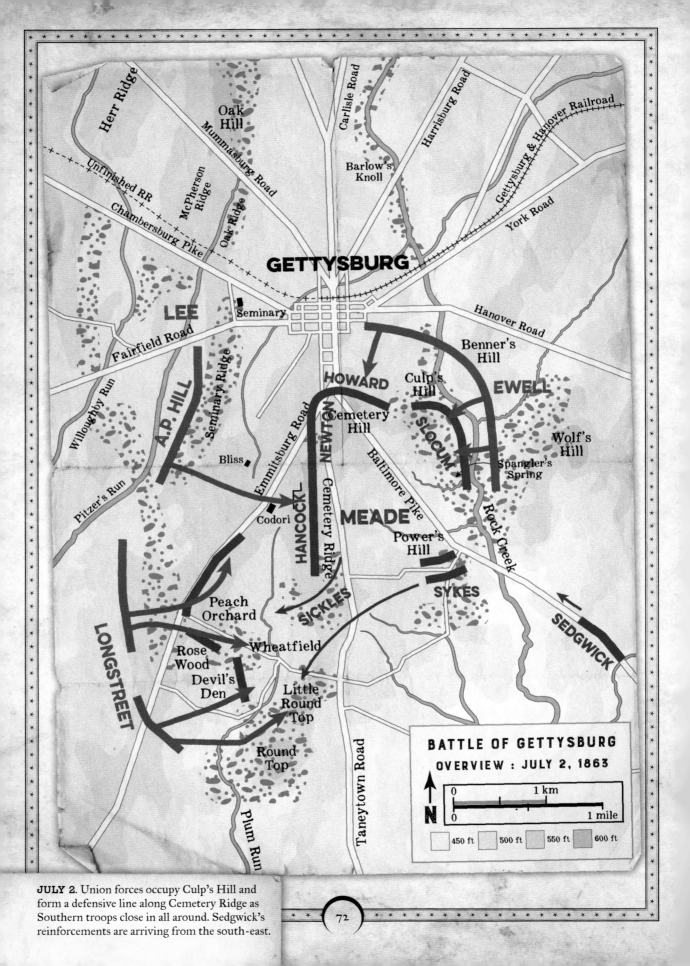

HERR RIDGE

Oak Hill

Mummasburg Road

Carlisle Road

Harrisburg Road

Gettysburg & Hanover Railroad

Unfinished RR

McPherson Ridge

Barlow's Knoll

York Road

Chambersburg Pike

Oak Ridge

GETTYSBURG

LEE

Seminary

Fairfield Road

Hanover Road

Benner's Hill

Seminary Ridge

HOWARD

Culp's Hill

EWELL

Willoughby Run

A.P. HILL

Cemetery Hill

SLOCUM

Wolf's Hill

Bliss

Spangler's Spring

NEWTON

Pitzer's Run

Codori

HANCOCK

Cemetery Ridge

MEADE

Power's Hill

Rock Creek

SICKLES

SYKES

Peach Orchard

SEDGWICK

Rose Wood

Wheatfield

LONGSTREET

Devil's Den

Little Round Top

Round Top

Taneytown Road

BATTLE OF GETTYSBURG
OVERVIEW : JULY 2, 1863

N

0		1 km

| 0 | | 1 mile |

| 450 ft | 500 ft | 550 ft | 600 ft |

Plum Run

JULY 2. Union forces occupy Culp's Hill and form a defensive line along Cemetery Ridge as Southern troops close in all around. Sedgwick's reinforcements are arriving from the south-east.

CHAPTER 5

SNIPERS AND SHARPSHOOTERS

Sunrise was 4:37 am, but Robert E. Lee was up well before then. After a quick breakfast he made off in the direction of the Seminary to overlook the enemy's deployment on Cemetery Hill, a mile and a quarter away, though all he could see was the flickering of their camp fires. He was joined there by General James Longstreet, who remembered the meeting:

On the morning of the 2nd I went to General Lee's headquarters at daylight and renewed my views against making an attack. He seemed resolved, however, and we discussed the probable results. The general is a little nervous this morning. He wishes me to attack; I do not wish to do so without Pickett. I never like to go into battle with one boot off.

> ## The enemy is here, and if we do not whip him, he will whip us.
>
> GENERAL ROBERT E. LEE

Foreign observer Major Justus Scheibert of the Prussian Royal Engineers said that Lee appeared 'care-worn' and was 'not at his ease' that morning. Francis Lawley of the London *Times* also wrote that Lee was 'more anxious and ruffled than I had ever seen him before, though it required close observation to detect it.'

PICKETT'S DIVISION

Major General George E. Pickett's Division was at Chambersburg, guarding the trains. It was only relieved in the early hours of July 2. After a march of twenty-five miles, it stopped around three miles outside Gettysburg to rest and it was not called up to fight that day. Indeed, Pickett did not join the

battle until 2:00 pm the following day, leading its most famous action.

Lee visited Ewell, but Union soldiers were already occupying Culp's Hill which Ewell had hoped to take. It was still dark and they could not ascertain the enemy's strength there. Returning to his headquarters Lee told Longstreet 'that it would not do to have Ewell open the attack.' Longstreet's Corps would have to attack from the right and at 11:00 am Lee 'ordered the movement.'

But Longstreet was not missing just one boot. His Second Division under Major General LaFayette McLaws was still on the road too and did not reach the battlefield until noon.

SKIRMISHES

While the generals were discussing tactics, the fighting had already started. According to Second Lieutenant Albert Peck of the 17th Connecticut:

As soon as it was light on the morning of the 2nd of July, we could see the Johnnies moving along the fences in our front, keeping out of sight as much as possible. It was not long before 'zip' came the bullets from them, and our boys promptly returned their fire, although it was difficult to see them. Our boys took shelter behind the rail and board fences and apple trees, and once in a while the bullets would peel the bark from the trees.

Sniping from both sides was a danger to the civilian inhabitants. Jacob Hollinger was determined to feed the animals in his barn, but when he went out he drew the fire of Union sharpshooters and complained to a Confederate officer. The officer appeared amused and said: 'Why, man, take off that gray suit. They think you are a Johnny Reb.'

Attorney William McLean took a peek out of a second-story window, a bullet came in through the crack of the shutter and lodged in the bed where his ailing wife had lain until he had moved her down to the safety of the cellar.

Henry Jacobs watched Confederate soldiers tear down a wall opposite his house to build a breastwork across the street. Other streets were blocked with wagons, boxes, and barrel. Nellie

Aughinbaugh remembered her father saying that he would do no more for the Rebels than he could help, but while he was out taking provisions to the Union hospitals, her mother would broil the raw fish some young Southern troops had looted. 'Mother would say those poor fellows were somebodies' sons,' Nellie said.

SHELLFIRE

When the 41st New York moved into position behind a stone wall on Cemetery Hill, they drew shellfire

SNIPER TACTICS

Anna Garlach watched Rebels put a hat on a stick over a barricade in Baltimore Street. When a Union sniper fired at it, Confederates hiding nearby would jump out and pick him off. Union sharpshooters worked in pairs. The first would cause the enemy sniper to duck. When he bobbed up again to retaliate, the second would be ready to pick him off.

But Confederate snipers got used to that tactic. Then the Yankees would work in threes. When the Rebel sniper had thought he had dodged the first two, the third would be on hand to take him out.

'Alas, how little we thought of human life as the stake for which this game was being played,' said one New Jersey soldier.

Dead sharpshooter, Gettysburg, July 1863. Photograph by Alexander Gardner.

James Longstreet

Lee's second in command at Gettysburg, James Longstreet was born in Edgefield District in South Carolina in 1821. His family owned a cotton plantation in Georgia. He was a poor student at West Point, graduating fifty-fourth out of a class of fifty-six in 1842. A brevet second lieutenant in the 4th US Infantry, he spent his first two years of service in Jefferson Barracks, Missouri with his friend from West Point Lieutenant Ulysses S. Grant.

Longstreet served with distinction in the 8th US Infantry during the Mexican-American War and was promoted to captain, then major. Wounded in the thigh while charging up a hill during the Battle of Chapultepec in 1847, he handed the colors to his friend Lieutenant George E. Pickett who reached the summit.

Longstreet resigned from the US Army in June 1861 to throw in his lot with the Confederacy. Promoted Brigadier General, he fought at the First and Second Battles of Manassas. By the Battle of Fredericksburg, he was a corps commander.

He opposed Lee's incursion into the north and claimed that he only acceded to it if they employed defensive tactics and only fought if the enemy attacked them when they were in a good defensive position. This was not the position at Gettysburg.

Lee denied giving any such assurance, but in his post-battle report admitted: 'It had not been intended to deliver a general battle so far from our base unless attacked, but coming unexpectedly upon the whole Union Army, to withdraw through the mountains with our extensive trains would have been difficult and dangerous.'

Longstreet has been blamed for losing the Battle of Gettysburg, for his delay in attacking and his slowness in organizing 'Pickett's Charge,' which he was opposed to. Others blame Lee for his poor handling of unwilling officers.

Normally Longstreet was not known for his reticence. He broke through the Union lines at the Battle of Chickamauga in September 1863. During the Battle of the Wilderness in May 1864, he was

accidentally shot through the shoulder by one of his own men, but returned with a paralyzed right arm to command a corps that October. Before Lee surrendered to Grant at Appomattox Court House, Longstreet told him: 'General, if he does not give us good terms, come back and let us fight it out.'

After the war, he was unpopular in the South because he joined the Republican Party and expressed his admiration for President Grant. He was appointed US minister to Turkey and later served as a commissioner of the Pacific railways.

from Confederate batteries. Union batteries returned fire, lobbing shells into the brickyard in Baltimore Street where Confederate snipers were taking cover.

From his headquarters in the wood-framed house belonging to the widow Lydia Leister on Taneytown Road, some nine hundred yards behind Cemetery Hill, Meade firmed up his defensive positions, but also planned to make a 'vigorous attack from our extreme right on the enemy's left.' But he was awaiting the Fifth Corps under Major General George Sykes, that arrived that morning, and the Sixth Corps under Major General John Sedgwick, that did not arrive until late in the afternoon. Meanwhile he sent General Warren to Culp's Hill to examine the ground there.

But Meade was a cautious man. He told his chief-of-staff Major General Daniel Butterfield:

> *Neither I nor any man can tell what the results of this day's operations may be. It is our duty to be prepared for every contingency, and I wish you to send out staff officers to learn all the roads that lead from this place.*

BLISS FARM

Two brigades from Pender's Division began extending the line southward down Seminary Ridge and sent out a skirmish line 150 yards to the east. The Union sent out skirmish lines too. One reached the Bliss Farm to the west of the Emmitsburg Road. The family had evidently fled the day before. A Yankee soldier entering the house noted in his diary that they had 'evidently left in a hurry as they left the doors open, the table set, the beds made.' The farm was occupied by the 1st Delaware who came under 'rattling fire from the enemy, which was repaid with interest.'

To the north, the Union skirmishers were being pushed back until the regimental headquarters in the basement of the barn was almost cut off. Lieutenant Colonel Edward P. Harris then made a precipitous withdrawal. In the confusion twenty-three-year-old Captain Martin W.B. Ellegood was mortally wounded. He died four days later.

Realizing that Rebel snipers at Bliss Farm could now hinder troop movements on Cemetery Ridge, the commander of the Second Corps' Third Division Brigadier General Alexander Hays sent ten companies from one Ohio regiment and two New York regiments

to take the Bliss Farm back. The following day it would find itself back in Rebel hands again. This time two hundred New Jersey soldiers were sent. They were armed with .69 smoothbore muskets loaded with 'buck and ball.'

'When we were within a short distance of the barn, our column halted, delivered their fire, then charged with a cheer, surrounding the barn and then the house,' said their color sergeant. They poured in through the doors and windows. Once they were face to face, the Rebels cried out: 'We surrender Yanks – don't shoot.' The New Jersey strike force had lost twenty percent of its number.

LITTLE ROUND TOP

Lee had sent out Captain Samuel R. Johnston, an engineering officer, on a reconnaissance mission. He reported back that he had reached Little Round Top, one of two rocky hills – Little and Big Round Top – more than a mile to the rear of Cemetery Hill and climbed part way up the slope without seeing any Union troops, except on the road.

But Johnston was mistaken. The Third Corps were just to the north-west of Little Round Top and Buford's cavalry were in Sherfy's Peach Orchard nearby. Johnston must have gone to Big Round Top instead. From what Lee could see from the top of Seminary Ridge, he also believed that the Union defenses extended down Emmitsburg Road, though the line bent backward, following Cemetery Ridge.

When McLaws arrived, Lee showed him a map with a line drawn perpendicular to Emmitsburg Road, near Sherfy's Peach Orchard, where he believed the Union position ended.

'General, I wish you to place your division across the road, and I wish you to get there if possible without being seen by the enemy,' said Lee. 'Can you get there?'

McLaws said he could and he asked to go out to reconnoiter the area with Johnston. Longstreet denied permission, saying the reconnaissance had already been done.

Visiting Ewell's headquarters again, Lee climbed to the top of the almshouse to view the Union positions on Cemetery Hill from the cupola there. They were not as disorganized as he had hoped. 'The enemy have the advantage of us in a short and inside line, and we are too much extended,' he said.

COLT ARMY MODEL 1860

Designed by Samuel Colt himself, the .44 'Army' Colt was the most popular Union Army revolver and much sought after by the Confederates. The six-shot pistol was carried in a holster on the belt by the cavalry as well as infantry and artillery officers. Its rapid rate of firing made it ideal for close quarter fighting.

The .454-inch-diameter lead ball was propelled by a thirty-grain charge of black powder ignited by a percussion cap containing fulminate of mercury which exploded on impact, firing the bullet out of the eight-inch barrel at over six hundred miles an hour. The ball could penetrate seven pine boards, each three-quarters of an inch thick, separated by a one-inch gap, at sixteen yards. Some 2,230 went to the South before the beginning of the war. The US government bought 127,157 before the Colt factory was put out of action by a fire in October 1864.

The lighter .36 'Navy' Colt was preferred by some officers. Both were loaded through the barrel and rammed home with a loading level. As the war progress the .44 Remington became more popular as the cylinder could be removed, though this had to be done by detaching the barrel. However, a soldier could carry one or more spare cylinders for quick reloading. There was also the matter of cost. The Colt was sold to the government for $25, the Remington for $12.

(Left) An unidentified Union soldier with Colt Army Model 1860 revolver. (Right) Colt Army Model 1860, caliber .44, with powder flask.

FLANKING ATTACK

His plan of attack was now complete. Longstreet would make a flanking attack to the right, with Hill and Ewell making opportunistic advances to the center and left. According to Lee:

> *It was determined to make the principal attack upon the enemy's left and endeavor to gain a position from which it was thought that our artillery could be brought to bear with effect. Longstreet was directed to place the divisions of McLaws and Hood on the right of Hill, partially enveloping the enemy's left, which he was to drive in. General Hill was ordered to threaten the enemy's center, to prevent reinforcements being drawn to either wing, and co-operate with his right division in Longstreet's attack. General Ewell was instructed to make a simultaneous demonstration upon the enemy's right, to be converted into a real attack should opportunity offer.*

Captain Jedediah Hotchkiss, Ewell's mapmaker, who was present noted: 'General Lee was at our quarters in the a.m. and there planned the movement, though not, in my opinion, very sanguine of its success. He feared we would only take it at a great sacrifice of life.'

ANOTHER DELAY

When Lee returned to Seminary Ridge, he learnt from Longstreet that McLaws' Division were ready to march and Longstreet's First Division under Major General John B. Hood was only awaiting its Alabama brigade. Longstreet asked to be allowed to delay his flanking movement until they arrived. Lee assented. They were delayed another forty minutes, according to Longstreet's account.

The delay was intolerable for some. Ewell had wanted to put his five regiments of 'Louisiana Tigers' pressed up as close to the Union lines as possible along a muddy ravine known as Winebrenner's Run. When daylight arrived, it was found that they were a sitting target for Union snipers and, behind them, there was open ground where they would be cut down by Union artillery if they tried to withdraw.

Lieutenant J. Warren Jackson said: 'If any one showed themselves or a hat was seen ... a volley was poured on us.' It was going to be a long hot day for the unwashed men who had the reputation of being 'wharf rats from New Orleans.'

Further down the run were three regiments of Carolinian Tarheelers under Avery who spent the day with 'enemy ... balls hissing around us.' When an aide suggested they move somewhere less exposed, Avery laughed and said there was no such place.

UNION PLANS

General Gouverneur Warren, Chief of Engineers, returned to Meade's headquarters from Culp's Hill to report that it would not be possible to launch an offensive there. There were a number of streams that had been dammed and would be useful for defense, and there were woods and marshes that it would be difficult to move artillery through.

Then Sickles arrived, saying that the Confederates were preparing to attack the Third Division's flank. 'I found that my impression as to the intention of the enemy to attack in that direction was not concurred in at headquarters,' he said.

Sickles asked Meade to come and see for himself, but Meade declined to leave his headquarters. So Sickles asked him to send Warren instead, only to be told that the engineering officer had other things to do. However, he would send the chief of artillery General Henry Hunt.

But when Hunt examined Sickles' position, he thought it would be a mistake to move the Third Corps forward onto the Emmitsburg Road as it would greatly extend the line. However, he suggested that Sickles check out Pitzer's Woods on the other side.

WAITING GAME

With an attack now out of the question, Meade packed Cemetery Ridge with the Second, Third, and Fifth Corps. Now they played a waiting game.

On Wolf Hill to the east, Joshua Chamberlain of the 20th Maine said: 'We knew the battle was to be fought, and a sharp one, but what most impressed our minds was the uncertainty of its plan. Indeed there seem as yet to be none.'

They had marched for thirty-six hours and were in need of rest. One soldier with the 44th New York said: 'We cooked breakfast and rested until noon. Then the most of us took our pants off and went for the graybacks for a while.' Graybacks were the lice that infested the ranks. The brigade was then issued with twenty cartridges on top of the forty they already had.

At noon Buford's men were sent back to Westminster to refit. Meade had given his permission for this on the tacit understanding that his cavalry chief Major General Alfred Pleasonton would bring up another mounted unit. When Sickles found that his flank had been left unprotected, Meade realized that Pleasonton had not followed through. A cavalry unit from the right was moved to the left, but they did not arrive in time to be any use that day.

There was frustration on the other side too.

'Nothing doing along our line,' said Lieutenant Colonel Henry Monier of the 10th Louisiana. 'Men getting restless; the hour of noon had passed; we heard chopping of trees on the hill ... the enemy were building a line of entrenchments.'

Randolph McKim, a Maryland officer in Brigadier General George H. Steuart's Brigade felt the same.

'Greatly did officers and men marvel as morning, noon, and afternoon passed in inaction,' he said. After a twenty-five-mile march, they had arrived at 7:30 pm the previous evening, only to be told that the attack on Culp's Hill was to be put off until the following day.

BOOTS AND SADDLES

Then 'Boots and Saddles' sounded and the 1,300 of Brigadier General Albert Jenkins' Brigade – Lee's largest cavalry force on hand – mounted up. They were to provide flank security to the east of town. They headed southwards down the Heidlersburg Road. Suddenly he halted them and moved off the road. He waited, as if for a signal.

After the report of a gun was heard, he took half-a-dozen of his staff, crossed Rock Creek and climbed Blocher's Knoll. Another officer from Jenkins' staff rode out to them with the dispositions of the army and they studied a map.

Two miles away on Cemetery Hill, an artillery officer spotted them and began firing. After a couple of rounds, Union gunners got the range. Before they could take cover, a fuzed shell burst overhead, knocking Jenkins and his horse to the ground.

Bleeding profusely from the head, the comatose Jenkins was carried back to the house where he had spent the night. Jenkins had not told anyone of his assignment. Nor was word sent to Lee. Still expecting Jenkins to relieve the unit, Ewell allowed Early to move Gordon's Georgia brigade from its position on York Road to the rear of the two brigades waiting to attack Cemetery Hill.

SHARPSHOOTERS TAKE AIM

With Longstreet making his flanking movement, Anderson's Division of A.P. Hill's Corps was to extend the Confederate right. Brigadier General Cadmus M. Wilcox marched his Alabama Brigade down to Pitzer's Woods. As the 10th and 11th Alabama regiments entered the woods, they were met with a burst of gunfire. At Hunt's suggestion Sickles had sent the 3rd Maine and Colonel Hiram Berdan's 1st US Sharpshooters there as a reconnaissance force.

The 10th Alabama had only just made contact with the Sharpshooters when the 11th unwittingly presented its flank to Berdan's men. Cut down by a murderous fusillade, the survivors fled back to the main column to reform. Forgetting their training, some of the Sharpshooters chased after them, offering easy targets to the 10th Alabama.

Holding their nerve, the 10th Alabama forced the Sharpshooters back to the reserve line held by the 3rd Maine.

There, Wilcox said, they had 'quite a spirited little fight.' By the time the 8th Alabama came to reinforce them, the 10th had worked their way around the Union flank and Berdan ordered a withdrawal.

SICKLES MAKES HIS MOVE

Wilcox's move confirmed in Sickles' mind that something was afoot on his flank. Without waiting for orders, he moved his First Division under Major General David B. Birney from the position Meade had assigned it on Cemetery Ridge up to the Emmitsburg Road. The Third Division under Brigadier General Andrew A. Humphreys moved forward behind the First, losing his connection to Hancock's corps to the right. Then Humphreys was ordered to detach three brigades to act as a reserve for Birney who was now too thinly spread to provide his own. Captain George E. Randolph then filled in the gaps with his artillery pieces.

Captain James E. Smith of the 4th New York Independent Battery was then told to put his guns

1ST US SHARPSHOOTERS

Soldier, inventor and world-renowned marksman, Colonel Hiram C. Berdan was given permission to form two sharpshooter regiments in the fall of 1861. He recruited men from New York City and Albany and from the states of New Hampshire, Vermont, Michigan, and Wisconsin. Recruits had to pass a marksmanship test with a rifle to qualify to be a member of the Sharpshooters. Each man had to be able to place ten shots in a circle of ten inches in diameter from two hundred yards away.

They were armed mostly with Sharps rifles. The first was bought by the legendary Union sniper Private Truman 'California Joe' Head and Berdan ordered two thousand for his Sharpshooters. They wore dark-green uniforms with leather leggings and were used to operating in small groups.

They fought in every battle in the Eastern Theater until the fall of 1864.

'California Joe' of the Berdan Sharpshooters.

on top of Devil's Den at the end of Houck's Ridge to the west of Little Round Top. This was no easy task.

'Its base boulders, some of them as large as a small house, rest in an irregular, confused mass, forming nooks and cavernous recesses suggestive of its uncanny name,' said one New York veteran.

The guns had to be manhandled to the ridge. Only four of them would fit there. The position offered a good field of fire to the west, but if the enemy attacked, it would be impossible to get the guns away. The other two guns were left behind the ridge in Plum Run Gorge.

FURTHER HOLD-UPS

There were further hold-ups with Longstreet's flanking movement. The guns under Colonel Edward P. Alexander were the first to move. He made his way unobserved by a Union signals officer on Little Round Top. The fighting in Pitzer's Wood was over when he halted his guns just beyond where Pitzer Run branched off Willoughby Run. Then he went back to look for McLaws who was supposed to be following.

He found him stopped just before an open clearing. Johnston had been sent along as a guide, but his earlier reconnaissance trip was to check out the enemy line, not to scout a route for the movement of a corps.

McLaws insisted on turning back to find another route where they would not have to cross open ground and risk being spotted by the enemy. However, Hood's Division which was following was already intermingled with his and it would take some time to separate them. Longstreet sent word that they simply about-face, but that would put Hood in the lead, a slight McLaws would not countenance. More time was wasted in the countermarch. 'There is no telling the value of the hours which were lost,' said Alexander.

Longstreet eventually caught up with McLaws when he was approaching Warfield Ridge to the west of Emmitsburg Road.

'How are you going in?' asked Longstreet.

'That will be determined when I can see what is in my front,' replied McLaws.

'There is nothing in your front,' said Longstreet. 'You will be entirely on the flank of the enemy.'

'Then I will continue my march in column of companies, and after arriving on the flank as far as is necessary will face to the left and march on the enemy,' said McLaws.

'That suits me,' said Longstreet, riding off.

LONGSTREET IS TO BLAME

Thinking himself clear of the enemy flank, McLaws turned, imagining that he could cross the Emmitsburg Road without opposition.

'The view presented astonished me, as the enemy was massed to my front, and extended to my right and left as far as I could see,' he wrote later. And he knew where the fault lay. 'General Longstreet is to blame for not reconnoitering the ground and for persisting in ordering the assault when his errors were discovered.'

McLaws sent his guns forward to challenge the Union forces in the Peach Orchard, drawing his men up into two lines with two brigades in each line.

Hood then threw off any pretense of concealment that the Confederate line extended to the south. An advanced party was sent to tear down any fences and clear the ground for battle, while Texas scouts were sent to find out how far the Union flank extended.

EXPECTING BATTLE

At 3:00 pm, Meade sent a telegram outlining the situation to Halleck, saying:

The army is fatigued. I have today, up to this hour, awaited the attack of the enemy, I having a strong position for defensive. I am not determined on attacking him till his position is more developed. He has been moving in on both my flanks, apparently, but it is difficult to tell exactly his movements. I have delayed attacking, to allow the Sixth Corps and parts of other corps to reach this place and to rest the men. Expecting a battle, I ordered all my trains to the rear. If not attacked, and I can get any positive information of the position of the enemy which will justify me in so doing, I shall attack. If I find it hazardous to do so, or am satisfied the enemy is endeavoring to move to my rear and interpose between me and Washington, I shall fall back to my supplies at Westminster ... I feel fully the responsibility resting upon me, but will endeavor to act with caution.

Coffee

The American addiction to coffee has its origins in the Civil War. Men fought over it, traded for it, and looted it from prisoners, the wounded, and the dead. The beans were ground between rocks, or crushed with rifle butts. The Union ration was twenty-eight pounds per man per year, while the Confederates got a ration of twenty-one pounds per man per year. Consequently, the Rebels would substitute chicory, peas, peanuts, roasted corn or rye, or even potatoes. Longstreet's artillery chief Colonel Alexander was said to have had a cup of sweet-potato coffee before the artillery barrage that raised the curtain for Pickett's Charge. Confederate soldiers would sometimes hurl their tobacco ration at a Union picket in the hope of getting a bag of coffee beans in return.

John D. Billings with the 10th Massachusetts Volunteer Artillery Battery said: 'What a Godsend it seemed to us at times! How often after being completely jaded by a night march ... have I had a wash, if there was water to be had, made and drunk my pint or so of coffee and felt as fresh and invigorated as if just risen from a night's sound sleep.'

A 'coffee cooler' became a term of abuse, meaning a coward or shirker who stayed behind, when their unit advanced, to cool their coffee.

Billings also described the distribution of the ration on active service: 'It was usually brought in an oatmeal sack; a regimental quartermaster receiving and apportioning it among ten companies ... Then the orderly sergeant must devote himself to dividing it. One method ... was to spread a rubber blanket on the ground – more than one if the company was large – and upon it were put as many piles of coffee as there were men to receive rations; and the care taken to make the piles of the same size to the eye, to keep the men from growling, would remind one of a country physician making his powders. The sugar that always accompanied the coffee was spooned out at the same time on another blanket. When both were ready they were given out, each man taking a pile ...'

'Every soldier of a month's experience in campaigning was provided with some sort of bag into which he spooned his coffee; but the kind of bag he used indicated pretty accurately ... the length of time he had been in service ... a raw recruit ... would take it up in a paper and stow it away in that well known receptacle of all eatables, the soldier's haversack, only to find it a part of a general mixture of hardtack, salt pork, pepper, salt, knife, fork, spoon, sugar and coffee by the time the next halt was made ... But your old veteran ... took out an oblong plain cloth bag, which looked immaculate as the everyday shirt of a coal-heaver, and into it scooped without ceremony both his sugar and coffee, and stirred them thoroughly together.'

Coffee and hardtack were standard soldier's fare.

He then called his corps commanders to his headquarters and held a council of war. Warren arrived to inform Meade that the position on Cemetery Ridge assigned to the Third Corps was not occupied. When Sickles turned up, Meade was furious. He stormed out of the Leister house and, before Sickles could dismount, ordered him to return to the position he had been ordered to take.

This would be difficult as the sound of artillery fire was coming from that direction, so Meade ordered the Fifth Corps into the position vacated by the Third. Meade then rode up onto Cemetery Ridge to see the position for himself and ordered Warren to attend to the situation.

THE RAILROAD

While the railroad played a key role in the Civil War, transporting troops and supplies, it was of little significance at Gettysburg. This was because the line from New Oxford had been disabled by the Confederates, who demolished the bridge over Rock Creek, and the extension of the line westward was halted by the Civil War. The line had opened in 1858 and the railroad station in Gettysburg was used as a hospital during the battle. When President Lincoln attended the consecration of the Soldiers' National Cemetery on November 19, 1863, he came by train.

The steam engine 'Firefly' on a trestle bridge of the Orange and Alexandria Railroad, Virginia, c. 1863.

PHOTOGRAPHING THE CIVIL WAR

The Civil War was the first war to be documented through the lens of a camera. Modern photography was less than a quarter-century old in 1861. However, the era's photographic process was far too elaborate for action shots. As a result, most images of the Civil War are portraits and landscapes. It was not until the twentieth century that photographers were able to take non-posed pictures on the battlefield.

The 1860s were the days before film as we know it, and the process was dependent on preparing glass or metal plates. Technological breakthroughs in the 1850s allowed images to be printed onto sensitized paper and mounted on card. Most importantly, this allowed mass production of photographs.

No photographers traveled with the Confederate armies, but photographic studios were common in Southern cities, towns, and even in military camps. As a result, Confederate photography consisted largely of portrait photographs of soldiers and their families, and some post-mortem images.

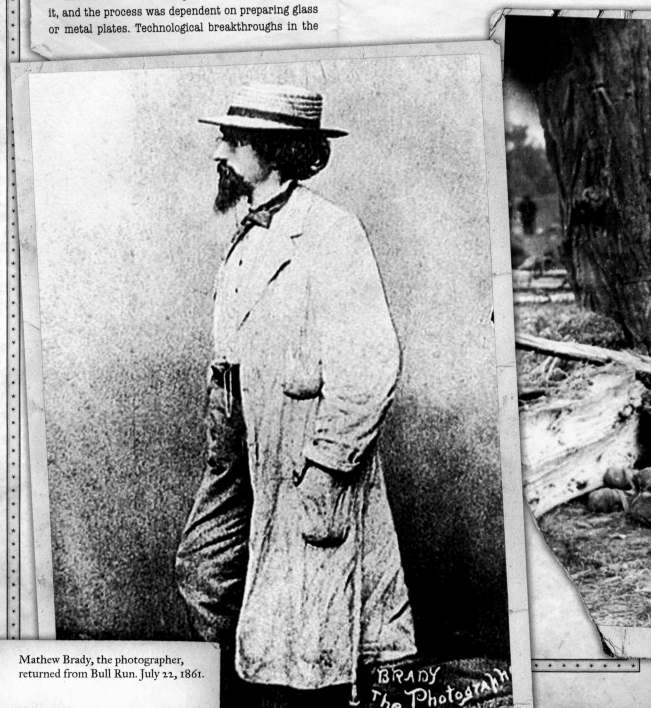

BRADY
The Photograph

Mathew Brady, the photographer, returned from Bull Run. July 22, 1861.

Northern photographers, however, notably Mathew Brady, Alexander Gardner, Timothy O'Sullivan, and George N. Barnard, traveled with the Union armies and photographed the scenery of the war and even the gruesome aftermath of battle.

Mathew Brady (1823 – 96), one of the most prolific photographers of the Civil War period, did not actually take many of the photographs attributed to him. More of a project manager, he spent most of his time supervising his team of traveling photographers, preserving their pictures and buying others from private photographers fresh from the battlefield. When photographs from his collection were published, they were all credited with 'Photograph by Mathew Brady', although they were actually the work of many different people.

In 1862, Brady shocked America by displaying Alexander Gardner's photographs of battlefield corpses – *The Dead of Antietam*. This exhibition marked the first time most people witnessed the carnage of war. The *New York Times* said that Brady had captured 'the terrible reality and earnestness of war'.

The Dead of Antietam. Photograph by Alexander Gardner, Battle of Antietam, 1862. A Union soldier regards the grave of Lt. John A. Clark, while a dead Confederate soldier lies unburied, looking as if his body has just been tossed aside.

CHAPTER 6

THE DEVIL'S CARNIVAL

UNEXPECTED STRENGTH

The gunfire heard at the Leister House was Sickles' own artillery opening up on McLaws. They were answered by the eighteen guns of Colonel Henry C. Cabell's Confederate artillery battalion.

Longstreet sent no less than three messengers to ask McLaws why he had not started his attack yet. McLaws told the third that he would start in five minutes, but before he could, another rode up telling him to hold off his attack until Hood was in position.

McLaws and Hood faced an enemy of unexpected strength. A frontal attack would be a costly one, but Longstreet arrived to tell them to get on with it. The Texas scouts, Hood had sent out had discovered that there were no Union troops on the south side of Big Round Top and suggested that they attack there. Longstreet would have none of it.

> ## The enemy's shells screamed and burst around us ...

'General Lee's orders are to attack up the Emmitsburg Road,' he said. 'We must obey the orders of General Lee.' Even though he did not agree with them.

While they continued to discuss the matter, the troops had to endure the artillery bombardment with no clear idea of what they were going to do. Captain Barziza of the 4th Texas said:

> *The enemy's shells screamed and bursted around us, inflicting considerable damage. It is very trying upon men to remain still and in ranks under a severe cannonading. One had time to reflect upon the danger and there being no wild excitement as in a charge, he is more reminded of the utter helplessness of his present condition. The men are all flat on the ground, keeping their*

places in ranks, and as a shell is heard, generally trying to bury themselves in the earth.

The last thing the 4th Texas wanted to do was to reflect on the dangers they faced. On the way to the battlefield that morning they had passed a field hospital where, a veteran said:

> *I saw a great many wounded soldiers, who were mangled and bruised in every possible way, some with their eyes shot out, some with their arms or hands, or finger, or feet, or legs shot off, and all seeming to suffer a great deal.*

In the line next to the Texans were the 3rd Arkansas. One of their number said:

> *It is very true that these men were tried and seasoned soldiers, with powers of endurance equal to any, yet they were not made of iron, and there is a limit to all human endeavor.*

The real problem was that, Sickles' line did not end at the Peach Orchard, rather it bent backwards. If Hood followed Lee's orders and attacked along the line of the road, his men would be subjected to enfilading fire from the side and rear. Eventually, Longstreet was persuaded to modify his plan a little. After all Lee's objective was to envelop the enemy's left and that is what Hood would be doing.

KEY TO THE WHOLE POSITION

When Warren reached Little Round Top, he saw immediately that it was a vital position that had to be held. But there was no artillery on it and the only soldiers there were a Signals Corps who, knowing the Confederates were coming, were about to evacuate. Warren explained:

I saw that this was the key to the whole position. Our troops in the woods in front of it could not see the ground in front of them; therefore, the enemy would come on them before they were aware. The woods west of the Emmitsburg Road furnished a concealed place for the enemy to form, so I requested a battery just in front of Little Round Top [Smith on Devil's Den] to fire a shot into those woods. The sound of the shot whistling through the air reached the enemy's troops causing them to glance up in that direction. This motion revealed to me the glistening gun barrels and bayonets of the enemy battle line, already formed and far outflanking our troops; his line of advance to Little Round Top was unopposed. This discovery was intensely thrilling and appalling.

Warren ordered the Signals Corps to stay and wave their flags to make it look like the summit of Little Round Top was occupied. Meanwhile, Warren sent an aide to inform Meade of the situation.

Major General LaFayette McLaws.

MEADE v SICKLES

Meade found Sickles in the Peach Orchard and again upbraided him for not being in the position he had been ordered to occupy, pointing out that he would not be able to hold such an extended line.

'I replied that I could not, with one corps, hold so extended a line against the Rebel army,' said Sickles, 'but that, if supported, the line could be held; and, in my judgment, it was a strong line, and the best one.'

Meade would not have it. Sickles had put his artillery so far out in front that he would lose it and, if he tried to support it, he would have to fight the whole battle out there where he was.

'You cannot hold this position,' Meade said, 'and the enemy will not let you get away without a fight.'

Meade got Warren's message just after he had left Sickles and ordered Humphreys' division to occupy Little Round Top. The order was countermanded after two brigades had been sent because a column from the Fifth Corps was already on its way.

When a messenger from Warren had reached Sickles, he had said he had no troops to spare. But when a messenger reached Sykes, he forwarded orders to Brigadier General James Barnes who was already moving westward with his First Division. The messenger was intercepted by Colonel Strong Vincent, commanding Barnes' Third Brigade. Without hesitation, Vincent moved his brigade off towards Little Round Top.

THE WORK OF THE DEVIL

At 3:40 pm, Alexander began pounding the Union positions with his fifty-four guns.

'The accuracy of the enemy's aim was astonishing,' said Smith on Devil's Den.

On the right, Captain Charles A. Phillips' 5th Massachusetts Battery said: 'As soon as the battery was in position, the guidon took his position on the right and the first shot was apparently directed at the flag and killed two horses on the right piece.'

Lieutenant John K. Buckley was with Battery E of the 1st Rhode Island Light Artillery in an exposed position in the road north of the Peach Orchard. 'I fired slow and carefully,' he said. 'Men and horses fell around me.'

'Our position was open and exposed,' said Captain John Bigelow with the 9th Massachusetts Battery. 'One man was killed and several wounded before we could fire a single gun.'

The volume of fire and tremendous noise was almost overwhelming. Bugler Charles Wellington Reed, attempting to describe it, wrote, 'such a shrieking, hissing, seething I never dreamed was imaginable, it seemed as though it must be the work of the very devil himself.'

Alexander was equally impressed by the opposition. 'They really surprised me, both with the number of guns they developed and the way they stuck to them,' he said.

Corporal William P. Ray of Virginia's Bath Artillery was lost in this return fire. 'He was killed while in the act of sighting his guns,' said his commanding officer Captain O.B. Taylor. 'He never spoke after receiving the shot, walked a few steps from his piece, and fell dead.'

Alexander himself had a near miss. 'I had had my right knee skinned by a bullet which passed behind one leg and in front of the other as I was walking between Gilbert's guns,' he said. 'It gashed both pants and drawers and let my knee stick out very disreputably, looking, not like a bullet hole, but like a big tear.'

Two of Gilbert's four guns were struck by the enemy's shot and dismounted, and of the seventy-five in action forty were killed or wounded.

STUART'S RETURN

Jeb Stuart had returned ahead of his men and reported to Lee. Instead of fulfilling the reconnaissance mission he had been sent on, he had clashed with two companies of Union cavalry on the Baltimore Road, then attacked another cavalry regiment in the streets of Hanover. Brigadier General Elon Farnsworth's brigade supported by Brigadier George A. Custer's Michigan Brigade counterattacked. Stuart was forced to disengage and return to Lee who told him to take up a position on the left wing.

He had to await his men though. As the gun battle on Lee's right began, Stuart's weary cavalry column under Brigadier General Wade Hampton was seven miles away in the village of Hunterstown. He had recently been fired at by a Yankee scout who emptied the entire magazine of his carbine at Hampton, merely grazing him, before escaping with a wound

Alabama troops in Confederate camp.

inflicted by Hampton with his pistol.

Stuart learnt that an outpost Hampton had left at Hunterstown had been run out by Custer and sent Hampton back to deal with him. Buying time for his horse artillery to deploy, Custer charged the oncoming cavalry column. But the first Confederate fusillade blew his horse out from under him and a trooper from the 1st Michigan had to ride to his rescue.

BENNER'S HILL

To the east of Gettysburg, Major General Edward Johnson ordered Major James W. Latimer to take his guns to Benner's Hill. Sixteen guns were sent 'streaming over the field in a bustle and busy speed and enveloped in clouds of dust.'

From there, they began pounding the First Corps on Culp's Hill, whose gunnery chief Colonel Charles S. Wainwright judged that the two sides were now evenly matched in the number of cannon. However, he added: 'In every other respect the Rebel guns had the advantage of us.'

One enemy shell exploded under one gun of Battery B of the 1st Pennsylvania Light Artillery, mortally wounding one man, who 'lost his right hand, his left arm at the shoulder, and his ribs so broken open that you could see right into him.'

HEAD KNOCKED OFF

While Alexander's gun were softening up Sickles' left flank, the enemy's overshoots began landing among the infantry concentrated behind ready for the assault.

Private John C. West of Company E, 4th Texas Infantry, wrote to his four-year-old son, saying:

> We were standing in an open field, under the shot and shell of these batteries, for half an hour, and a good many soldiers were killed all around me. One poor fellow had his head knocked off in a few feet of me, and I felt all the time as if I would never see you and little sister again.

In a letter to his wife, West recalled that 'the infernal machines came tearing and whirring through

the ranks with a most demoralizing tendency.'

The men were ordered to lie down.

Hood was still concerned that Longstreet had not formally verified the orders that Lee had given. He sent his adjutant general Major Harry Sellers, who was told: 'You will execute the orders you have received.' Hood recalled:

After this urgent protest against entering the Battle of Gettysburg according to instructions – which protest is the first and only one I ever made during my entire military career – I ordered my line to advance and make the assault.

However, he was still determined to obey the spirit rather than the letter of his orders. 'When we get under fire, I will have a digression,' he told Sellers.

LANCES OF STEEL TIPPED WITH FIRE

Pickett's Division could already hear the roar of battle as they approached. This seemed to inspire them, though they were tired after the long march from Chambersburg. 'The roads were hard and firm, and we made good time,' said a soldier with the 7th Virginia, 'but the day was terribly hot and clouds of dust stifling. Water was scarce and we suffered much.'

Another Virginian said: 'The vertical rays of the sun seemed like real lances of steel tipped with fire.' But William Cocke of the 9th Virginia was anxious to see the young lady who had jeered at them for retreating just a few days earlier.

The men were allowed to rest when they reached Marsh Creek, while Pickett went to report his arrival with Longstreet, and his adjutant checked in with Lee. They learned that the Sixth would not be needed that day.

NO COMMUNICATION

What Hood said to his men before they went into battle around 4:10 pm is disputed.

'Forward, my Texans, and win this battle or die in the effort,' is what Colonel Phillip A. Work commanding the 1st Texas heard him say.

'Forward – Steady – Forward,' is all a private in the 4th Texas recalled, while another remembered Hood saying: 'Fix bayonets, my brave Texans; forward and take those heights.'

Work then yelled: 'Follow the Lone Star flag to the top of the mountain.' Clearly, he thought they were on their way up the Round Tops.

To the right of the Texans were the Alabama brigade under Brigadier General Evander M. Law. Lieutenant Colonel William Oates, commanding the 15th Alabama, said: 'No communication as to what was intended to be done was made to the regimental commanders until after the advance began.'

Law's adjutant Captain Leigh R. Terrell spurred his horse to the front and gave the order: 'Attention! Shoulder – Arms ... Guide Center. Forward. March!'

The British observer Arthur Fremantle said the troops on the march were 'queer to look at. They carry less than other troops; many of them have only got an old piece of carpet or rug as baggage; all are ragged and dirty, but full of good humor and confidence in themselves and in their general, Hood.'

The first to move out were the skirmishers, followed by the double-ranked lines of men, their shoulders almost touching, with the Confederate flag held proudly aloft in the center of each regiment.

'We moved quietly forward and down the steep decline, gaining impetus as we reached the more level ground below,' said a soldier from the 1st Texas. A comrade from the 4th said: 'We could see the Federals on the hills to our left, and the Stars and Stripes waving at us.' Every Union gun was targeted on them.

AIMING POINT

Colonel Vincent had reached the summit of Little Round Top with Private Oliver W. Norton carrying the brigade's flag, which proved to be the perfect aiming point. Vincent was just deciding how to position his regiments when a shell crashed into some nearby rocks.

'Down with that flag, Norton,' he shouted. 'Damn it, go behind the rocks with it.'

They could already see the Confederate lines advancing below. So could Smith from Devil's Den five hundred yards to the west.

'The four guns were now used to oppose and cripple this attack and check it has far as possible,' said Smith. 'I never saw the men do better work; every shot told; the pieces were discharged as rapidly as they could be with regard to effectiveness, while the conduct of the men was superb.' This was not easy as every round had to be carried from the foot of the ridge.

'Man after man went down,' said a watching infantryman, 'but still the exhausting work went steadily on.' General Hunt visited and warned them that they were likely to lose their guns. On leaving, he found Plum Valley behind their position blocked by a herd of horned cows driven crazy by the shelling.

'All were stampeded, and were bellowing and rushing in their terror, first to one side and then to the other,' he said.

Guns from the Peach Orchard and the Wheatfield to the north also bombarded the advancing Confederates. They were also harassed by the 2nd US Sharpshooters in four-man cells in a loose line to the west of Big Round Top. Some penetrated the enemy lines and began picking off Confederate gunners. Companies had to be detached from the Alabama regiments and the Georgians following them to handle the threat. But this weakened the main assault force.

HOOD FALLS

Hood moved forward behind his men. He had reached the orchard of Bushman's Farm when a Yankee shell burst in the air above him. 'I saw a spiracle [spherical] case shot explode twenty feet over Hood's head,' Colonel Work said: 'I saw him sway to and fro in the saddle and then start to fall off his horse, when he was caught by one of his aides.' Hood was wounded in the arm, but he was 'utterly prostrated and almost fainting.' 'It evidently gave him intense pain and utterly unnerved him, so that I could get no orders from him,' said Major John C. Haskell.

Hood was taken away in an ambulance. Now his division was 'without a leader and ignorant of where the enemy is.'

However, the commander of the Texas brigade Brigadier General Jerome B. Robertson believed that he was to keep the Emmitsburg Road on his left and pivot to the left so the two brigades faced north. However, he found that the road ran north-north-east and Law's brigade to his right were plowing on eastward, showing no sign of turning. Meanwhile his brigade was breaking up, with the 1st Texas and the 3rd Arkansas moving north-east, while the 4th and 5th Texas headed straight on eastward. Robertson then abandoned the idea of

turning northward. Deciding to stick with Law, he ordered the 1st Texas and 3rd Arkansas to close up, but they ignored him. They were heading straight for Smith's guns in Devil's Den.

THE HORNET'S NEST

When the Alabama line reached the open land before the Slyder farm, the Sharpshooters gathered behind a stone wall. Their fire was so intense, this was known as the Hornet's Nest. But when the Alabamians outflanked the line, the Sharpshooters split up into their four-man units again.

Law then decided that it was time to wheel north into Plum Run Gorge. However, Colonel Oates would not comply. He was determined to chase the Sharpshooters up the Big Round Top. Oates said:

> *I received an order from Brigadier General Law to left-wheel my regiment and move in the direction of the heights to my left, which order I failed to obey, for the reason that when I received it I was rapidly advancing up a mountain.*

SWATHED IN SMOKE

On Little Round Top, Colonel Vincent had decided to deploy his four regiments along the lower slopes to the west and south of the hill to give the enemy less room to maneuver. Skirmish lines were sent out. Below and to the right, Houck Ridge was swathed in smoke from Smith's cannon.

Vincent moved along the line giving instructions. When he reached the 20th Maine on the extreme left, he told Colonel Joshua L. Chamberlain that they were expecting a 'desperate attack' and he was to hold that position 'at all hazards.' Chamberlain's two brothers were also serving in the regiment. He put them at either end of the line. As they had ridden up to Little Round Top, a Rebel shell had screamed past them.

'Boys,' said Chamberlain, ordering his brother to separate. 'Another such shot might make it hard for mother.'

The 1st Texas and 3rd Arkansas were closing on Smith's guns. The Second Brigade under Brigadier General J.H. Hobart Ward alongside them held their fire until the Confederates were two hundred yards away. The first volley was so effective that they managed to fire a second before the Rebels could make an effective reply.

Smith switched to canister and Ward swung his two right regiments to the left to attack the Confederates with enfilading fire. They were joined by the Third Brigade under Colonel Philippe Regis de Trobriand on the western edge of the Wheatfield to the north.

Robertson's men were being hit from the front and left. He called for reinforcements. Law sent the 44th and 48th Alabama.

RAIN OF DEATH

Smith now realized that the Confederates were approaching from his left and making for Plum Run Gorge to his rear. He tried to persuade Colonel Elijah Walker commanding the 4th Maine to move off the ridge and block the gorge. When he refused, Smith went over his head to Ward.

The second wave of Confederates, Georgians under Brigadier General Henry L. Benning, were now advancing. Smith called for spherical case, but was told that they had run out of the long-distance ammunition.

'Give them shell!' yelled Smith. 'Give them solid shot! Damn them, give them anything!'

Benning's men were to follow some four hundred yards behind the first wave. But instead of following the line taken by Law, he followed Robertson into the face of Ward's guns. 'We had not got out of the woods before the guns from the hill top were turned on us,' said one Georgian.

'Down the plunging shot came, bursting before and around and everywhere, tearing up the ground in a terrific rain of death,' said a reporter for the *Savannah Republican*. 'Still the old brigade moved on.' As they approached the Yankee guns 'the rain of grape and canister began, mingling their sharp cries with the shrill whistle of the mad Minié balls which seemed to come in showers.'

TEXANS CHARGE

Once Smith's attention had turned to the second wave, the 1st Texas charged, bringing them out into the open below Smith's guns.

'When the enemy approached to within three hundred yards of our position the many obstacles in our front afforded him excellent protection for his sharpshooters, who soon had our guns under control,' said Smith.

The Texans scrambled up the hill, scattering the gunners. The 124th New York came to the rescue. Two volleys from them sent the Texans rushing for cover. The New Yorkers then charged down the hill

FROM LITTLE ROUND TOP TO DEVIL'S DEN, GETTYSBURG

The view overlooking Devil's Den from Little Round Top, *c.* 1910.

after them, straight into a volley of gunfire. A bullet hit twenty-two-year-old Major James Cromwell in the heart and he fell lifeless.

'My God! My God men!' yelled Colonel Augustus van Horne Ellis, commanding the 124th. 'Your major's down; save him, save him.'

They made a second downhill charge. It was no more successful than the first. This time Colonel Ellis was killed. Though the 1st Texas withdrew out of range, the 44th Alabama appeared on their left no more than 150 yards away and started pouring down enfilading fire.

'No troops could long stand such a storm,' said one New Yorker.

INVISIBLE ENEMY

A second brigade of Georgians under Brigadier General George T. Anderson were also coming to Robertson's help, heading toward the center of Sickles' line alongside Benning. Meanwhile the 44th and 48th Alabama had reached the mouth of Plum Gorge.

'The enemy were as invisible to us as we were to them,' said Colonel William F. Perry, commanding the 44th Alabama. 'The presence of a battery of artillery of course implied the presence of a strong supporting force of infantry.'

Law rode forward to speak to Oates, whose 15th Alabama were now on the extreme right of the line. He told Oates 'to hug the base of Great Round Top and go up the valley between the two mountains, until I found the left of the Union line, to turn it and do all the damage I could.'

While the left of the 44th Alabama were enfilading the 124th New York, the right then came up against the 4th Maine, blocking the entrance to the gorge. Even though they were supported by the 48th Alabama, Colonel Walker considered them nothing more than 'a strong skirmish line' which was easily stopped.

The left wing, however, charged up onto the crest and took Smith's guns in Devil's Den, though some of the 1st Texas who had held their position on the ridge, claimed it was they who had taken the guns.

Smith's gunners fled with their equipment, denying the Confederates the use of their guns for the time being, and they soon came under fire from other Union batteries.

COUNTERATTACK

The 99th Pennsylvania under the command of Major John W. Moore moved from the right of the line to support a counterattack by the 4th Maine and 124th New York. They had watched as a dark mass of Confederate infantry headed toward Devil's Den.

Color-Sergeant Harvey M. Munsell said: 'My heart was in my mouth ... Frightened almost to death, and not a soul in the regiment knew it but myself ... I would have sooner died two hundred thousand times than to continue in the terrible suspense when seconds seemed hours.'

Moore led the charge, crying: 'Pennsylvania and our homes!' They quickly recaptured the guns and, from their position on the top of the ridge, poured volley after volley into the gorge below.

With the 4th Maine involved in the action on the ridge, the 48th Alabama managed to push past them into an open area in Plum Run Gorge. However, the two guns Smith had left in Plum Run Gorge came into their own.

'The enemy are taken by surprise,' said Smith. 'Their battle flag drops three different times from the effect of our canister. Thrice their lines wavers and seeks shelter.'

The Alabama men melted into the woods and the Union held Houck's Ridge. Benning's Georgia brigade tried again, but stalled just before the crest. On his way up the slope, Private J.W. Lokey of Company B, 20th Georgia, was told by a comrade: 'Don't go up there; you'll get shot.'

At the top of the hill, he was just taking aim with his Enfield when a Minié ball went through his right thigh. As he hobbled down the hill again he saw a Yankee sergeant running in the same direction. As he was behind Confederate lines, Lokey called to him for help. Lokey recalled:

Coming up, he said: 'Put your arm around my neck and throw all your weight on me; don't be afraid of me. Hurry up; this is a dangerous place.' The balls were striking the trees like hail all around us, and as we went back he said: 'If you and I had this matter to settle, we would soon settle it, wouldn't we?' I replied that he was a prisoner and I a wounded man, so I felt that we could come to terms pretty quick.

J.E.B. 'Jeb' Stuart

James Ewell Brown 'Jeb' Stuart was born in Patrick County, Virginia, in 1833. His great-grandfather Major Alexander Stuart had commanded a regiment during the American Revolutionary War. His father was a veteran of the War of 1812, a Democratic politician and a slave-owner.

Stuart attempted to enlist in the US Army in 1852, but was rejected for being underage. Two years later he went to West Point, where he befriended Robert E. Lee who became superintendent there in 1852. Stuart graduated thirteenth in his class of forty-six in 1854.

Commissioned as a brevet second lieutenant, he joined the US Regiment of Mounted Riflemen in Texas, later transferring to the newly formed 1st Cavalry Regiment as quartermaster and first lieutenant. When he married, he and his wife owned two slaves – one inherited, one purchased.

He served in 'Bleeding Kansas' and frontier actions against Native Americans, where he suffered a minor wound when shot in the chest by a Cheyenne during a cavalry charge with saber drawn. His patent for a saber hook – 'an improved method of attaching sabers to belts' – was licensed to the US Government.

Following the secession of Virginia, he resigned from the US Army and was commissioned as a lieutenant colonel of the Virginia Infantry. Within two months, he was commanding the 1st Virginia Cavalry Regiment, promoted to full colonel.

In June 1862, he achieved fame by riding all the way round the Army of the Potomac, capturing 165 Union soldiers and various supplies on the way. The master of public relations, he cultivated a cavalier image, wearing red-lined gray cape, yellow sash, hat cocked to the side with an ostrich plume, and a red flower in his lapel. In Lee's eyes, he did wonders for morale.

Promoted Major General in July 1862, he commanded the upgraded Cavalry Division. At the Second Battle of Manassas, he again circled the Union army, returning with twelve-hundred horses. At the Battle of Fredericksburg Stuart's horse artillery checked the Union attack on General T.J. 'Stonewall' Jackson's corps and at the Battle of Chancellorsville, Stuart was appointed by Lee to take command of the 2nd Army Corps after Jackson had been wounded.

He led a cavalry charge against Union cavalry at Brandy Station on June 9, 1863. Sent on a reconnaissance mission, he got involved in a number of raids and was delayed. He did not arrive at Gettysburg until the second day of the battle when his exhausted troops were of little use.

After the battle, Stuart continued providing useful information about Union troop movements, but at Spotsylvania Courthouse on May 11, 1864, his cavalry were defeated by that of General Philip Sheridan and he was mortally wounded. He died the following day, aged 31.

George A. Custer

Long before he would meet his fate at Little Bighorn, Custer, as a newly appointed Brigadier General, commanded a brigade of Michigan cavalry regiments. At Gettysburg, when he was only 24 years old, he displayed his dynamic ability to lead men in battle, leading regiment after regiment in desperate charges that eventually won the day in the cavalry battle east of the battlefield.

Born in 1839 and raised in Michigan and Ohio, Custer went to West Point Military College in 1858, but came last in his class. With the outbreak of the Civil War, he joined the Union Army and developed a strong reputation during the Civil War. He fought in the First Battle of Bull Run. His association with several important officers helped his career, as did his success as a highly effective cavalry commander. At the conclusion of the Appomattox Campaign, in which he and his troops played a decisive role, Custer was present at General Robert E. Lee's surrender.

After the Civil War, Custer was dispatched to the west to fight in the American Indian Wars and appointed lieutenant colonel of the US 7th Cavalry Regiment. He and all his men were killed at the Battle of the Little Bighorn in 1876, fighting against a coalition of Native American tribes. The battle is popularly known as 'Custer's Last Stand'. Custer and his men were so decisively beaten that the Battle of Little Bighorn has diminished all his other previous achievements.

A DEVIL'S CARNIVAL

While fighting was still underway on Devil's Den, the Confederates were approaching Little Round Top. The skirmishers fell back, bringing with them the men of the 2nd US Sharpshooters. Then the 4th and 5th Texas appeared out of the wood. Before them they saw their objective.

'We had to fight the Yankees on a mountain where it was very steep and rocks as large as a meeting house,' one soldier from the 4th Texas recalled. The Southerners scrambled up the slope attacking Vincent's right in what one Texan called 'a devil's carnival.'

'In an instant a sheet of smoke and flames burst from our whole line, which made the enemy reel and stagger, and fall back in confusion,' said an officer of the 83rd Pennsylvania. The Confederates did their best to hold out.

'For the first time in the history of the war, our men began to waver,' said a Texan with the 5th. He recalled the balls 'whizzing so thick around us that it looks like a man could hold out a hat and catch it full.'

Unwilling to withdraw, many Texans lay down where they were. The Union troops held their fire, while others moved forward to take prisoners. This had its own difficulties. Union soldier Oliver W. Sturdevant said:

> *The scene where our first volley struck the enemy's line was one of sickening horror. Their dead and wounded were tumbled promiscuously together, so that it was difficult to cross the line where they fell without stepping on them.*

Captain A.N. Husted, taking a prisoner, said the Texan 'stood directly in front of me begging me not to shoot him, when a bullet, from the musket of a brother Texan, entered his back. Probably he saved my life, or, at least, protected me from a severe wound.' Despite this, the Texans who had retreated to the tree line, reformed, and tried to take the hill a second time.

Dead on Little Round Top.

BONES CRASH LIKE GLASS

As Anderson advanced, his men were pounded from the front by Ward's men on the ridge and from the left by de Trobriand's men by the Wheatfield.

'For nearly an hour the enemy were on three sides of us, and a battery of sixteen guns enfilading us with grape,' said Captain George Hillyer of the 9th Georgia. 'If it had not been for the shelter of rocks and trees behind which we fought, not one of us would have escaped.' A Confederate major with the 59th Georgia said:

Grape, canister, and musket balls fell in a shower like hail around us. I could hear bones crash like glass in a hailstorm. The ground was covered with the dead and the dying, Federals and Confederates lying in piles together. Our regiment was literally cut to pieces, the Federals suffered equally.

De Trobriand's brigade was reinforced by Humphrey's division. Barnes' Third Brigade under Vincent was already engaging the enemy on Little Round Top. Now his First under Colonel Joseph S. Tilton and Second under Colonel Jacob B. Sweitzer also moved forward to support de Trobriand.

Private John Haley was with the 17th Maine holding a stone wall on the left. As Anderson's brigade approached, he said:

Our fire began to tell on their ranks, which were more dense than usual. We peppered them well with musketry while Randolph's battery, which was on a gentle rise in rear of us, served a dose of grape and canister every few seconds. There was a dreadful buzzing of bullets and other missiles, highly suggestive of an obituary notice for a goodly number of Johnny Rebs, and we could see them tumbling around right lively. A great number of our own men were sharing the same fate.

FIRING DOWN ON US

The 15th and 47th Alabama had climbed to the top of Big Round Top in the face of the Sharpshooters who were 'taking shelter and firing down on us from behind the rocks and crags which covered the side of the mountain thicker than gravestones in a city cemetery.'

Terrell caught up with them and told Oates to 'press on, turn the Union left, and capture Little Round Top, if possible, and to lose no time.' His men scarcely had time to rest before they were clambering down the north side of Big Round Top.

Meanwhile the six ten-pounder Parrotts of Battery D, 5th US (Light) Artillery under Lieutenant Charles E. Hazlett had been manhandled to the summit of Little Round Top. Thanks to the trees and boulders, this took considerable effort. But once they were on the summit, Warren told Hazlett that it was not a good place for them. The slope was too steep, so it would be impossible for the guns to hit anything in front of them.

'Never mind that,' said Hazlett, 'the sound of my guns will be encouraging to our troops and disheartening to the others, and my battery's of no use if this hill is lost.'

They began shelling Plum Run Gorge when two Georgia regiments were being held up by the 40th New York from de Trobriand's brigade and the 6th New Jersey from Colonel George C. Burling's Third Brigade of the Second Division. Meanwhile, to the south, Company B of the 20th Maine under Captain Morrill were out skirmishing when some Sharpshooters warned them that Confederates were coming down from Big Round Top. They took shelter behind a stone wall.

The 47th Alabama, now under the command of Lieutenant Colonel Michael J. Bulger, were leading the descent from Big Round Top. Meeting a staff officer of Evander Law, who had now taken command of Hood's Division, Bulger was ordered to charge the Union line.

Without waiting for the 15th, they hit the line at the meeting of the 83rd Pennsylvania and the 20th Maine, who had been warned by their skirmisher. A well-aimed volley cut down the 47th. Bulger was hit. He took shelter in a rocky crevice with blood gushing from his mouth and nostrils where he was captured. Mangled and leaderless, the 47th withdrew.

Hearing the din of battle, the 15th Alabama marched toward it. Oates ordered them to 'swing around, and drive the Federals from the ledge of rocks ... gain the enemy's rear, and drive him from the hill.' However, they were spotted as they attempted to move around the 20th Maine's left flank. Chamberlain then made an unconventional move. He compressed the usual double-rank on musketers into a single long rank, then bent – or 'refused' – the left end back to prevent the Confederates getting round it.

CHAPTER 7
THE RED FIELD OF BATTLE

GAP IN THE UNION LINE

To the left of McLaws' Division, Brigadier General Joseph B. Kershaw, with five South Carolina regiments and battalions, spotted a gap in the Union line between Stony Hill to the west of the Wheatfield and Wheatfield Road. He intended to exploit it. However, when he moved forward towards Emmitsburg Road with Longstreet at his side, he found that half of Hood's men had headed off in the direction of the Round Tops. Then he heard the drum of Brigadier General William Barksdale's Mississippian brigade to his left beating assembly, so he knew he would have no support from them.

He split his brigade in two. Three regiments would head on toward Stony Hill, while the two regiments and battalion on the right would turn northward to attack the Peach Orchard salient. They faced a terrible slaughter at the hands of the artillery there.

'You could constantly see men falling on all sides and terrible missiles of death were flying thick and fast everywhere,' said a soldier with the 2nd South Carolina. Shells were cutting down trees, plowing up the earth, and 'cutting off the arms, legs and heads of our men, cutting them in two, and exploding in their bodies, tearing them to mincemeat.'

The left went to ground, trying to pick off the gunners. Then they suffered from a terrible mistake. The right had got bunched up and the units intermingled. To cure this they were ordered to move to the right and open the line. But the order reached the left instead. The South Carolinians pulled back from the guns and turned their flank and rear to

them. Franklin Gaillard with the 2nd South Carolina saw what happened:

> We were in ten minutes or less time, terribly butchered. I saw half a dozen at a time knocked up and flung to the ground like trifles. In about that short space of time we had about half of our men killed or wounded. It was the most shocking battle I have ever witnessed. There were familiar forms and faces with parts of their heads shot away, legs shattered, arms tore off.

John Coxe remembered 'the awful deathly surging sounds of those little black balls as they flew by us, through us, between our legs and over us.'

General Kershaw lamented: 'Hundreds of the bravest and best men of Carolina fell, victims of this fatal blunder.' Nevertheless, his right took Stony Hill which had been held by Barnes. This meant that the Union line had to fall back to defend the battery in the middle of the Wheatfield.

Missiles of death were flying thick and fast everywhere.

WITHDRAWAL FROM DEVIL'S DEN

To hold Sickles' unauthorized line, the Fifth Corps and the Second Corps had been called in to save the day. Despite the damage they had inflicted on the Confederates, Ward's brigade on Houck's Ridge had lost 781 men out of the two thousand or so engaged, with the 4th Maine suffering fifty percent casualties.

It was now time to withdraw from Devil's Den. The last regiment to leave was the 99th Pennsylvania. Out of the eight color-guard, only two of the enlisted men were left – Corporal George Setley and Private Charles W. Herbster. When the order came to withdraw, Sergeant Munsell remembered:

Nothing would move them. There they were riveted to the ground, avenging the lives of their comrades, and there we left them. Setley was frothing at the mouth with excitement and anger, and Herbster was taking it as cool as a cucumber.

Herbster died later than day. Setley was captured and died in captivity the following year. Munsell escaped with the flag, returning it to the regiment, and earning himself a Medal of Honor.

The Confederates took Devil's Den. Much good it did them as it now became a favorite target for the Union artillery on the surrounding hills.

'All the while the summits were blazing with cannon,' said the reporter from the *Savannah Republican*, 'The shells and shrapnel shot descended, exploding in the earth and hurling the rocks to an amazing height, but in spite of all, our men held their places firmly.'

Dead Confederate sharpshooter in Devil's Den.

PADDY, GIVE ME A REGIMENT

Back at Little Round Top, Oates thought he spotted a weakness. At the left, the line was so stretched that each man sought his own individual cover. Oates ordered a charge. In the face of their concentrated force, a section of the Union line broke, but the flanking fire forced the 15th Alabama back. Chamberlain remembered the enemy came within a dozen yards before the fire of the 20th Maine forced them to break and take cover.

From his position on Little Round Top, Warren could see the Third Corps being driven from their positions and rode out to find reinforcements. He ran into Captain Patrick O'Rorke of the 140th New York heading the column of the Third Brigade of the Second Division, Fifth Corps, under Brigadier General Stephen H. Weed who were headed for the Wheatfield. Warren knew O'Rorke and said: 'Paddy, give me a regiment.'

O'Rorke was awaiting orders from General Weed and hesitated, but Warren assured him that he would take responsibility. Leaving the rest of the column to go on its way, O'Rorke led the 140th New York up Little Round Top, where the situation was getting desperate. Oates was keeping up pressure on Chamberlain's left. Fighting there became hand to hand.

To the left, the 4th Alabama and the 4th and 5th Texas, who had already been beaten back several times, tried again, this time with the assistance of the 48th Alabama. They had to advance across a battlefield already strewn with the dead and the dying. It was too much for some. Private William A. Fletcher of the 5th Texas recalls:

> *We forwarded without a murmur, until we struck the danger point. The men about-faced near as if ordered and marched back. The command 'Halt!' was not heeded.*

Nevertheless some stalwarts continued the advance. Then it was the time for the Union to suffer a blunder. A junior officer in the 16th Michigan, without authority, ordered the colors to the rear. A third of the men fell back with them. The regimental commander, Lieutenant Colonel Norval E. Welch, assumed a general retreat had been ordered and led them off the hill.

Soldiers from Alabama and Texas now swarmed up the slope. The 44th New York to their left turned first to the right. Colonel Vincent rushed to the scene. He threw himself into the breach and rallied his troops – at the cost of his own life. Hit in the groin and mortally wounded he was carried from the field.

'This is the fourth or fifth time they have shot at me,' he said, 'and they have hit me at last.' Command passed to Colonel James C. Rice of the 44th New York.

The gap in the line was now occupied by the Confederates, but the 350 men of the 140th New York turned up in the nick of time. O'Rorke gave the order to open fire. In the resulting fusillade from both sides, O'Rorke fell, mortally wounded in the throat. But the arrival of the 140th put new heart into the other Union units and the Confederates fell back.

THE WHEATFIELD

Sickles sent his aides out to direct reinforcements to the Wheatfield. First to arrive were the First Brigade of Brigadier General John C. Caldwell's division of Hancock's Second Corps, commanded by Colonel Edward E. Cross. Entering the fray in the wrong orientation, they had to quickly reform. Then Cross led them across the eastern edge of the Wheatfield to attack the ragged Confederate battle line in the woods to the south-west.

They bent the line, but before it broke, Cross was shot in the stomach and fell mortally wounded. As he was stretchered off to a field hospital, he said: 'I think the boys will miss me. Say goodbye to all.'

Then came Caldwell's Third Brigade under Brigadier General Samuel K. Zook. He led his men against Kershaw's men on Stony Hill. But the Confederates had good cover there and Zook was shot and killed, and his brigade staggered to a halt.

Then Caldwell's Second Brigade – the Irish Brigade – under Colonel Patrick Kelly took the field. Lieutenant Colonel Elbert Bland of the 7th South Carolina remarked to his commanding officer: 'Is that not a magnificent sight?' In the Wheatfield their almost perfect line was preserved, though Confederate enfilading fire from the woods decimated their front line. Gaps were filled by each file moving closer.

As they closed on the enemy, the Irish Brigade

found their heads level with the Confederates' feet, shooting down on them. Soon the ground was littered with men who had been shot in the head or upper body.

Nevertheless the situation for the defenders grew desperate. Kershaw called on the Georgian brigade of Brigadier General Paul J. Semmes, though he was mortally wounded in the thigh as they went into action. Despite these reinforcements, he could only halt the Irish Brigade, not throw it back.

TO THE LEDGE!

At Little Round Top, Oates tried one more assault, sure that if he could get his boys to the end of the line he might be able to turn it. He pulled out his pistol, waved it in the air and cried: 'Forward men, to the ledge!'

Pausing along the way for his men to catch up, he drew his saber and led the charge. They had only progressed about twenty yards before they were hit with a deadly round of fire and Oates' beloved brother John was cut down.

The 15th Alabama held their ground and exchanged musket and pistol fire with the enemy. The line had thinned as Oates had anticipated, but the Union forces knew what he was planning. They quickly reinforced and counterattacked. The 15th Alabama tried to stave off the counterblow using their muskets as clubs. They were within a few feet of their objective, but hand-to-hand fighting and point-blank fire was too much for them.

Captain De Bernie Waddell of Company G, serving as regimental adjutant, took fifty men from the right wing to try and outflank the enemy. The move further depleted the 15th's strength. They were now taking fire from the 2nd US Sharpshooters and the 20th Maine's Company B from behind a stone wall to the rear. Oates sent a message asking the 4th Alabama for reinforcements. They should have been no more than two hundred yards away, but they could not be found.

The Union troops were about to overrun the 15th's right flank. 'There never were harder fighters than the 20th Maine men and their gallant colonel,' Oates said years later. Then Captain Frank Park and Captain Blant Hill told Oates that they had seen more enemy troops advancing on their rear. When Oates looked round, he saw the toll the Sharpshooters,

protected by the wall, were having on his men.

'While one man was shot in the face, his right-hand or left-hand comrade was shot in the side or back,' he said. 'Some were struck simultaneously with two or three balls from different directions.'

THE BLOOD OF THE BRAVE

It was late afternoon and the shadows were getting longer. All around lay dead Alabamians, mixed with the corpses of men from Maine and Pennsylvania, and the wounded, crying out for water.

'My dead and wounded were then nearly as great in number as those still on duty,' said Oates. 'They literally covered the ground. The blood stood in puddles in some places on the rocks; the ground was soaked with the blood of as brave men as ever fell on the red field of battle.'

Park and Hill urged Oates to order a retreat, but he still hoped for reinforcements. 'Return to your companies,' said Oates. 'We will sell out as dearly as possible.' Park snapped a salute. 'All right, sir,' he said. Hill was too stunned to reply.

But Oates soon had misgivings. The 15th were exhausted and almost out of ammunition. The units were hopelessly disorganized. The men could keep up fire from behind rocks and trees, but organizing another uphill charge would be impossible.

Oates ordered a retreat. They would have to abandon their dead and wounded, including Oates' own brother. As he gave the signal to retire, amid a monstrous clamor of clanking metal and shouting, Union soldiers swept down the hill with bayonet's fixed. 'We ran like a herd of wild cattle,' said Oates.

FIELD OF FIRE

On the way down the slope, some of Oates' men turned and fired. Others were too tired and surrendered, begging their captors for a sip of water. Waddell's detail were chased off to the east, in the direction of Taneytown Road. Others ran straight into the field of fire of the Sharpshooters behind the stone wall.

The flag disappeared into the tree line. But the color-bearer fell wounded. A Yankee soldier tried to pry the flag from his hand. As he did so, Sergeant Patrick O'Connor of the 15th Alabama bayoneted him in the side of the head, grabbed the flag and fled the field.

LAST HOME OF A REBEL SHARPSHOOTER

Like other Civil War photographers, Alexander Gardner sometimes tried to communicate both pathos and patriotism with his photographs, reminding his audience of the tragedy of war. Sometimes, the most effective means was to create a scene – by posing bodies – and then draft a dramatic narrative to accompany the picture.

Contemporary analysis confirmed that the type of weapon seen in this photograph was not used by sharpshooters. Moreover this particular firearm was seen in a number of Gardner's scenes at Gettysburg and probably was the photographer's prop. Such a rifle would not have survived the hordes of relic hunters who swarmed over the battlefields. But Gardner's photo succeeded in transforming this soldier into a particular character in the drama, a man who suffered a painful, lonely, unrecognized death.

Gettysburg, Pa., Dead Confederate soldier in the Devil's Den. Photographed by Alexander Gardner, July 1863.

Oates remembered fleeing through what he thought were a line of dismounted cavalry and taking three of them prisoner. He also remembered a man near him who had been wounded in the throat. His breath whistled as he breathed through his trachea and blood sprayed out of his neck every time he exhaled.

DEFENSIVE LINE

Waddell came across Captain Francis Shaff's Company A, which had been sent to pursue Union Sharpshooters that had been harassing the regiment as they moved forward. They went on to capture several Union wagons and remained detached from the regiment for the rest of the day. Hastily they formed a defensive line to halt the 20th Maine who were now in hot pursuit.

Oates tried to reform his line, but it was impossible. His men were too disorganized, terrified, or preoccupied with helping the wounded. In the heat, the exhausted Oates passed out. Two of his burliest men carried him to the summit of Big Round Top, where the regiment's assistant surgeon revived him.

As he rested there, he wondered whether he could have turned the flank if he had had just one more company with him. One company had been left behind at the starting line, filling canteens. They had been captured trying to catch up. He had also detached Company A. While it was clear that the loss of these two units had played a role in their failure to take Little Round Top, he said to himself: 'The men did their best for me, and I did my best for them. We all fought hard here today. I will not dwell on what might have been.'

Reconsidering the matter years later, he realized that, even if he had taken Little Round Top, there was no way that he could have held it for more than a few minutes.

FIRE AT WILL

With fighting in the Wheatfield now at a standstill, Caldwell committed his Fourth Brigade under Colonel John R. Brooke. Leading his men into the middle of the field, Brooke ordered his men to fire at will. 'The din was almost deafening,' said a Union officer. 'The men were firing as fast as they could load.'

However, they got mixed up with the other Union units fighting there and the Confederate riflemen began to find their range. It was clear that they would either have to go forward or back.

'Fix bayonets!' Brooke ordered.

Seizing the colors, he moved forward. The men were soon charging toward the south-west corner of the field. The onslaught overwhelmed Anderson's men and forced Kershaw off Stony Hill and back to Rose farm.

Brooke now found himself supported by two brigades of regular US Army troops, part of Brigadier General Romeyn B. Ayres' Fifth Corps and Colonel Jacob B. Sweitzer's brigade covering his left flank. They advanced to the northern end of Houck's Ridge, where they were harassed by Confederate snipers on Devil's Den.

BARKSDALE'S CHARGE

The momentum seemed to be with the Union, but Barksdale had assembled 1,400 Mississippians and marched them on a narrow front toward the Peach Orchard. The artillery there was depleted by long counter-battery actions. But Battery E of the 1st Rhode Island Light Artillery under Lieutenant John K. Bucklyn on the western side of the road blasted them with canister. Other Union guns turned on them.

Colonel Benjamin G. Humphreys gave the order: 'Double quick, charge!' Private McNeily of the 21st Mississippi on the right said:

At top speed, yelling at the tops of their voices, without firing a shot, the brigade sped swiftly across the field and literally rushed the goal; our men began to drop as soon as they came to attention, and were well peppered in covering the distance to the enemy.

Barksdale's line tore through the fields without breaking ranks even when exploding shells blew holes in them. Their blood was up and they wanted to exact revenge on the Union cannon that had outgunned theirs. The Mississippi veterans were invigorated, unleashed at last to get to grips with the Yankees. They were unstoppable. The artillerymen began towing their guns away, while support regiments fell back in disarray. One eyewitness reported:

Daniel E. Sickles

Sickles was a controversial figure. Born in New York in 1825, he studied law at the University of the City of New York and won a seat in the New York State Assembly as a Democrat in 1847. When he was thirty-three, he married Teresa Bagioli, who was fifteen or sixteen. The following year he was censured by the legislature for bringing a known prostitute into the chambers. He also took her with him when he became secretary to the US delegation in London and introduced her to Queen Victoria, using as her alias the surname of a political opponent. He caused more scandal by snubbing the Queen at an Independence Day celebration.

Returning to the US, he was elected to the New York Senate, then the US House of Representatives. In 1859, he shot dead his wife's lover in Lafayette Square, across the street from the White House. He was the first person in the US to use the defense of temporary insanity and was acquitted.

Already a major in the New York National Guard, he raised four volunteer regiments for the Union Army, becoming colonel of one of them, though he had to relinquish command when Congress refused to confirm his commission. Using his political connections, he regained his rank and commanded the 'Excelsior Brigade,' comprising the four regiments he had raised, at the Battle of Seven Pines and the Seven Days Battles. President Lincoln nominated him for promotion to Major General in November 1862.

He distinguished himself at the Battle of Chancellorsville. His failure to follow Meade's orders as Gettysburg, effectively ended his career in active service. He also lost a leg there. After the war he served as military governor of North and South Carolina, then as US minister to Spain. He retired from politics after a final term in Congress and died in 1914.

The shattered line was retreating in separate streams, artillerists heroically clinging to their still smoking guns, and brave little infantry squads assisting them with their endangered cannon over soft ground. The positions of these batteries showed broken carriages, caissons and wheels, while scores of slain horses and men lay across each other in mangled and ghastly heaps.

Mississippian Private Henley said the Yankees 'ran in crowds. You could not shoot without hitting two or three of them.'

WHERE ARE MY MEN?

Once they had taken the Peach Orchard, the Confederates stopped to reform, but Barksdale urged them on. 'We have them on the run,' he ordered. 'Move your regiments.'

The fleeing Union artillery streamed past Sickles' headquarters at the Trostle farm. As the 68th Pennsylvania fell back, Colonel Andrew H. Tippin was stopped by Brigadier General Charles K. Graham who ordered him 'at once to engage the enemy coming down on our right flank, which was promptly done under his directions.'

The 68th Pennsylvania, 2nd New Hampshire, and 3rd Maine formed a second line along Wheatfield Road before being pushed back again. The last of General Graham's regiments to leave the field was the 141st Pennsylvania. As Colonel Henry J. Madill trudged to the rear, he was met by Sickles, who said: 'Colonel, for God's sake can't you hold on?' All Madill could say, with tears in his eyes, was: 'Where are my men?'

The 141st Pennsylvania had lost 151 out of the 209 engaged, the highest casualty rate in Graham's brigade.

With Barksdale's charge into the Peach Orchard, the Trostle farm became too hot for a corps headquarters, not because of direct fire at it, but shots flying over the ridge and landing there. It was decided to move the headquarters behind the buildings for added protection. While Sickles was doing this, a shot glanced off his legs without even spooking his horse.

His mangled leg was bound with handkerchiefs, then with a strap from a saddle. Command was passed to Birney. Sickles was stretchered to the Third Corps hospital on Taneytown Road, puffing on a cigar. His leg was amputated that afternoon. On July 4, he was taken back to Washington, DC, bearing news of victory. President Lincoln and his son Tad visited him the next day. Sickles received the Medal of Honor for 'most conspicuous gallantry on the field.' The shattered bone of the leg, along with a cannonball of the type that had hit it, are on display in the National Museum of Health and Medicine in Silver Spring, Maryland.

TO DO MY DUTY

Throughout the day, there was an artillery duel between Latimer's Confederate guns on Benner's Hill and the Union guns on Culp's Hill and Cemetery Hill. One of the first casualties on Latimer's line was Captain William D. Brown of the Chesapeake Artillery. He had ridden round to the front of the guns to exhort his men to fight manfully for the honor of Maryland. Just as he finished, a solid shot hit his right leg, went through his horse, and shattered his left leg.

The disemboweled horse toppled over, breaking three of the captain's ribs and pinning him to the ground. Some of his men managed to extricate him. As they carried him to the rear, he passed the 1st Maryland and said to Captain John W. Torsch: 'Captain, if you should get home, tell my poor father I died endeavoring to do my duty.' Then he added: 'We are making out badly up there.'

At first, the Confederates cheered because the Union gunners shot high. But these were only ranging shots. Soon Rebel casualties began to mount. When Private Jacob F. Cook, who was serving as Number One cannoneer with Brown's battery, went to find out what was delaying the ammunition, he asked Sergeant Robert A. Crowley, chief of the piece, where the rest of the crew were. Crowley showed him. Corporal Daniel Dougherty had been cut in half. Private Frederick Cusick's head had been taken off. The rest were lying about wounded. As they talked, another shell landed, disemboweling the driver of the gun carriage Private Thaddeus Parker and killing the two lead horses. Crowley and Cook carried the dying Parker to the rear where he begged to be put out of his misery.

GETTYSBURG PEACH ORCHARD
BY EDWIN FORBES (1894)

Union General Daniel Sickles spurs ahead of his officers to inspect the front lines of his threatened Third Corps at the tip of the Peach Orchard salient. Confederates can be seen massing for an attack by the fringe of trees in the distance.

African-Americans at Gettysburg

Before the Civil War, some 190 African-Americans lived in Gettysburg. One free black resident of Gettysburg, Randolph Johnston, had been 'training a local colored militia for such an emergency.' Now that it was at hand, David Wills, a white lawyer who would host President Lincoln at the dedication of the Soldiers' National Cemetery at Gettysburg that November, telegraphed Governor Curtin informing him of the availability of Johnston's sixty men. The offer was declined.

Johnston was determined to fight anyway. He and local teacher Lloyd Watts joined the 24th US Colored Troops, both becoming sergeants.

A black unit of thirty-day volunteers organized in Philadelphia after June 15, 1863 made it all the way to Harrisburg to take part in the Gettysburg campaign, but upon arriving, were told by their white commander that he could only accept sixty-day volunteers; by the time he was overruled, it was too late for them to take part in the battle.

As the Confederate army moved into the North, they seized African-Americans – whether runaway slaves or free men and women – as 'contraband.' Those in Gettysburg fled, hid, or feigned infirmity so they would not be attractive to slave owners. Mary Fastnacht, a white woman who was twelve at the time, said: 'They, of course, were badly frightened and, with their bundles tried to leave town.'

Two refugees, a mother and a daughter appealed to Mary's mother because 'they were alone and did not know what to do.' 'Mother told them to come to our house,' said Mary, 'that she would hide them in the loft over the kitchen, take the ladder away and they would be safe.' Some were not so lucky, one eyewitness said they 'saw "a number of colored people" corralled together and marched away.'

Others were forced to cook and clean for the Confederate officers. The Confederate army used black teamsters, slaves hired out by their white owners. Some sixty-four were captured and taken to Fort McHenry in Baltimore. Not until December 18, 1863, did the US War Department issue orders about how to handle those still there. They said:

> Those who wish to take the oath of allegiance can be discharged, and if they so choose, continue as private servants of officers, or serve the Government as Cooks, Teamsters, Laborers or in any other capacity in which they can be useful. Those who refuse to take the oath of allegiance will be detained as prisoners of war, and will be employed or not, as the Commanding Officers of the Post where they are confined, may deem expedient and proper.

Researching the role of African-Americans at Gettysburg, Harvard Professor Henry Louis Gates could only find one who had fought there, Charles F. Lutz. He was with the 8th Louisiana – a Confederate infantry regiment. Apparently he could pass for white in census records. He was wounded on East Cemetery Hill on the second day of the battle.

One free black Gettysburgian Basil Biggs led a crew of black men to rebury more than 3,500 soldiers from disparate hospital sites to the new Soldiers' National Cemetery. However, such service seems to have done local African-Americans little good. The book *The Colors of Courage* points out:

> Of the thirty-six hotels and boardinghouses in the area in the early 1950s, none accepted guests of color and only three (out of fourteen) restaurants served them food, 'depending on the situation.'

Company E, 4th U.S. Colored Infantry at Fort Lincoln, District of Columbia, c. 1863.

GOING TO BALTIMORE

Corporal Samuel Thompson was dealing out ammunition from the ammunition chest of his piece. Sam was a carefree fellow who often spoke longingly of returning to his home in Baltimore. But he was careless about closing the metal lid of the chest after removing rounds from it. When a cannoneer warned him that he was running a risk, but Sam said: 'Oh nothing's going to hurt Sam. Sam's going to Baltimore!'

A few seconds later a shell exploded nearby, scattering sparks. Some fell into Sam's open ammunition chest. The chest exploded in 'a sheet of flame, a terrible report.' Sam was found lying nearby on the ground. Cannoneer John Hatton remembers it well:

Clothing scorched, smoking and burning, head divested of cap and exposing a bald surface where used to be a full suit of hair, whiskers singed off to the skin, eyebrows and eye-lids denuded of their fringes, and the eyes set with a popped gaze, and facial expressions changed to a perfect disguise. Was he breathing? No! The body was warm and flaccid, but the spirit had flown from the care and scenes of strife to seek his 'Baltimore.' It was the body of Sam Thompson, the jovial soul.

TWO OR THREE YARDS OF MEN

From his vantage point on Culp's Hill, Wainwright watched as a single shell from Latimer's gun 'struck in the center of a line of infantry who were lying down behind the wall. Taking the line lengthways, it literally plowed up two or three yards of men, killing or wounding a dozen or more. Fortunately it did not burst.'

Fearing for his infantry, General Geary called for the Twelfth Corps guns to counter it. Lieutenant Edward D. Muhlenberg sent a section of Napoleons plus three ten-pounder Parrotts under the command of Lieutenant Edward R. Geary, the general's son, to the summit. They had to cut down some trees to clear the field of fire. In a letter to his mother, Lieutenant Geary described how they had disabled the enemy battery eight-hundred yards to their front, blowing up two of its caissons, dismounting one of its pieces, and killing twenty-five of its horses. In the action three of his own men were wounded. Geary described the scene:

One had a piece of his head knocked off, all the flesh between his shoulder and neck taken away, and his right hand almost knocked off. He was still living when we left Gettysburg. He was a terrible sight when first struck, and when I had him carried to the rear, it almost turned my stomach, which is something that, as yet, has never been done. The other two were not so severely wounded. I made one very narrow escape from a shell. One of the gunners, who saw the flash of one of the rebel guns, hallowed to me to 'look out, one's coming,' and I had just time to get behind a tree before the shell exploded within a foot of where I had been standing.

PERMISSION TO WITHDRAW

From his vantage point in the cupola of the Roman Catholic church, Ewell assumed that Longstreet was making steady Confederate progress on the right and ordered an attack.

No sooner had the orders to move reached General Johnson on the far left than a sergeant major of Latimer's command arrived to tell him that 'the terrible fire of the enemy's artillery rendered his position untenable.' Johnson gave his permission for Latimer to withdraw, provided he left four guns in place to cover the advance of his infantry.

To the east of Benner's Hill was Brinkerhoff's Ridge. All day, the Confederate and Union forces had been skirmishing there. This was important because the ridge was bisected by the Hanover Road, which ran directly into Ewell's flank. The 2nd Virginia of Brigadier General James A. Walker's veteran Stonewall Brigade was sent to hold it.

DISMOUNTED CAVALRY

In the late afternoon, the Union skirmishers were replaced by dismounted cavalrymen who had been sent to Gettysburg to intercept Stuart. Brigadier General Walker ordered the 2nd Virginia forward. They pushed back four companies of the 10th New York Cavalry north of the road. The four companies of the 10th south of the road also pulled back. Together they counterattacked but could do nothing more than slow the 2nd Virginia's advance.

Two companies of Pennsylvania dismounted cavalry then turned up and double-quicked it up to a stone wall. From there, they emptied their carbines into the enemy, aided by a two-gun battery behind them on the road, and stopped them.

It was getting dark and Colonel John Quincy Adams Nadenbousch, commanding the 2nd Virginia, concluded that he was facing a number of infantry and cavalry regiments, backed by artillery. This was reported back to Walker.

When Johnson began his assault on Culp's Hill, he asked Walker whether the Hanover Road was secure enough for him to move the Stonewall Brigade up. Walker said it wasn't. So Johnson went into action without the 1,300 battle-hardened veterans of the Stonewall Brigade.

SENSING VICTORY

With no attack coming on the right, Meade had shifted as many men as possible over to the left. Major General George Sykes' Fifth Corps and Major General John Sedgwick's Sixth Corps had been sent there. Then Meade ask Major General Henry W. Slocum to send as many men as he could spare from the Twelfth Corps. He ordered two divisions from Culp's Hill to head for the left flank. He thought Meade wanted him to send the whole of the Twelfth Corps if at all possible.

Indeed the situation on the left was perilous. The collapse of Birney's position in the Peach Orchard, left Humphrey's Second Division exposed to the left and rear. Birney, now corps commander, sent word that he should bend back his flank to form a new line with the men on the Big and Little Round Tops. This was impossible as there was a gap in the line where Birney's men had been. Nevertheless Brewster angled his Second Brigade backwards to protect his left. But the Confederates now sensed victory. One of Humphrey's aides recalled clearly:

The crash of artillery and the tearing rattle of our musketry was staggering, and added to the noise in our side, the advancing roar and cheer of the enemy's masses, coming on like devils incarnate ... our thin line showed signs of breaking. The battery enfilading us redoubled its fire, portions of Birney's command were moving to the rear broken and disordered. Our left regiments took the contagion and fled, leaving a wide gap through which the enemy poured in upon us. In vain did staff officers draw their swords to check their flying soldiers ... For a moment the rout was complete.

DANGER WARNINGS

Longstreet led the all-Georgian brigade of Brigadier General William T. Wofford along Emmitsburg Road until he was warned of the danger of being 'shot down by our own troops'. He dismounted and went to the back.

Wofford then made for Stony Hill. This reinvigorated the South Carolinians of Kershaw's Brigade and Georgians under Anderson and Semmes. They forced back the Union troops of Brooke, Zook, and the Irish Brigade. The five small regiments of regular US troops under Colonel Sidney Burbank in Ayres' Fifth Division moved in to extricate Sweitzer's brigade, taking heavy loses.

One volunteer said: 'For two years the US regulars taught us how to be soldiers; in the Wheatfield at Gettysburg, they taught us how to die like soldiers.'

Breaking away from Barksdale's Brigade, the 21st Mississippi engaged the 2nd New Hampshire who reeled back to Cemetery Ridge. Brigadier General Charles K. Graham, hit in the shoulder by a musket ball and in his hip by shrapnel, tried to escape by lying down on his horse's neck. The Rebels simply shot his horse out from under him, extricated the general and took him prisoner.

PULLING BACK

The Union batteries down Wheatfield Road were pulling back. The last of them to leave was the 2nd Battery of the New Jersey Light Artillery under Captain A. Judson Clark. They were just about to make their getaway when some Mississippians jumped on board.

'Halt, you Yankee sons of bitches,' one yelled. 'We want those guns.'

'Go to hell,' said the Northerner. 'We want to use them yet awhile.'

Another retreating Union unit opened fire on the Rebels and Clark's men made off with the gun.

THREE 'JOHNNIE REB' PRISONERS, CAPTURED AT GETTYSBURG, 1863. PHOTOGRAPH BY MATHEW BRADY

Mathew Brady arrived at Gettysburg nearly two weeks after the fighting, around July 15, by which time the battlefield and bodies had been largely cleaned up and most Confederate prisoners were long gone. So who were these three men? No one knows for sure, but after Gettysburg, many of Robert E. Lee's conscripted hired soldiers became disaffected, so there is a good chance that they may have been Southern deserters. It is ironic that Brady's resulting famous photograph has made them into one of the Civil War's most iconic images of Confederate soldiers.

CHAPTER 8

BULLETS AS THICK AS HAILSTONES

FINISH THE WAR

Seeing the gap in the Union line at the Peach Orchard, Longstreet's artillery officer Colonel Alexander also thought the battle was won. He urged his men forward, telling them that they would 'finish the whole war this afternoon.' However, a thousand yards further on he saw 'a ridge giving good cover behind it and endless fine positions for batteries. And batteries in abundance were showing up and troops too seemed to be marching and fighting everywhere.' This did, however, give him plenty of targets to shoot at.

Longstreet, too, was not convinced the battle was won. Every thrust forward had been met with a riposte. 'To urge my men forward under these circumstances would have been madness,' he said.

> **Take your brigade ... and knock the hell out of the Rebs.**

HILL'S SECTOR

Onus now turned to Hill's sector. The next along the Confederate line was Major General Richard H. Anderson's Division which had seen no action the previous day. On his right was Brigadier General Cadmus M. Wilcox's Brigade of Alabamians.

However, Wilcox could not advance straight ahead without becoming entangled in men from McLaws' Division who had veered to the left in their charge. So Wilcox had to move his brigade four hundred yards to the north before turning to the east.

Meade ordered Hancock to take over command of the Third Corps, but when he caught up with Birney, he was told 'the Third Corps had gone to pieces and fallen to the rear.' Nevertheless, he turned to Colonel George L. Willard of the so-called Harpers Ferry Brigade and ordered him to prepare for battle.

Hancock decided to send the Third Division to support Birney. When the order reached Hays, he turned to Willard and said: 'Take your brigade over there and knock the hell out of the Rebs.'

The Harpers Ferry Brigade advanced, not in conventional fashion, but in line abreast and, unusually, with fixed bayonets, which made reloading a musket more difficult.

Barksdale's Mississippians continued their advance in a loose formation until they were suddenly hit on the front and left by the Harpers Ferry Brigade. But while the Union men were fresh, the Southerners were a spent force. Shouting and swearing Barksdale sought to rally his men. Yankee guns turned on him and he was hit several times. The Union line passed over the fallen Confederate leader and he was captured and died in captivity the following day.

THE UNSTOPPABLE REBELS

The remaining Union guns on Wheatfield Road did not have enough horses left to tow the guns away. Those hitched up were shot by the Confederates. The guns had to be moved by prolonge – an arrangement of ropes that allowed the gun to be manhandled backward during recoil. The guns were then used to fill holes in the line where there was not enough infantry. They fired canister shot with the fuse cut so they would explode at short range from the muzzle of the cannon. Private David Brett of the 9th Independent Battery, Massachusetts Light Infantry recalls the scene:

HARPERS FERRY BRIGADE

The US armory at Harpers Ferry, West Virginia, played a key role in the Civil War. The raid on the arsenal there by the radical anti-slavery activist John Brown in 1859, while failing in its aim to provoke an armed slave uprising, polarized the national debate on the abolition of slavery and propelled the nation toward Civil War. Brown was captured, tried for treason, and hanged.

Between 1861 and 1865, Harpers Ferry changed hands eight times. Because of its strategic position, both Union and Confederate armies frequently moved through the town.

When Virginia seceded in April 1861, the US garrison tried to burn the arsenal and destroy the weapons-making equipment there. In the Battle of Harpers Ferry in September 1862, Major General Thomas J. 'Stonewall' Jackson surrounded the town, which was virtually indefensible as it was enclosed on three sides by high ground. Colonel George L. Willard

commanded the 125th New York Volunteer Regiment there; men who had been in the Army for just twenty-one days. Lacking even the most basic combat skills, they failed to hold an exposed position. Few were killed, but over twelve thousand surrendered.

The captured regiments were paroled early in 1863, exchanged for Confederate prisoners, and were assigned to the defense of Washington, DC, where Alexander Hays put them through rigorous training. Nevertheless when they turned up at Gettysburg under the command of Willard, the Harpers Ferry Brigade were greeted as the 'Harpers Ferry Cowards' until they proved themselves in combat – which is what they did.

They halted the advance of Barksdale after he had taken the Peach Orchard, charging into action with the cry 'Remember Harpers Ferry!' Willard was shot in the face by an artillery round and died instantly.

Harpers Ferry, West Virginia, *c.* 1860.

We fought with our guns until the Rebs could put their hands on [them]. The bullets flew as thick as hailstones ... it is a miracle that we were not all killed ... nor a man ran, four of five fell within fifteen feet of me.

The Union were taking a terrible beating. It seemed to many on both sides that the Confederates were unstoppable. However, the Union troops were making the Rebels pay a very high price for their gains.

At the southern edge of the battlefield, the Confederates tried to break the Union line by pushing across the northern neck of Little Round Top. This was prevented by the Fifth Corps, supported by the Sixth who had just arrived on the battlefield, and the Pennsylvania Reserves – with six members winning a collective Medal of Honor when they rushed a cabin and captured the Confederate sharpshooters sheltering there.

THE IRISH BRIGADE

Irishmen fought on both sides during the Civil War. However, new immigrants in New York, Boston, and Philadelphia made up most of the Irish contribution – 144,000 men fighting for the Union.

The formation of the Irish Brigade was authorized by the Secretary of War in September 1861. It originally consisted of the 63rd, 69th, and 88th New York Infantry. The 28th Massachusetts and the 116th Pennsylvania joined later.

They fought in all the major battles of the war. In early training in 1862, they mustered some three thousand men. A year later, only three hundred were left. They had lost seven hundred in the Seven Days Battles, 540 at Antietam, and 545 at Fredericksburg. After the Battle of Chancellorsville, Brigadier General Thomas F. Meagher wrote to his divisional headquarters, saying: 'I beg most respectfully to tender you ... my resignation as Brigadier General commanding what was once known as the Irish Brigade. That Brigade no longer exists.'

However, the brigade was not disbanded. Several hundred of its injured recovered in time for the Battle of Gettysburg, where it fielded 532 officers and men – making it the smallest of the fifty-eight Union brigades. It lost thirty-seven percent of that strength in the battle. Nevertheless, it continued fighting and took part in the victory parade in Washington, DC, at the end of the war. It lives on as the 'Fighting 69th' of the New York National Guard.

Lt. Col. James J. Smith and officers of 69th New York Infantry (Irish Brigade), 1862.

George L. Willard

George Willard was the son and grandson of generals. He had served as an enlisted man in the Mexican War, received a commission in 1848, and was a captain in the 8th United States Infantry at the outbreak of the Civil War.

Promoted to major of the 19th US, he took leave to become colonel of the 125th New York. Willard and his men surrendered at the Union debacle at Harpers Ferry, earning them the nickname of the 'Harpers Ferry Cowards'.

The brigade was paroled, and exchanged for Confederate prisoners, after spending a miserable winter in a Union prison camp. General Hays rebuilt their shattered morale, and by Gettysburg they were spoiling for a chance to erase their bad name.

On July 2, Willard led the brigade in a counter-attack against Barksdale's Mississippi Brigade, who had punched a half mile deep hole in the Union lines. Shouting 'Remember Harpers Ferry!' the brigade threw back the Mississippians, recaptured several Union cannon, and mortally wounded General Barksdale. It was doubly sweet revenge, as the Missippians had been one of the brigade's foes at Harpers Ferry.

But Willard was also killed, struck in the head by an artillery shell as the brigade was pulling back to Union lines. His body was carried to a farmhouse on Taneytown Road, where it was wrapped in linen and sent home for burial.

A small monument to Colonel George Willard stands south of Gettysburg in Plum Run swale between the State of Pennsylvania Monument and the Codori Farm. It was erected in 1888 by the survivors of the 125th New York Infantry Regiment.

ADVANCED TOO FAR

The 21st Mississippi were still on the rampage and captured the guns of Battery I of the 5th US Light Cavalry under Lieutenant Malbone F. Watson before they had even been fired. But the Rebel commander Colonel Benjamin G. Humphreys quickly realized that they had advanced too far. The Confederate lines on both sides had been checked and he beat a hasty retreat when the 39th New York – the so-called Garibaldi Guard – recaptured Watson's guns.

Colonel George L. Willard's Harpers Ferry Brigade had shown their mettle by preventing the collapse of the Union center, going on to recapture the three guns of the 3rd US Light Artillery abandoned during the Third Corps' retreat from Emmitsburg Road. Their success brought them the attention of the Confederate guns and they fell back.

Though Colonel Willard had restored the reputation of his men, he would not live to enjoy it. According to the regimental history written by Ezra D. Simons, chaplain of the 125th New York Volunteers in 1888, on their way back across Plum Run, Willard was struck by a shell that 'carried away part of his face and head ... and the colonel fell from his horse instantly killed.'

Willard's body was quickly carried from the field, to avoid demoralizing the troops. The loss of such a promising leader was keenly felt. Hancock later stated that Willard was 'one of the best officers of his rank and age.'

THE GARIBALDI GUARD

The 39th New York Volunteer Infantry Regiment were the most polyglot of all the Union Army. Also known as the 1st Foreign Rifles they comprised Hungarians, Spaniards, Italians, French, Swiss, and British veterans of the Crimean War and the India Mutiny – some eleven nationalities in all. They got their nickname the 'Garibaldi Guard' because, before they received the full uniform, they paraded in the red shirts associated with Giuseppe Garibaldi's Republican Army that united Italy in 1860.

The regiment's full uniform consisted of a blue frock coat, blue pants trimmed with red cord, red undershirt, and a felt hat decorated with feathers and green leaves. Their knapsacks were said to contain blankets and comfortable under clothing, while their haversacks 'were crammed with bread, cheese, bologna sausages, etc.'

They were mustered in New York City for three-years service in May 1861 by George D'Utassy, a Hungarian Jew who served in the Austrian Army before defecting to the Hungarian revolutionaries in 1848. Captured and sentenced to death, he escape to Turkey, moving on via England to Nova Scotia, where he worked as a cavalry instructor, dancing teacher, and a language professor – he claimed to speak twelve languages.

The Garibaldi Guard was initially attached to the 1st Brigade of the Fifth Division under Colonel Louis Blenker, a German-American soldier. But D'Utassy did not get on with Blenker because of his hatred of Germans. He tried to Americanize his unit and refused to accept orders in German. Blenker went on to command the German Division.

The 39th New York was at Harpers Ferry, but D'Utassy was cleared of any fault. However, he was court-martialed again in 1863 for forging muster rolls and accounts, defrauding the government, and selling the rank of major to a fellow officer. He ended up in Sing Sing prison.

Captain Schwartz, sharpshooter, 39th New York Regiment (Garibaldi Guard), 1861.

NO SUPPORT CAME

Meanwhile General Cadmus Wilcox continued to advance, though 'grape and canister were poured into our ranks.' They were approaching Cemetery Ridge, Wilcox wrote later:

> *This stronghold of the enemy, together with his batteries, were almost won, when still another line of infantry descended the slope in our front at a double-quick. Seeing this contest so unequal, I dispatched my adjutant-general to the division commander to ask that support be sent to my men, but no support came. Three several times did this last of the enemy's lines attempt to drive my men back and were as often repulsed. The struggle at the foot of the hill on which were the enemy's batteries, though so unequal, was continued for some thirty minutes. With a second supporting line, the heights could have been carried. Without support on either my right or my left, my men were withdrawn to prevent their entire destruction or capture.*

For the Union, this was little short of a miracle. The men of the 1st Minnesota had been moved onto the ridge just an hour earlier, just in time to witness Caldwell's disastrous engagement. Their commander, Colonel William Colvill, had tried to muster enough stragglers to form a line. Hancock had to order him to stop, for fear of demoralizing the troops.

Though his force was pitifully small, Hancock had no alternative but to commit them. 'Colonel, do you see those colors?' Hancock asked Colvill, pointing to some Confederate flags in Wilcox's lines. 'Then take them'.

SUICIDE MISSION

It was a suicide mission. 262 Minnesotans charged down the hill at nearly 1,600 Alabamians. A sergeant of the 1st Minnesota described the scene in a letter published in the *Saint Paul Pioneer* on August 9, 1863:

> *Now their cannon were pointed to us, and round shot, grape and shrapnel tore fearfully through our ranks, and the more deadly Enfield rifles were directed to us alone. Great heavens, how fast our men fell. Marching as file-closer, it seemed as if every step was over some fallen comrade.*

Cadmus Wilcox

In an army of bearded men, Wilcox's strong jaw was clean-shaven; he was six feet tall, with high cheekbones and a well-tended mustache, and no hint of gray in his short, dark hair. His careful barbering bespoke his 'no nonsense' approach to soldiering.

Yet no man wavers; every gap is closed-up – and bringing down their bayonets, the boys pressed shoulder to shoulder and disdaining the fictitious courage proceeding from noise and excitement, without a word or a cheer, but with silent, desperate determination, step firmly forward in unbroken line ... Three times [our] colors were shot down – and, three times arising go forward as before. One fourth of the men have fallen, and yet no shot has been fired at the enemy, who paused a moment to look with awe upon that line of leveled bayonets, and then, panic-stricken, turned and run; but another line took their place – and poured murderous volleys into us, not thirty yards distant.

Sergeant Mat Marvin of Company K, 1st Minnesota, was one of those who went down during the charge. But he did not stay down. In his journal he wrote:

We had not fired a musket and the Rebs were firing rapidly. I dropped to the ground with a wound somewhat I picked myself up as quick as possible, where I saw blood on my shoe, the heel of which was tore out. I thought it a slight one, and run to ketch up, thinking no Rebel line could stand a charge of my Regiment, and if the bayonet must be used I wanted a chance in, as it was free to all, I had just ketched-up again when I fell a second time, too faint to get up.

Marvin was unable to stand and walk after this second fall. After drinking from his canteen and pouring water over his head and wrists, he crawled back to the Union lines on his hands and knees.

PLUM RUN

The 1st Minnesota reached the dry bed of Plum Run, spurred on their way by the 19th Maine. There they took enfilading fire from the Florida Brigade under Colonel David Lang. The Union survivors then hightailed it back to Cemetery Ridge. They had lost between 170 and 178 of their number. Wilcox wrote:

The enemy did not pursue, but my men retired under a heavy artillery fire, and returned to their original position in the line, and bivouacked for the night, pickets being left on the pike ... In the engagement of this day

I regret to report a loss of 577 men killed, wounded, and missing.

OUR BLEEDING RANKS

A final attempt to capture Cemetery Ridge was undertaken by the Georgia brigade under Brigadier General Ambrose R. Wright with a thousand men. They attacked at the north of the line, under six guns. One of Wright's Georgian brigade wrote later:

Wild with enthusiasm and ardor, on we pressed, while every instant the enemy thundered their shot and shell in our midst. Shells amongst us, shells over us, and shells around us tore our bleeding ranks with ghastly gaps. A comrade shrieks and falls. A hasty glance shows that his right leg was torn off by a shell. Many of us saw the shell just before it struck. Another comrade falls, and the third drops by his side. A shell comes bouncing along, skips one of the two friends lying side by side in agony and strikes the other and tears him in two. The ground roared and rumbled like a great storm, and the shower of Minié balls was pitiless and merciless. We pressed on, knowing that the front was safer now than to turn our backs and with a mighty yell, we threw ourselves upon the batteries and passed them, still reeking hot.

The Union gunners managed to save four of the guns, abandoning just two to the Confederates. But though Union soldiers were massing on the ridge, the Rebels charged on catching up with the four guns that had originally eluded them. The problem was that the Georgians had driven into the Union lines like a wedge, so they were exposed on both flanks. Ambrose Wright and his men were forced to pull back as quickly as they had come and had to abandon three of the guns they had taken.

CHARGED DOWN ON THEM

The 13th Vermont charged down on them, urged on by the commander Colonel Francis V. Randall, whose horse was shot out from under him.

'Go on boys,' he shouted. 'I'll be at your head as soon as I get out of this damned saddle.'

It was an opportunity lost.

'I have not the slightest doubt,' Wright wrote in

his after-action report, 'that I should have been able to maintain my position on the heights ... if there had been a protecting force on my left, or the brigade on my right had not been forced to retire.'

CULP'S HILL

Thinking things were going well on the right, General Ewell decided to attack on the left. He sent in the Second Corps under General Johnson, minus the Stonewall Brigade which was still on Brinkerhoff's Ridge, protecting the left flank. Johnson's first objective was to be Culp's Hill, which was now poorly defended as General Slocum had sent two divisions to the left flank.

The Virginia Brigade under Brigadier General John M. Jones were already in front of Benner's Hill to the east, as security for Latimer's gun. The Louisiana Tigers and the mixed North Carolina-Virginia-Maryland brigade under Brigadier General George H. Steuart were to cross the Hanover Road and extend Jones's flank.

As they moved forward, they had to ford Rock Creek where the water was waist deep. The far bank, though, was occupied by Union skirmishers.

'At about 7:00 pm they began to advance with their line of battle,' said Union General George S. Greene, 'I immediately withdrew my line to this side of the brook, and threw forward every man of my reserve. We held this point with the briskest fire we could concentrate.'

'Scarcely had we reached the creek that runs by the foot of the mountain,' said one Southerner, 'when we were fired upon by the enemy who were 'ambushed' nearby. Four of Company B fell wounded and many others along the line.'

Private Benjamin A. Jones of the 44th Virginia recalled the objective as being 'a ditch filled with men firing down on our heads.' It was dark and the terrain was rough. 'All was confusion and disorder,' said Captain Thomas R. Buckner.

General Jones had been hit in the thigh and had to pass the command to Lieutenant Colonel Robert H. Dungan of the 48th Virginia. The Louisiana Tigers managed to get within a hundred yards of Greene's line, but 'were attended with more loss than success,' lamented Colonel Jesse M. Williams.

AUTUMN LEAVES

Two of Steuart's regiments had stumbled into a cul de sac where they took fire from Greene's men to the front and the 137th New York to their left. They 'reeled and staggered like drunken men,' said one observer. 'Men fell like autumn leaves,' said another. And in the darkness there were numerous incidents of friendly fire.

However, when General Steuart joined the fray at Culp's Hill with three regiments, they found themselves confronting a section that had been unmanned by Slocum and unreinforced by Greene. After clearing a couple of outposts, they moved up the empty trenches until they met the 137th New York under Colonel David Ireland. He pulled back his rightmost company to defend the flank, while Steuart attempted to move round behind it.

The 137th and 149th New York maneuvered to face the enemy. The 149th had to be rallied when they assumed a general retreat was going on. A squad from the 137th then made a bayonet charge on the 10th Virginia led by Captain Joseph H. Gregg, who was mortally wounded. Higher up the hill the 6th Wisconsin, 14th Brooklyn, and 157th New York, kept up a steady barrage of fire. Exhausted, Jones and Nicholls pulled back. Steuart broke off contact, but held on to the trenches he had taken.

ATTACK ON CEMETERY HILL

George Greene called for reinforcements to support the Union troops on Cemetery Hill. Although they made adjustments, it was late and they assumed that they would be spared an attack that day.

They were wrong. General Early had issued orders to advance on Cemetery Hill, sending up the North Carolina brigade under Colonel Avery and Hays' Louisianans.

When he saw the Confederate battle lines directly in front of his positions, Colonel Andrew L. Harris with the Second Brigade on Cemetery Hill said: 'We could not have been much more surprised if the moving column had raised up out of the ground amid the waving timothy grass of the meadow.'

Avery's three regiments came under fire from the 5th Maine Light Artillery, who had spent valuable time registering the distances on their front. Lieutenant Edward N. Whittier wrote:

All comrades of the old Fifth know how quickly and how well our guns opened the artillery fire that evening, for the order, 'Case 2½ degrees, three seconds time', had barely been heard before up went the lids of the limber-chests, the fuses were cut in another moment, and the gun were loaded as if on drill. Slap went the heads of the rammers against the faces of the pieces, a most welcome sound, for at the same moment came the order, 'Fire by battery,' and at once *there was the flash and roar of our six guns, the rush of the projectiles, and along the front of the enemy's charging line every case shot – 'long range canister' – burst as if on measured ground, at the right time and in the right place and in front of their advance.*

A prisoner of war at the nearby German Reformed church recalled with horror and fascination the Confederate advance up the hill:

Confederate General Jubal Anderson Early's attack on East Cemetery Hill, July 2, 1863. Originally published in *The Century Magazine*, 1884.

I could see hands, arms, and legs flying amidst the dust and smoke. It reminded me much of a wagon load of pumpkins drawn up a hill, and the end gate coming out, and the pumpkins rolling and bouncing down the hill.

HIT THEIR OWN MEN

As Confederates approached the Union lines, the Union gunners had to depress their muzzles so much that some of them hit their own men. However, in the midst of this pandemonium Lieutenant Milton Daniels of the 17th Connecticut noticed two cool-headed privates, George Wood and William Curtis:

While the Tigers were coming across the meadows George and Bill were sitting down behind the stone wall, and you would have supposed they were shooting at a target. I saw George shoot, taking a dead rest, and heard him say, 'He won't come any further, will he, Bill?' Then Bill shot, and said: 'I got that fellow, George.' And they kept it up that way, perfectly oblivious to danger themselves.

But eventually the fighting turned to vicious, hand to hand combat.

'Soon, along the whole line, the fighting was obstinate and bloody,' said Colonel Harris, 'The bayonet, club-musket, and anything in fact that could be made available was used, by both the assailing and assailers.'

A GOOD MAN KILLED

The Louisianans rammed through a gap between the 25th Ohio and 75th Ohio in Harris's right center. Sergeant Oscar Ladley of the 75th found himself face to face with a Confederate officer carrying his regiment colors and a pistol.

'I had no pistol nothing but my sword,' he said. 'Just as I was getting ready to strike him, one of our boys run him through the body so saved me. There was a good man killed in that way.'

As Avery's Tarheels closed on Brickyard Lane, the colonel was shot through the throat and mortally wounded. He quickly scribbled some last words for his friend, Major Samuel McDowell Tate commanding the 6th North Carolina: 'Major: Tell my father I died with my face to the enemy. I.E. Avery.' The original note is now in the State Archives in Raleigh.

Command passed to Colonel Archibald C. Goodwin.

A USELESS SACRIFICE OF LIFE

The Louisianans and North Carolinians were now making inroads. Part of the Union line collapsed. This fighting was increasingly ferocious. Rocks were used to break open heads.

The Rebels managed to silence the Union batteries. Confederate reinforcements could now

reach Cemetery Hill without facing Union fire. However, in the darkness it was not easy to know what was going on. Rodes, to Ewell's right, did not believe that there had been a breakthrough and considered sending men to support the action on Cemetery Hill 'a useless sacrifice of life.' There would be no reinforcements that night.

The fighting continued on the eastern part of Cemetery Hill. In the darkness and smoke, the Confederate force appeared much larger than it was. However, Hancock sent over a brigade. Eventually, superior numbers told and the Confederates withdrew. There was only one thing left to do that night.

'We gathered up the dead and cared for the wounded of both friend and foe,' wrote Colonel Harris.

EVERYTHING IS WELL

According to Arthur Fremantle, General Lee only received one report and sent one message the whole day. That evening though, he was visited by General Hill and received reports from Ewell and Longstreet. A visitor to his headquarters that night said that he was himself again. They concluded that: 'Everything is well.'

There could be no doubt that they had inflicted considerable damage on the Army of the Potomac. Though there had been no great breakthrough, Longstreet had gained ground along the Emmitsburg Road and, according to Lee's report: 'Ewell also carried some of the strong positions he assailed.'

Jeb Stuart's three brigades of cavalry had arrived and Lee had a fresh division under Pickett on hand. However, he made no report to Richmond and did not know that there had been some Union raids to the north of the city, causing some panic. Nor did Lee know that on the Union side, Major General John Sedgwick's Sixth Corps had arrived. But John Beauchamp Jones, author of *A Rebel War Clerk's Diary* was sanguine about the enemy's attacks. 'He cannot take Richmond,' he wrote, 'nor draw back Lee.'

OVERNIGHT DECISIONS

That night, Colonel Joshua Lawrence Chamberlain and the 20th Maine took Big Round Top, which was then held by the 83rd Pennsylvania and the 44th

New York. Meanwhile Colonel George H. Sharpe of the Union Army's Bureau of Military Information began compiling the regiment, brigade, and division of the captured Confederates.

He concluded, not entirely accurately, that, with the exception of Pickett, Lee had committed his entire force to the battle, but he had also learned that Pickett's Division had now come up, was bivouacked nearby, and would be ready for action the next morning.

When Sharpe informed Meade and his staff of this, Hancock said: 'General Meade, don't you think Sharpe deserves a cracker and a drink.' Whiskey was provided.

In his report to Washington that night, Meade said he would hold his present position, but until he was advised better of the condition of his army he had not decided whether his actions would be offensive or defensive. He also wrote to his wife, telling her that their son had had two horses shot out from under him.

Afterward there was a council of war. It was generally agreed that, though they were getting short of supplies, the Army of the Potomac was better off staying where they were. The consensus was also that they should remain on the defensive – at least for the next day. Meade was convinced that Lee would attack again.

DEATH AND JOURNALISM

Gettysburg was dark that night. No one dared light lamps to avoid attracting gunfire. The improvised hospitals did what they could, digging out bullets and amputating limbs. The churchyard of the Luther church was full of severed arms and legs that had been thrown out of the windows. But most of the dead and dying still lay where they had fallen.

The wife of General Francis Barlow appeared in the town. On hearing that her husband had been wounded, she had crossed the lines to try and find him. Journalists had also turned up.

'In front of some of our brigades, who had good protection from stone walls or fences,' wrote Lorenzo Crounse of the *New York Times*, 'the rebel dead laid piled in lines like windrows of hay.'

G.W. Hosmer of the *New York Herald* noted: 'Everyone is exhausted and there is great misery for want of water.'

SLEEPING WITH THE DEAD

Local resident Jacob Hollinger argued with Confederate soldiers about food. They asked his daughter Julia to sing for them. She agreed, but would only sing Union songs in the hope that Union soldiers would hear them and be heartened. For each Union song she sang, the Rebels answered with Confederate anthems.

Some Union soldiers sought solace among their fallen comrades. A soldier from the 1st Minnesota said:

> *The sun had gone down and in the darkness we hurried, stumbled over the fields in search of our fallen companions, and when the living were cared for, laid ourselves down on the ground to gain a little rest, for the morrow bid far more stern and bloody work, the living sleeping side by side with the dead.*

Alfred R. Waud, artist of *Harper's Weekly*, sketching on the battlefield.

Council of War. General Meade (standing 2nd from left) meeting with his commanders on the evening of July 2, 1863 at the Leister Farm.

HE HAS SOUNDED FORTH THE TRUMPET THAT SHALL NEVER SOUND RETREAT.

PART 3

THE THIRD DAY

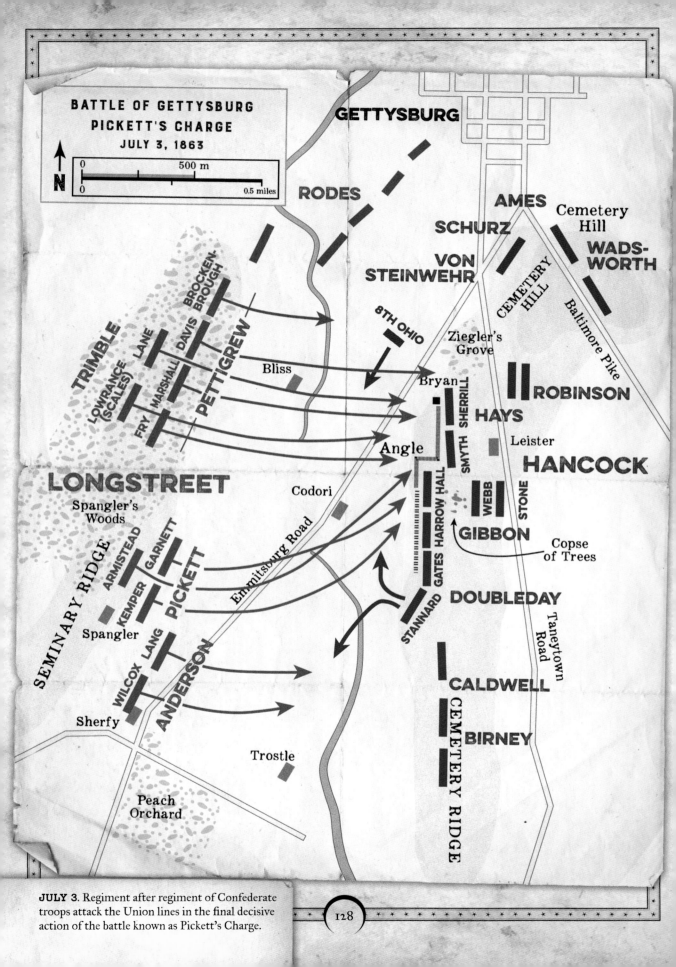

BATTLE OF GETTYSBURG
PICKETT'S CHARGE
JULY 3, 1863

N

0 — 500 m

0 — 0.5 miles

GETTYSBURG

RODES

AMES

Cemetery Hill

SCHURZ

WADS-WORTH

VON STEINWEHR

CEMETERY HILL

Baltimore Pike

8TH OHIO

Ziegler's Grove

Bryan

Bliss

ROBINSON

TRIMBLE

BROCKEN-BROUGH

LANE

DAVIS

PETTIGREW

SHERRILL

HAYS

LOWRANCE (SCALES)

MARSHALL

SMYTH

HANCOCK

FRY

Angle

Leister

LONGSTREET

Codori

HARROW HALL

WEBB

STONE

Spangler's Woods

GIBBON

Copse of Trees

ARMISTEAD

GARNETT

GATES

KEMPER

PICKETT

Emmitsburg Road

STANNARD

DOUBLEDAY

SEMINARY RIDGE

Spangler

Taneytown Road

WILCOX

LANG

ANDERSON

Sherfy

CALDWELL

BIRNEY

Trostle

CEMETERY RIDGE

Peach Orchard

JULY 3. Regiment after regiment of Confederate troops attack the Union lines in the final decisive action of the battle known as Pickett's Charge.

CHAPTER 9

NOTHING LESS THAN MURDER

Lee issued orders to Ewell that he was to attack the enemy's right in the morning. In Ewell's mind though, there was no point in attacking Cemetery Hill again. Instead he could concentrate on Culp's Hill where George Steuart still held a line of trenches.

Meanwhile Colonel Alexander, reporting to Longstreet's bivouac, had also been told that they would renew their attack. Pickett's Division would assault the enemy's line. Longstreet did not know exactly where, but somewhere in the vicinity of the Peach Orchard. He reconnoitered positions for his guns then, with 'my saddle for a pillow and with dead men and horses of the enemy all around, I got two hours of good sound and needed sleep.'

But things did not bode well. During the night the arrival of Jeb Stuart's cavalry and Sedgwick's Sixth Corps had not gone unnoticed. Lieutenant Colonel David Zable of the 14th Louisiana said: 'We could hear and see the arrival of heavy reinforcements of the enemy in our front.'

I felt satisfied that the enemy would attack again.

GENERAL GEORGE MEADE

FORWARD WITH BEATING HEARTS

Out on the Chambersburg Pike that morning, the 5,830 men of Pickett's Division formed up after a frugal meal. Lieutenant William Wood of the 19th Virginia said: 'The usual jests and hilarity were indulged in, and soon after, when ordered into line, we again took up the march, no gloomy forebodings hovered over our ranks.' A captain in temporary command of one of Brigadier General James L. Kemper's regiments had heard from Lee's headquarters that the Union Army was broken and their regiment was at Gettysburg merely to mop up.

However, as they marched toward the battlefield, John Dooley with the 1st Virginia spotted a figure on horseback who he took to be General Robert E. Lee.

'I must confess that the general's face does not look as bright as though he were certain of success,' he said. 'But yet it is impossible for us to be any otherwise than victorious and we press forward with beating hearts.'

With Pickett in place, Longstreet had been ordered to attack according to the 'general plan' of the previous day. This would involve attacking Cemetery Ridge with Alexander's artillery somewhere in the vicinity of the Peach Orchard. However, Longstreet remembered Lee's original plan of enveloping the enemy's left. It now sat on Big Round Top and Longstreet ordered reconnaissance in the area.

MURDER AT SUNRISE

When Union General Alpheus Williams woke at 4:30 am, after what he reckoned was just half-an-hour's sleep, he ordered Lieutenant Muhlenberg commanding the Twelfth Corps' artillery to open fire on Culp's Hill again. Twenty-six guns poured fire onto the Confederate lines some six-hundred to eight-hundred yards away. However, George Steuart's 1st Maryland were well protected by the Union earthworks.

'The whole hillside seemed enveloped in a blaze,' said Major William W. Goldsborough of the 1st Maryland Battalion, 'and the balls could be heard to strike the breastworks like hailstones upon the roof tops.'

When the bombardment lifted, General Geary,

who had returned to the summit of Culp's Hill, was supposed to attack, but General Johnson's Rebels got in first, moving forward searching for a chink in the enemy's lines.

The Louisiana Tigers and the Stonewall Brigade attacked Greene's trenches. 'I think it was the hardest battle we ever had,' said a soldier from the 33rd Virginia. Private Louis Leon of the 53rd North Carolina recalled the carnage:

> It was truly awful, how very fast, did our poor boys fall by our sides – almost as fast as the leaves that fell as cannon and musket balls hit them ... You could see one with his head shot off, others cut in two, then one with his brain oozing out, one with his leg off, others shot through the heart. Then you would hear some poor friend or foe crying for water, or 'For God's sake' to kill him.

'It was nothing less than murder to send men into that slaughter pen,' lamented Major Goldsborough.

A TREMENDOUS BLOW

The Condeferates found themselves up against the entire Twelfth Corps. The 66th Ohio climbed out of their trenches and took a line at right angles, behind rocks, logs, and tree, and poured fire onto the enemy. On the opposite flank the 147th Pennsylvania did the same.

Brigadier General William Smith's Virginia Brigade from Jubal Early's Corps were sent as reinforcements. They were led into place by Johnson's adjutant, Major Henry Kyd Douglas on horseback:

> There came little puffs of smoke, a rattle of small arms, the sensation of a tremendous blow and I sank forward on my horse, who ceased his prancing when my hold was loosened on his bridle reins.

Douglas was carried to the rear and survived to write the book *I Rode With Stonewall: The Experiences of the Youngest Member of Jackson's Staff.*

RUSH THE LINE

General Slocum bypassed General Wright and instructed General Ruger of the 3rd Brigade of the Twelfth Corps who were south of Culp's Hill to attack the Confederate flank which he considered

'shaky.' Ruger thought it better to send a small force to probe the enemy line before committing the entire brigade.

Orders were sent to Colonel Silas Colgrove. He picked two regiments – the 2nd Massachusetts and the 27th Indiana. There was little cover so they were ordered to rush the Rebel line. When the message reached Lieutenant Colonel Charles Mudge commanding the 2nd Massachusetts, he asked: 'Are you sure that is the order?'

Assured that it was, Mudge said: 'Well, it is murder, but it's the order.' The regiment formed

Jennie Wade

Sniper fire between Confederate troops barricaded in Gettysburg town and Union troops on Cemetery Hill continued throughout the day. At 8:30 am twenty-year-old Mary Virginia 'Jennie' Wade was shot by a stray bullet in her sister's kitchen on Baltimore Street as she made biscuits for Union soldiers. She was the only civilian casualty of the battle.

up and Mudge shouted: 'Up men, over the works! Forward, double quick!'

The men let out a Yankee cheer, sprang over the wall and trotted forward double quick. Then Colgrove ordered the 27th to charge. The line was anything but shaky. They ran straight into a volley by Steuart's men in the trenches and Smith's troops behind a stone wall on the exposed flank of the attacking columns. Mudge was shot in the throat and killed, while five men carrying the regimental colors were struck down.

The Hoosiers turned up a few minutes later to their right, allowing the Bay Staters to fall back. The 27th Indiana were then forced to retreat as well. The 2nd Massachusetts suffered forty percent casualties, the 27th Indiana thirty-two percent.

CHARGE OF MARYLAND INFANTRY (C.

CHARGE OF THE 2ND MARYLAND INFANTRY, CSA, AT GETTYSBURG

The 2nd Maryland was a Confederate infantry regiment made up of volunteers from Maryland who, despite their home state remaining loyal to the Union, chose instead to fight for the Confederacy. Strangely, some of the Union troops opposing them at Gettysburg, were the 1st Maryland Infantry, Potomac Home Brigade, a bizarre instance of soldiers from the same state fighting each other.

STRIKING AT THE ENEMY

Having seen Pickett's Division was running behind schedule, Lee informed Ewell, then set out for Longstreet's headquarters in the schoolhouse by Willoughby Run. Longstreet told him that he had had scouts out all night and had found a way around Meade's right. Lee was not interested. He pointed to Cemetery Ridge.

'The enemy is there,' Lee said, 'and I am going to strike him.'

Longstreet stated that they had tried to defeat the enemy there the day before when they had more fresh men. Meade would be expecting them to attack there again and could strike against the flank of any assault force and get around its rear. But Lee was adamant.

'I am going to take them where they are on Cemetery Hill,' he said.

Lee and Longstreet then set out for a point where they could get a better view of the enemy lines and called for General Hill to join them.

LEE'S MADNESS

It was decided that Pickett should lead the charge, supported by Hood and McLaws, with as much other force as Hill could spare from his command. Longstreet repeated his objections, saying it would be madness to commit the two divisions from the corps that had suffered so badly the day before.

Hill volunteered the whole of his corps, but Lee pointed out that it occupied a vital position in the center. Nevertheless it was agreed that Heth's Division should join the attack. It was opposite the Union's center and there was a concealed position to the right where there was enough room for Pickett.

Longstreet was given command of the assault force. He then felt that it was his duty to 'say a word against the sacrifice of my men.' He famously said to Lee: 'General, I have been a soldier all my life. I have been with soldiers engaged in fights by couples, by squads, companies, regiments, divisions, and armies, and should know, as well as anyone, what soldiers can do. It is my opinion that no fifteen-thousand men ever arrayed for battle can take that position.'

Lee was irritated.

Longstreet said no more and began preparing for the attack.

COME OVER TO THEIR LINES

Meanwhile, Alexander Hays made another attempt to take back Bliss Farm for the Union. Thirty men from the 12th New Jersey and 1st Delaware charged, but were forced back when Union artillery fire drew counter-battery fire from the Confederate guns on Seminary Ridge.

Rebel gunners in the Peach Orchard realized that they would soon become involved. They walked out onto the battlefield and told any wounded Union soldier that could walk, to come over to their lines. Some did. Then the gunners began firing.

Two hundred Union troops were sent from the same two regiments. This time they took the farm, but there was not enough of them to set up an effective perimeter. The farmhouse was quickly encircled and, when the Confederates attacked in force, the Union troops pulled back to Cemetery Ridge again. They had lost another twenty-eight men and the Bliss Farm was still in Confederate hands.

Later sixty men of the 14th Connecticut armed with breech-loading Sharps rifles tried again. They were driven from the house by Confederate artillery fire and muskets, but managed to hold the stone-and-brick barn for nearly an hour in the July heat.

The Confederates kept moving more men up to the farm, until Alexander Hays feared that he might have a full-scale engagement on his hands. So he sent orders for the house and barn to be set on fire. The Connecticut sharpshooters did as they were told and, pausing only to grab a couple of chickens, withdrew.

MURDEROUS FIRE

Ewell and Johnson were still convinced that Culp's Hill could be taken. At 8:00 am, O'Neal's Alabama brigade were sent in. They had to climb the hill already strewn with the bodies and body parts of the Rebels, 'under a terrific fire of grape and small-arms, and gained a hill near the enemy's works.' There they hugged the ground, 'exposed to murderous fire,' and were pinned down for the next three hours. A soldier with the 7th Ohio give his account of holding back the assault:

> *We lay behind our solid breastworks, obeying the command to reserve our fire until the first line of battle was well up the slope and in easy range, when the command, 'Front rank ... Ready ...*

> *Aim Low ... Fire!' was given and executed, and immediately the rear rank the same, and kept up as long as the* [enemy's] *line remained unbroken.*

When they had fired sixty rounds, they would quickly be replaced by a reserve regiment who did the same, while they reformed, cleaned their guns, and replenished their ammunition boxes until it was their turn again.

The Alabama brigade managed to extricate itself just before noon. O'Neal recorded: 'Officers and men fought bravely, and held their ground until ordered to fall back.' Lieutenant Colonel Goodgame was more forthright in his report. 'Engaged the enemy at an early hour, but were unable to dislodge him from his fortified position,' he wrote. He then listed the regiment's losses for the entire battle – seven killed, fifty-eight wounded, and sixty-five missing (mostly captured). Two-thirds of that tally came from around Culp's Hill.

Long before O'Neal's men fell back from Culp's Hill, Meade was confident enough of the position there that he ordered General Sedgwick's Sixth Corps to move so that it was in position to reinforce Hancock on Cemetery Ridge.

BLOW HIS OWN BRAINS OUT

Further Confederate attacks were ordered by Johnson, though both Steuart and Daniel strongly disapproved of making the assault. The carnage was horrifying. Union soldiers watched as a badly wounded Confederate agonizingly reloaded his gun, then used the ramrod to push the trigger and blow his own brains out.

A stray dog limped across the battlefield to be cut down alongside the Confederates. Though 'perfectly riddled,' it managed to lick someone's hand. 'Regarding as the only Christian-minded being on either side, I ordered him to be honorably buried,' said Union General Thomas L. Kane.

Eventually Johnson conceded that 'the enemy were too strongly intrenched and in too great numbers to be dislodged by the force in my command ... No further assault was made; all had been done that it was possible to do.'

STAGGERING LOSSES

Culp's Hill had cost the Union's Twelfth Corps 1,082 casualties, though only 204 of those were killed. On the Confederate side, Johnson's division alone had suffered some 2,002 casualties. Added to that were losses of around four hundred each for O'Neal's and Daniel's brigades with another 213 for Smith's. The 2nd Virginia of the Stonewall Brigade had four dead, thirteen wounded and three missing. One of the dead Virginians was John Wesley Culp, whose Pennsylvanian family had lent their name to the hill.

TEAR HIM LIMBLESS

Preparing for the next attack Longstreet told Alexander to used his artillery to cripple the enemy – 'to tear him limbless, as it were' – then the infantry would charge, with the artillery advancing to aid the attack. So Alexander deployed seventy-six guns along a 130-yard line from the Peach Orchard to Spangler's Wood, reserving just two batteries to protect the extreme right of the First Corps' line.

This was done in the face of the Union guns that, Alexander said, 'had ammunition in abundance – literally to burn – and plenty more close at hand.' He could not understand how they got away with it. 'We lay exposed to their guns, and getting ready at our leisure, and they let us to do it,' he said.

The only casualty was a horse that had a haunch taken off by a Union shell while maneuvering a turn. 'I never saw so much blood fly or so much grass painted red before,' Alexander said.

Lee's artillery chief Brigadier General William Pendleton had procured thirty-three guns from Ewell and fifty-five from Hill. One-hundred-and-sixty-four were now aimed at targets on Cemetery Ridge.

But Alexander had his worries. The Borman fuses they were using had a high failure rate and his men were not adept at the long-range shooting that would be required that day. Due to powder shortages, they had never had target practice. All the firing had been in the heat of battle.

NOT TWENTY-FIVE CENTS FOR MY LIFE

Soon after 9:00 am, Pickett's division began arriving at the southern end of Seminary Ridge. As space was limited there, Brigadier General Lewis A. Armistead's brigade formed up behind those under Brigadier General James L. Kemper and Brigadier General Richard B. Garnett.

Alongside them were Heth's division, still under the command of Pettigrew after Heth was wounded in the head on the first day. They were to advance abreast.

Some of the men shared Longstreet's gloomy assessment of the situation. After speaking with the artillerymen, one soldier said: 'I would not give twenty-five cents for my life if the charge is made.'

But others had no such misgivings. It was rumored that Virginians had been selected because they were 'expected to be successful where others had failed.'

While Longstreet had his doubts, Pickett insisted that his men could do the job. To the left, Brigadier General William Mahone begged Anderson to come and observe the situation. He could not understand why 'General Lee would insist on such an assault after he had seen the ground':

I said to him what was plain to my mind. That no troops ever formed a line of battle that could cross the plain of fire to which the attacking force would be subjected, and live to enter the enemy's works … in any organized force.

But Anderson refused to take the matter up with Lee. According to Mahone, Anderson replied that 'we had nothing to do but to obey the order.'

Meanwhile, for the men of Pickett's division, there was fun to be had. John Dooley said: 'While we are resting here we amuse ourselves by pelting each other with green apples. So frivolous men can be even in the hour of death.'

CALM BEFORE THE STORM

Up on Cemetery Ridge, the troops were similarly relaxed. Lieutenant Franklin Haskell said:

The men on the crest lay snoring in their blankets, even though some of the enemy's bullets dropped among them, as if bullets were the drops of dew around them. As the sun arose today the clouds became broken, and we had once more glimpses of sky, and fits of sunshine – a rarity, to cheer us. From the crest, save to the right of the Second Corps, no enemy, not even his outposts, would be discovered, along all the position where he so thronged on the Third Corps yesterday. All was silent there.

Hancock's Second Corps packed five infantry brigades and twenty-eight guns into half-a-mile ending to the north in Ziegler's Grove where two of Hays' three brigades took cover behind a stone wall.

A HEARTY LUNCH

As nothing seemed to be happening, around noon General Gibbon decided it would be a good idea to have lunch. An officer managed to procure a few chickens, some butter, and a huge loaf of bread.

'I think an unprejudiced person would have said of the bread, that it was good – so of the potatoes, before they were boiled,' said Haskell. 'Of the chickens, he would have questioned their age, but they were large and in good running orders, the toast was good, and the butter – there were those who when coffee was given them, called for tea, and vice versa, and were so ungracious as to suggest that the water was used in both might have come from near a barn.'

General Hancock was invited to partake in the enormous pan of chicken stew, potatoes, toast, bread and butter, and tea and coffee. General Meade also dropped by. Afterward they smoked cigars and Meade said he thought the enemy would attack to his left again toward evening. Hancock thought he would attack at the Second Corps' position. Then the officers returned to their commands, leaving Gibbon, Haskell, and Gibbon's other staff officers to doze in the heat.

Meanwhile the Army of the Potomac's artillery chief, General Hunt – now satisfied with the situation at Culp's Hill rode over to Cemetery Ridge to observe the scene there.

'Our whole front for two miles was covered by batteries already in line or going into position,' he said. 'Never before had such a sight been witnessed on this continent, and rarely, if ever, abroad.' Quickly, he began moving forward support units.

RELY ON YOUR JUDGMENT

Longstreet was still convinced that the Confederate charge would be a disaster and end with a cruel slaughter. Nevertheless, he did everything he could to make it a success. He wrote later. 'Divisional commanders were asked to go to the crest of the ridge and take a careful view of the field, and to have their officers there to tell their men of it, and to prepare them for the sight that was to burst upon them as they mounted the crest.' Then he wrote to Alexander, saying:

If the artillery fire does not have the effect to drive off the enemy or greatly demoralize him, so as to make our effort pretty certain, I would prefer that you should not advise General Pickett to make the charge. I shall rely a great deal on your judgment to determine the matter and shall expect you to let General Pickett know when the moment offers.

Then Longstreet said: 'I rode to the woodland hard by, to lie down and study for some new thought that might aid the assaulting column.' Alexander quickly wrote a reply to Longstreet.

Union Headquarters on Cemetery Ridge.

General, I will only be able to judge the effect of our fire upon the enemy by his return fire, for his infantry is but little exposed to view and the smoke will obscure the whole field. If, as I infer from your note, there is an alternative to this attack it should be carefully considered before opening our fire, for it will take all of the artillery ammunition we have left, and if the result is unfavorable, we will have none left for another effort.

Longstreet still wanted to save his men and felt that, if the artillery was not effective, he would be justified in holding Pickett back. So he tried again:

Colonel: The intention is to advance the infantry if the artillery has the desired effect of driving the enemy's off, or having other effect such as to warrant us in making an attack. When that moment arrives advise General Pickett and of course advance such artillery as you can use in aiding the attack.

WHOLE INFERNAL YANKEE ARMY

Alexander passed the note over to Brigadier General Ambrose R. Wright, who observed that Longstreet had put the onus back on Alexander. So Alexander asked Wright, who had penetrated the line the previous day, what he thought of the attack.

'It is mostly a question of supports,' said Wright. 'It is not as hard to get there as it looks ... The real difficulty is to stay there after you get there – for the whole infernal Yankee army is there in a bunch.'

Alexander then went to Pickett to find out what he thought, and found him 'in excellent spirits and sanguine of success.' The artillery officer now had no choice.

'General Lee had originally planned it,' he said, 'and half the day had been spent in preparation. I determined to cause no loss of time by any indecision on my part.'

He wrote to Longstreet, saying: 'General: When our fire is at its best, I will advise General Pickett to advance.'

Longstreet then sent a note to Colonel James B. Walton, commanding the First Corps' artillery. It said: 'Let the batteries open ...'

The first shot was fired at 1:07 pm. The number two gun misfired, then another cannon fired the second round. Then the entire line of Confederate artillery opened up with a roar that shook the earth.

WILDEST CONFUSION

The noise shook Gibbon's staff from their torpor. Seconds later, shells were falling on them.

'The wildest confusion for a few moments obtained among us,' said Lieutenant Haskell. 'The shells came bursting about. The servants ran terror-stricken for dear life and disappeared. The horses, hitched to the trees or held by the slack hands of orderlies, neighed out in fright, broke away and plunged riderless through the fields.'

All except for Haskell's own horse.

'I found him tied to a tree near by, eating oats, with an air of the greatest composure, which under the circumstances, even then struck me as exceedingly ridiculous. He alone of all beasts or men near was cool. I am not sure but that I learned a lesson then from a horse.'

Meanwhile around 1:00 pm Jeb Stuart had led his Confederate Calvary around to confront the Union rear, including Brigadier General George Armstrong Custer, along Cemetery Ridge.

ADMIRABLE SHOOTING

General Hunt's plan was to respond to the Confederate bombardment, sparingly, if at all. He wanted to reserve his guns for the enemy infantry. While the Confederate gunners had got the range right, their elevation was somewhat high and most of the shells were passing over the Union gunners' heads. However, the twenty-pounder Parrotts of Virginia battery under Captain E. Raine on Benner's Hill hit them perfectly from the north-east.

'It was admirable shooting,' said Major Thomas Osborn, commander of the Eleventh Corps' artillery. 'They raked the whole line of batteries, killed and wounded men and horses, and blew up caissons rapidly. I saw one shell go through six horses standing broadside.'

He wheeled three batteries toward them. The Union gunners quickly got the range and elevation and soon reduced the Rebel fire, which then became wild.

Battery A, 4th US Artillery under Lieutenant Alonzo H. Cushing was in the middle of Meade's line. A member of his battery said: 'The fire we were under was something frightful, and such as we had never experienced before ... Every few seconds a shell would strike right in among our guns, but we could not stop for anything. We could not even close our eyes when death seemed to be coming.'

Alexander could detect no restraint in the Union response. 'The whole line from Cemetery Hill to Round Top seemed in five minutes to be emulating a volcano in eruption,' he said. One estimate put the number of shells fired along the whole line by both sides at 1,500 rounds a minute.

The Confederate batteries were taking punishment too. Sergeant John L. Marye of the Fredericksburg Artillery said:

The uproar was terrific. Round shot whistled by and plowed the ground. The air was alive with screaming, bursting shells and flying fragments ... Cannoneers with jackets off and perspiration streaming down their faces, blackened with powder, kept the guns cool by plunging spongeheads in buckets of water, and as fast as a man fell another took his place; guns were dismounted, limbers and caissons blown up and horses ripped open and disemboweled.

Nor were the Confederate batteries having the desired effect. Optimistically, Robert E. Lee had thought that fifteen minutes of intense fire would be enough to suppress the Union batteries. It was taking longer than that. An integral part of Lee's plans was that the artillery should advance with the infantry to give them support. But between 2:00 pm and 3:00 pm the Confederate guns were in danger of running out of ammunition before they could do that.

Brigade officers of the Horse Artillery commanded by Lt. Col. William Hays.

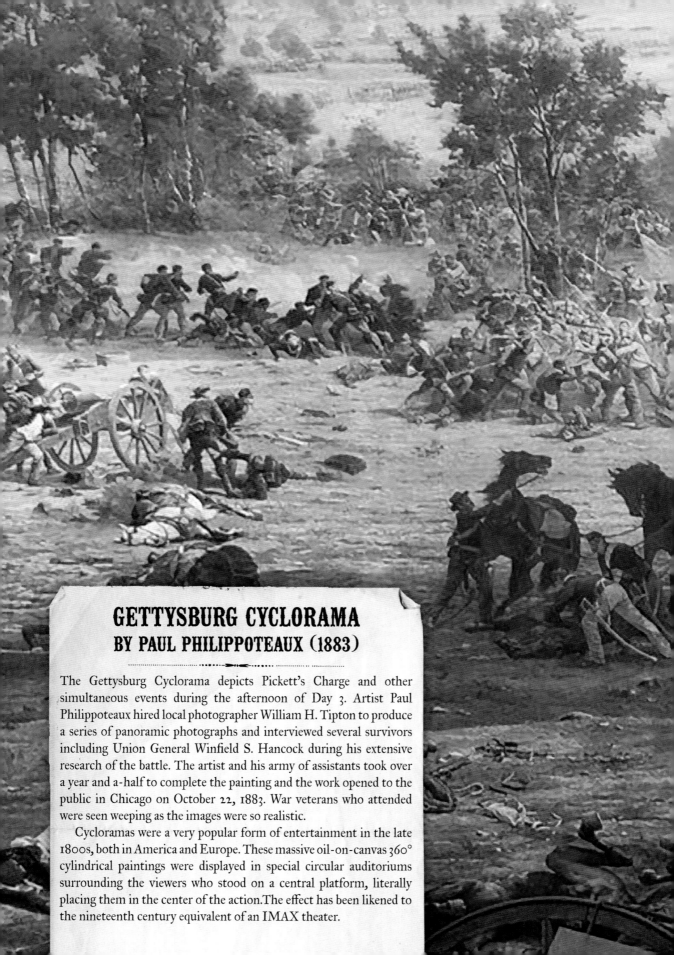

GETTYSBURG CYCLORAMA
BY PAUL PHILIPPOTEAUX (1883)

The Gettysburg Cyclorama depicts Pickett's Charge and other simultaneous events during the afternoon of Day 3. Artist Paul Philippoteaux hired local photographer William H. Tipton to produce a series of panoramic photographs and interviewed several survivors including Union General Winfield S. Hancock during his extensive research of the battle. The artist and his army of assistants took over a year and a-half to complete the painting and the work opened to the public in Chicago on October 22, 1883. War veterans who attended were seen weeping as the images were so realistic.

Cycloramas were a very popular form of entertainment in the late 1800s, both in America and Europe. These massive oil-on-canvas 360° cylindrical paintings were displayed in special circular auditoriums surrounding the viewers who stood on a central platform, literally placing them in the center of the action. The effect has been likened to the nineteenth century equivalent of an IMAX theater.

CHAPTER 10

A TEMPEST OF DEATH

OVERSHOOTING THE TARGET

The reason that the Confederate fire was ineffective was because they were overshooting. Several shells landed near the Leister house, forcing General Meade to move his headquarters to Powers Hill.

There, Meade was buttonholed by an irate citizen who complained that his house was being used as hospital, his garden as a graveyard, and amputated limbs littered his grounds. Were the government going to pay for the damage, he wanted to know.

'Why, you craven fool,' said Meade. 'Until this battle is decided, you do not know, neither do I, if you will have a government to apply to ... If I hear any more from you, I will give you a gun and send you to the front line to defend your rights.'

Other overshooting shells were hitting a medical post in a barn off Taneytown Road. Chaplain Erza D. Simons of the 125th New York remembered seeing Hiram D. Clark 'lying unconscious, with leg just amputated, on the operating bench, midway on the floor of the barn, as the storm of shell burst around the place. But he aroused from the effects of the chloroform administered, with a smile on his lips, and remained uncomplainingly all that fearful afternoon.'

THE AGONIES OF DEATH

Sergeant George Scott of Company G of the 13th Vermont said: 'We hardly dared rise on our elbows, even, for just above our heads raged a tempest of orchestral death. Shot and shell struck, rent and tore the bank just back of us ... On that hot and sultry day we were exposed to the full glare of the sun. Many overcame with heat.'

He even noticed a sergeant, who had just had

> ## Shot and shell struck, rent and tore the bank just back of us ...

a near miss with a shell, fall asleep. This was not unusual at Gettysburg. Colonel Wheelock G. Veazy said: 'The effect of the cannonade on my men was the most astonishing thing I ever witnessed in any battle. Many of them, I think the majority, fell asleep, and it was with the greatest effort only that I could keep awake myself.'

DUG INTO A FOXHOLE

While the Confederate shells overshot the Union lines, the Rebel troops were massed for an infantry attack. Private Erasmus Williams of the 14th Virginia quickly dug a foxhole with his bayonet. A lieutenant laughed at him, saying good-naturedly: 'Why Williams, you are a coward. I am going to stand right up here and witness the whole proceeding.'

The lieutenant got another laugh when shot landed nearby, covering Williams with dirt. It would be his last laugh. 'Presently, indeed almost instantly, the defiant lieutenant was swept away by a shot or shell, and his blood sprinkled all over me,' said Williams. 'A shell stuck in the ground right by me with the fuse still burning. I had just time to stretch my hand and pull out the fuse, else both I and others might have been killed by the explosion.'

John Dooley recorded:

> *In one of our regiments alone the killed and wounded, even before going into the charge amounted to eighty-eight men; and men lay bleeding and gasping in the agonies of death all around, and we unable to help them in the least. Ever and anon some companion would raise his head disfigured and unrecognizable, streaming with blood, or would stretch his full length, his*

limbs quivering in the pangs of death. Orders were to lie as closely as possible to the ground, and I, like a good soldier, never got closer to the earth than on the present occasion.

APPALLING SCENES

Things were much the same for Heth's Confederate division. Lieutenant William Peel of the 11th Mississippi recalled:

In the hottest of the cannonading I heard a shell strike in the right of the regiment and turning over, as I lay on my back, I looked just in time to witness the most appalling scene that perhaps ever greeted the human eye. Lieutenant Daniel Featherstone from Noxubee County, was the unfortunate victim. He was a large man – would have weighed perhaps two hundred pounds. He was lying on his face, when the shell struck the ground near his head and ricocheted, entered his breast, exploded about the same time and knocking him at least ten feet high and not less than twenty feet from where he was lying.

COME AT ONCE

The prolonged shelling made General Alexander anxious that he would not have the ammunition to support the infantry charge, so he sent a note to Pickett and Pettigrew that said:

General: If you are to advance at all, you must come at once or we will not be able to support you as we ought. But the enemy's fire has not slackened materially and there are still eighteen guns firing from the cemetery.

However, as soon as he had sent this note, Alexander did notice a slackening in the rate of Union fire. He saw some guns being hauled away. They were not being replaced and 'I began to believe that we stood a good chance for the day.' Quickly he dispatched another note to Pickett, saying: 'For God's sake come quick. The eighteen guns have gone. Come quick or my ammunition will not let me support you properly.'

On Cemetery Ridge, Hancock was determined that the artillery fire should continue, to keep up the morale of his infantrymen. But Hunt had decided that, if they ceased firing, they might fool the Rebels

into believing that they had suppressed the Union's guns and they would bring their infantry out into the open. Meade had a similar thought and sent orders authorizing Hunt to stop firing. They were both now convinced that Lee intended to attack in the center. When the gunfire ceased Meade returned to Cemetery Ridge.

SHALL I ADVANCE?

When George E. Pickett received Alexander's first note, he showed it to Longstreet and said: 'General, shall I advance?'

This was the moment that Longstreet had been dreading. 'My feelings had so overcome me that I could not speak for fear of betraying my want of confidence to him,' he recalled. 'I bowed affirmation and turned to mount my horse.'

Pickett said: 'I shall lead my division forward, sir.'

Longstreet rode over to the wood where Alexander was stationed with his artillery. When he got there, Alexander told him seven guns that were to have led the charge with Pickett were out of action, and he did not have enough ammunition to support the charge. He could not replenish it as to avoid counter-fire, the train carrying reserve ammunition had been moved well out of range.

'I then saw that there was no help for it, and that Pickett must advance under his orders,' said Longstreet. 'He swept past our artillery in splendid style, and the men marched steadily and compactly down the slope.'

As they started up the ridge, over one hundred cannon from the breastworks of the Union army hurled a rain of canister, grape and shells down upon them; still they pressed on until halfway up the slope, when the crest of the hill was lit with a solid sheet of flame as the masses of infantry rose and fired. When the smoke cleared away Pickett's Division was gone. Nearly two-thirds of his men lay dead on the fields, and the survivors were sullenly retreating down the hill.

THE CATASTROPHE OF GETTYSBURG

'The artillery fight over, men began to breathe more freely, and to ask: "What next I wonder," ' said Haskell on Cemetery Ridge.

The gunners wiped the sweat from their sooty faces. Ammunition boxes were replenished. Reserve guns were brought up to replace the disabled ones and the smoke gradually cleared from the crest.

'There was a pause between acts,' recalled Haskell, 'with the curtain down, soon to rise upon the great final act, and the catastrophe of Gettysburg.'

General Gibbon said he believed that the Confederates were falling back and that the cannonade was simply a noisy way of disguising their movement. Meanwhile Hunt galloped about on horseback giving fresh orders to his batteries. Then Captain Wessels said, excitedly: 'General, they say the enemy's infantry is advancing.' Haskell noted that Wessels was pale.

'To say that none grew pale and held their breath at what we and they saw, would not be true,' said Haskell. 'Might not six thousand men be brave and without shade of fear, and yet, before a hostile eighteen thousand, armed, and not five minutes' march away, turn ashy white?'

The number is now thought to have been more like eleven thousand. Lieutenant Frank Haskell saw them coming:

None on that crest now need be told that the enemy is advancing. Every eye could see his legions, an overwhelming, resistless tide of an ocean of armed men, sweeping upon us! Regiment after regiment, and brigade after brigade, move from the woods, and rapidly take their places in the lines forming the assault ... More than half a mile their front extends – more than a thousand yards the dull gray masses deploy, man touching man, rank pressing rank, and line supporting line. Their red flags wave; their horsemen gallop up and down; the arms of eighteen thousand men, barrel and bayonet, gleam in the sun, a sloping forest of flashing steel. Right on they move, as with one soul, in perfect order, without impediment of ditch, or wall, or stream, over ridge and slope, through orchard, and meadow, and cornfield, magnificent, grim, irresistible.

Gettysburg battlefield, scene of Pickett's charge.

NO NEED TO ISSUE COMMANDS

On Cemetery Ridge, everything was quiet. There was no noise or confusion. There was no need to issue commands. The men were in their places. They were veterans of a dozen battles and they knew what they would have to do. Frank Haskell described the scene:

The click of the locks as each man raised the hammer, to feel with his finger that the cap was on the nipple; the sharp jar as a musket touched a stone upon the wall when thrust, in aiming, over it; and the clinking of iron axles, as the guns were rolled up by hand a little further to the front, were quite all the sounds that could be heard. Cap-boxes were slid around to the front of the body; cartridge boxes opened; officers opened their pistol holsters ... The trefoil flags, colors of the brigades and divisions, moved to their places in the rear; but along the lines in front, the grand old ensign that first waved at the Battle of Saratoga in 1777, and which these people coming would rob of half its stars, stood up, and the west-wind kissed it as the sergeants sloped its lance towards the enemy.

General Gibbon rode coolly down the lines. In a calm voice, he said to the men: 'Do not hurry, men, and fire too fast. Let them come up close before you fire, and then aim low, and steadily.'

PICKETT'S CHARGE

To the Union troops on Cemetery Ridge, the Confederate advance seemed orderly and effortless, but Kemper's Brigade found itself diverting from the main axis of the advance. Although they had been told to save their strength for the final rush, Kemper's men had to make a series of quick maneuvers to catch up with the right flank of Garnett's Brigade.

Over on the left flank Colonel John M. Brockenbrough's brigade had been divided, with half being put under the command of Colonel Robert M. Mayo of the 47th Virginia who did not hear the order to advance and his men had to run to catch up.

Pickett's artillery commander Major James Dearing raced his empty caisson to the rear to get fresh ammunition. As he passed the advancing 8th Virginia, he cried to their commander Colonel Eppa Hunton: 'For God's sake, wait till I get some ammunition and I will drive every Yankee from the heights.'

Meanwhile behind the 3rd Virginia, Pickett encouraged his men to 'charge the enemy and remember Old Virginia.'

Alexander rode around his batteries. If they had more than fifteen long-range projectiles they were told to limb up and follow the columns. Shorter-range weapons were sent up too. Those with less than fifteen rounds were told to wait until the infantry had got a good way ahead, then aiming well over their heads, fire at the Union batteries that were firing on the infantry.

In all, some eighteen cannon moved up behind the infantry. On the left, Hill's artillery commander Colonel R. Lindsay Walker did not advance any of his thirty-six guns with the infantry because he had not been told of this part of Lee's plan.

EXCITING ADMIRATION

'The Confederate approach was magnificent, and excited our admiration,' said Hunt, who was in charge of the Union artillery.

As the Rebels advanced, oblique fire from the batteries under Lieutenant Colonel Freeman McGilvery, reinforced by that of the six rifles of Hazlett's battery, now under the command of Lieutenant Benjamin F. Rittenhouse, caused Pickett's men to drift to the left, so their weight fell on the position occupied by the batteries under Captain John C. Hazard. But due to Hancock's admonition to keep firing, they had exhausted their long-range ammunition during the initial artillery battle.

'Had my instructions been followed here, as they were by McGilvery, I do not believe that Pickett's Division would have reached our line,' said Hunt. 'We lost not only the fire of one-third of our guns, but the resulting crossfire, which would have doubled its value.'

Nevertheless, according to Captain Patrick Hart, commanding a battery on McGilvery's line: 'The exploding shells took out four, six, eight men, sometimes more than that ... the gaps we made were simply terrible.'

At the other end of the line, directing fire from Cemetery Hill, Major Osborn said: 'Each solid shot or unexploded shell cut at least two men in half.'

TOSSED IN THE AIR

Colonel Franklin Sawyer of the 8th Ohio, also on Cemetery Hill, recalled the scene:

> [The Confederates] ... *were at once enveloped in a dense cloud of smoke and dust. Arms, heads, blankets, guns and knapsacks were thrown and tossed into the air. Their track, as they advanced, was strewn with dead and wounded. A moan went up from the field, distinctly to be heard amid the storm of battle, but on they went, too much enveloped in smoke and dust now to permit us to distinguish their lines or movements, for the mass appeared more like a cloud of moving smoke and dust than a column of troops. Still it advanced amid the now deafening roar of artillery and the storm of battle.*

Confederate after-action reports played down the role of the artillery as the Union artillery held back at first, either under Hunt's instructions or because Hancock's batteries had exhausted their long-range ammunition. But as they approached, a captain in the 18th Virginia said: 'The enemy's big guns were now loaded differently, and they tore great gaps through our ranks.'

A ravine around halfway between their starting line and the enemy allowed the two halves of Brockenbrough's Brigade to reunite. But then, as they advanced further a soldier with 22nd Virginia Battalion remembered: 'The enemy's batteries soon opened upon our lines with canister, and the left seemed to stagger.' An officer with the 40th Virginia said:

> *We came so close to the serried ranks of the Yankees that I emptied my revolver upon them, and we were still advancing when they threw forward a column to attack our unprotected left flank. I feel no shame in recording that out of this corner the men, without waiting for orders, turned and fled, for the bravest soldiers cannot endure to be shot at simultaneously from the front and side. They knew that to remain, or to advance, meant wholesale death or captivity. The Yankees had a fair opportunity to kill us, and why they did not do it I cannot tell.*

Colonel Arthur Fremantle, the British observer, recalled the spooked brigade in full retreat, 'flocking through the woods in numbers as great as the crowd in Oxford Street [London] in the middle of the day.'

With Brockenbrough's Brigade on the left of the Confederate line disposed of, Major Osborn shifted his fire onto Pettigrew's Fourth Brigade under Brigadier General Joseph R. Davis. Gaps began opening up there too.

THE WORK OF DEATH BEGINS

Enfilading fire from Rittenhouse's guns on Little Round Top caused similar trouble. Rittenhouse recalled: 'Many times a single percussion shell would cut out several files, and then explode in the ranks. Several times almost a company would disappear, as the shell would rip from right to left.'

But as the Confederates drifted northwards, they moved out of the firing arc of all but Rittenhouse's two rightmost tubes.

On McGilvery's line, Captain James Thompson said: 'Their lines and columns stagger, reeled and yelled like demons ... We mowed them down like ripe grain before the cradle.'

Colonel Franklin Sawyer, 8th Ohio Infantry.

George Edward Pickett

Pickett was born to one of the 'first families' of Virginia in Richmond in 1825. His entrance to West Point was secured by Congressman John T. Stuart, a law partner of Abraham Lincoln. Graduating last in his class of fifty-nine, Pickett served with distinction in the Mexican War, carrying the colors over the parapet at the Battle of Chapultepec when Longstreet was wounded.

In 1853, he challenged Winfield Scott Hancock to a duel; the challenge was declined. Pickett served with the 9th US Infantry in Texas, rising to the rank of captain in 1855. The following year, he was posted to Washington Territory where he took a Native American woman named Morning Mist as his second wife. Their son became a newspaper artist.

Picket was a combatant in the so-called Pig War, a bloodless confrontation with the British over the islands that lie between Vancouver and the North American mainland.

Although Pickett personally abhorred slavery, he resigned his commission when Virginia seceded and joined the Confederate Army. By October 1862, he was promoted Major General and given command of a Virginia division.

Despite proving himself an able commander, his name will always be associated with Pickett's Charge, though his was not the only division involved and the action was actually commanded by Longstreet.

At the time, he was wooing a teenager, eighteen years his junior, who became his third wife and gave him two children.

Though he was criticized and even accused of cowardice, he was retained as a divisional commander. However, eight days before the surrender at Appomattox, his division was nearly wiped out while he was attending a shad bake.

Fearing as a former officer in the US Army, he might be arrested and executed after the war, he fled to Canada, though he later returned and worked as an insurance agent in Norfolk, Virginia. Asked why Pickett's Charge failed, Pickett frequently replied: 'I've always thought the Yankees had something to do with it.'

A year before his death in 1875, Congress granted him a full pardon.

Down below in the 1st Virginia, Dooley remembered: 'Some are actually fainting from the heat and dread. They had fallen to the ground overpowered by the suffocating heat and the terrors of the hours ...'

Then there were the constant barrage of orders –

... Onward – steady – dress to the right, give way to the left – steady, not too fast – don't press upon the center – how gentle the slope! – steady – keep well in line – there is the line of guns we must take – right in front – but how far they appear.

They were still nearly a third of a mile away, almost in a semicircle on Cemetery Ridge. They had to march on the center. Behind the guns, they could see lines of infantry. Dooley described the frightening view in front of them:

To the right of us and above the guns we are to capture, black heavy monsters from their lofty mountain sites belch forth their flame and smoke and storms of shot and shell upon our advancing line, while directly in front, breathing flame in our very faces, the long-range of guns which must be taken, thunder on our quivering melting ranks. Now truly does the work of death begin. The line becomes unsteady because at every step a gap must be closed and thus from left to right much ground is often lost.

A PERFECT STORM

As the first of his men reached Emmitsburg Road, Pickett himself stopped well out of harm's way. He sent a note to Kemper about the small force of Union troops stretching out from the enemy's lines, hoping to catch his brigade in enfilading fire, and Lieutenant Robert A. Bright was sent to Longstreet, asking for reinforcements. Little is known of Pettigrew's movements during the charge and Lee seems to have returned to his headquarters at the opening of the cannonade.

On Pickett's left flank, Davis's Brigade was now taking fire from skirmishers to the north and double-quicked in an attempt to escape them. To their left was Lieutenant Peel, who recalled:

We were now advancing in the face of a perfect tempest of maddened shells that plowed our line and made sad havoc in our ranks. As we moved onward we were greeted, as we came successively within range of these less far-reaching, but far more destructive projectiles, with showers of grape and canister, and at the distance of about two hundred yards the infantry opened on us from behind the stone fence. Pressing onward, we returned fire. Our line was now melting away with an alarming rapidity. It was already reduced to a mere skeleton of the line of one hour ago. Still on it pushed, with a determination that must ever be a credit to the Confederate soldier.

Junction of Baltimore Pike and Emmitsburg Road, Gettysburg, July 1886.

Gettysburg Cyclorama – Caisson Exploding.

CHAPTER 11

GRAIN BEFORE THE REAPER

When they reached the Emmitsburg Road, Davis's Brigade was well ahead of the rest of Pettigrew's left wing. Battery I of the 1st US Artillery under Lieutenant George A. Woodruff was blasting canister at them. To the left were Union soldiers in an enfilading position. Ahead were the 12th New Jersey who opened up on them with .69 smoothbores loaded with buck and ball.

'They fell like grain before the reaper,' said one New Jerseyman, 'and after repeated efforts to capture the guns, broke and fled in great disorder ... All that came as far as our line of battle came as prisoner.'

The Union soldiers were behind a stone wall. 'Here we were subjected to a most galling fire of musketry and infantry,' wrote Davis. 'So reduced were our already thinned ranks that any further effort to carry the position was hopeless, and there was nothing left but to retire to the position originally held, which was done in more or less confusion.'

Confederate Lieutenant Peel was not so lucky:

> The state of my feelings may be imagined, but not described, upon seeing the line broken, and flying in full disorder, at the distance of about one hundred and fifty yards from us. There were but two alternatives: to surrender, or become the 'flying target' of a thousand muskets. We preferred the former, and in a moment more a white flag floated from behind the corner, around which the moment before our accurately aimed muskets had belched their deadly contents into the ranks of the enemy. An old sergeant came out and took charge of us, and ordered us through the gate that was open on the left of the house. As we passed through, all unarmed of course,

> a Yank soldier brought down his musket, and, with its muzzle right at the breast of one of our party, was on the point of firing. I cringed for the safety of my brave comrade; and shuddered at the thought of seeing him thus butchered, but just at this critical juncture, our sergeant sprang forward, knocked up the musket and, with a word of reproach, asked the soldier if he did not see that these men had surrendered.

LONGSTREET AND FREMANTLE

Lieutenant Bright found Longstreet sitting on a fence with Arthur Fremantle who was saying, 'General Lee sent me here, and said you would put me in a position to see this charge. I would not have missed it for the world.'

'I would,' said Longstreet. 'The charge is over Colonel Fremantle.'

Then Longstreet turned to Bright. 'Captain Bright, ride back and tell General Pickett what you heard me tell Colonel Fremantle.'

But before Bright rode off. Longstreet stopped him and added: 'Tell General Pickett that Wilcox's Brigade is in that Peach Orchard, and he can order him to his assistance.'

When Bright returned to Pickett, the general sent orders for Wilcox to advance with three separate officers, in the hope that one would get through. All three did.

THE WHITES OF THEIR EYES

As Davis's Brigade fell back, Archer's Brigade now under the command of Colonel Birkett D. Fry of the 13th Alabama linked up with the left of Pickett's line. As Fry was hit in the thigh, he urged his men on,

> ### Steady men! Close up! A little faster! Save your strength!

saying: 'Go on, it will not last five minutes longer.'

To their right, Garnett riding at the rear of his line said: 'Steady men! Close up! A little faster; not too fast! Save your strength!'

To the left of the Third Brigade was Pettigrew's Brigade, now commanded by Colonel James K. Marshall. As they charged up the slope from Emmitsburg Road, Marshall paused to wave the men forward. At that moment, two bullets hit him in the head and killed him.

Colonel Henry K. Burgwin commanding the 26th North Carolina said: 'The smoke was dense and at times I could scarcely distinguish my own men.'

Ahead were four Pennsylvania regiments taking cover behind two stone walls. Colonel Dennis O'Kane commanding the 69th Pennsylvania reminded his men that they were defending the soil of their native state. 'Should any man flinch in his duty,' he said, 'the man next to him would kill him on the spot.' In an order reminiscent of Bunker Hill, he also told his men to hold their fire 'until the enemy came so close to us that we could distinguish the white of their eyes.'

TUMBLING VICTIMS

When Garnett's men reached the Emmitsburg Road, they found their way impeded by a fence that was too stout to push down, so they had to climb over.

'As soon as the top of the fence was lined with troops, the whole line tumbled over, falling flat into the bed of the road, while the enemy's bullets buried themselves into the bodies of the falling victims,' an observer said.

Confederate dead gathered for burial, Gettysburg, 1863.

Garnett's Brigade was then thrown into confusion when the 8th Virginia had to divide to get around the farm buildings there. They faced the wall where Lieutenant Alonzo Cushing had stationed two guns. Despite being hit twice – once painfully in the genitals – Cushing continued ranging his guns. He was then knocked from his feet, and when he yelled another order, a bullet entered his mouth and killed him. Sergeant Frederick Fuller assumed command, but the ammunition was soon exhausted.

VOLLEYS BLAZE AND ROLL

To the right, Kemper's Brigade broke in two. Some men took cover in the rough ground just south of the copse there and sniped at the Union gunners on the other side of the wall. The rest moved left to join Garnett's and Archer's Brigades on their assault on the wall where Cushing's guns had fallen silent.

They were within fifty feet of the wall when the 69th Pennsylvania popped up and loosed off a volley. There was an angle in the wall there. On the other side was the 71st Pennsylvania.

'All along each hostile front,' said Haskell, 'the volleys blaze and roll; as thick the sound as when a summer hail-storm pelts the city roofs; as thick the fire as when the incessant lightning fringes a summer cloud.'

Under intense pressure from Archer's Brigade, the 71st pulled back behind a second wall thirty yards to the rear. Confederate troops quickly scrambled over, taking control of the angle.

DON'T LET ME BLEED

Hancock had witnessed how General Hays had seen off Davis's Brigade by flanking it and wanted General Stannard on his left to do the same. He rode over to him. Words were exchanged, when Hancock suddenly toppled from his horse. He had been hit in the thigh.

'Don't let me bleed to death,' said Hancock.

Stannard produced a neckerchief and his aide Lieutenant George G. Benedict fashioned a tourniquet. That was the end of Hancock's participation in the battle, but as he lay bleeding on the ground he said to one of his aides, Major William G. Mitchell: 'Tell General Meade that the troops under my command have repulsed the enemy's assault and that we have gained a great victory. The enemy is now flying in all directions from my front.'

A flanking action by the 13th and 16th saw Kemper's Brigade off. Kemper himself was hit in the groin and captured.

Lt. Alonzo Cushing (back row, center), Antietam, Maryland, 1862. Cushing died heroically at Gettysburg defending the Union position against Pickett's Charge.

ANGEL OF DEATH

On the Union right, Hays was preparing to withstand Pettigrew and Pender's division, now under the command of Major General Isaac R. Trimble.

'When within a hundred yards of our line of infantry, the fire of our men could no longer be restrained,' said Hays, 'four lines arose from behind the stone wall, and before the smoke of our first volley had cleared away, the enemy, in dismay and consternation, were seeking safety in flight; many attempts to rally them by their officers were in vain. In less time than I can recount it, they were throwing away their arms and appealing most piteously for mercy.'

The Confederates were subjected to an incessant stream of grape, canister, Minié, and buck and ball. The 14th Connecticut were firing their Sharps breech loaders so fast they had to pour water from their canteens over the barrels to cool them.

'No longer could the measured tread be heard, no longer were the orders of the commanding officers audible, for the shrieks of the wounded and groans of the dying filled the air,' said the regimental history of the 14th.

Major J. McLeod commanding the 7th North Carolina said: 'Our loss in this vicinity was fearful, the dead and wounded lying in great numbers both in the field and road.'

Hays said: 'The angel of death alone can produce such a field as was presented.'

But still the Southerners came on, even trying to scramble over the wall in the face of the single remaining cannon of the Rhode Island battery that was now loaded with canister.

ON THE SIDE OF THE LORD!

Of the eight hundred men of the 26th North Carolina who had joined battle with the Iron Brigade on the first day, only three hundred were left for the assault on Cemetery Ridge where another hundred were lost. Among those captured were First Sergeant James M. Brooks and Private Daniel Boone Thomas, who was wounded and carrying the tattered pieces of the regimental flag. Looking to their left, they saw the flag of the 47th North Carolina go down within ten feet of the wall. Suddenly the men of the 12th New Jersey stopped firing. One of them yelled: 'Come over on this side of the Lord!'

Hands were extended and the two young men were hauled to safety. The torn and bloodstained flag was captured. Both men would be imprisoned with Daniel's older brother Nathaniel and all would fight in later battles.

CRAWLING FROM THE CARNAGE

Longstreet had sent a message to Brigadier General James H. Lane to move Pender's Third Brigade across the Emmitsburg Road to clear the Union flankers. When the order reached Colonel Clarke M. Avery, he said: 'My God, General, do you intend rushing your men into such a place unsupported, when the troops on the right are falling back?'

'Seeing it was useless to sacrifice my brave men, I ordered my brigade back,' said Lane.

Looking on, Trimble was shot through the left leg. His aides lifted him out of the saddle and laid him on the ground. 'General, the men are falling back,' said one. 'Shall I rally them?' 'No,' said Trimble. 'Let them get out of this, it's all over.'

Survivors of Pettigrew's and Trimble's command trudged back to Seminary Hill. Some men lay on the battlefield unhurt, waiting to retreat under the cover of darkness. Others were too badly wounded to return quick and 'crawled from the field of carnage'.

Back on Seminary Hill, Lee passed among the men, saying: 'The fault is mine.' But assured them it would be all right in the end. He ordered Pettigrew to rally his division to protect the artillery in case of a Union counterattack. Then he noticed Pettigrew's bloody arm. His horse had been killed and his hand shattered by a shell.

'General, I am sorry to see you wounded,' said Lee. 'Go to the rear.'

HAVE THEY TURNED?

On the way back to Cemetery Ridge, General Meade met his son George, whose horse had been killed.

'Hello, George,' his father said. 'Is that you? I am glad you are here. You must stick by me now, you are the only officer left.' He remarked that it was 'a pretty lively place' and told his son to take one of his orderly's horses. 'Let's go up here and find out what is going on,' he said

Meade kept asking his son if he saw anyone he recognized. They came across Lieutenant John Egan of the 1st US Artillery, who Captain Meade did know. General Meade asked him if the attack had been repulsed. Egan replied that it had and that General Hays had one of their flags.

'I don't care for their flag,' Meade snapped. 'Have they turned?'

Egan repeated that they had. Meade and his son then rode on.

Then they came across a large body of prisoners being taken to the rear. Recognizing him as an authority figure, the Confederates asked him where they should go. He laughed, as he was now in fine spirits.

'Go along that way and you'll be well taken care of,' he said, pointing.

Just then Confederate shells began raining down. The prisoners scattered and ran away, some of them cheering the show of force from their side. The two officers then rode on toward the Copse of Trees, where fighting was still raging.

THE BLOODY ANGLE

Once in possession of the 'bloody angle' in the wall abandoned by the 71st Pennsylvania, Garnett sent word for Brigadier Lewis A. Armistead's Brigade that were following them to come up immediately.

The 72nd Pennsylvania then appeared near the top of the ridge and loosed off a volley. Private Robert

H. Irvine, one of General Garnett's couriers, said: 'Just as the general turned his horse's head slightly to the left he was struck in the head by a rifle or musket ball and fell dead from his horse, and almost at the same moment a cannon shot from a Union battery on the right struck my horse immediately behind the saddle, killing him and throwing his body over the general's body and me upon the ground.'

To the Rebel's right, the 69th Pennsylvania had lost several men to friendly fire from Captain Andrew Cowan's 1st New York Independent Battery of six three-inch ordinance rifles. They cracked and ran, some back through Cowan's battery, others into the Copse of Trees. Those that remained at the wall found the enemy behind them.

'It looked as though our regiment would be annihilated, the contest here became a hand-to-hand affair,' said Private Anthony W. McDermott of the 69th. 'Company F completely hustled over the stone wall into the enemy's ranks.' Their commander Colonel Dennis O'Kane was also mortally wounded.

The Rebels now seized the opportunity to rush Cowan's battery. Above the din of battle, Cowan heard a Confederate officer yell: 'Take that gun!'

The charging Confederates were brought down by double charges of canister. General Henry Hunt, in charge of the Union artillery, appeared behind the

Hancock's Corps Assaulting the Works at the 'Bloody Angle.' Drawing by William B.T. Trego, 1887.

guns as the Rebels charged again. He fired his pistol and shouted: 'See 'em! See 'em!'

Five bullets struck his horse, which reared and collapsed, trapping Hunt under him. Members of Cowan's battery pried him free and he mounted one of the battery's horses.

OATHS, CURSES & YELLS

When Lewis Armistead's men arrived, they finished off Company F. Captain George Thompson was killed. The survivors were taken prisoner. Then, with his hat on the tip of his saber, Armistead jumped over the wall and led his troops up the ridge. Some of Garnett's men followed. But after just a couple of yards, Armistead's luck ran out. He was hit in the chest and arm.

His men could see the Union troops massing for a counterattack. Those who did not flee, found themselves overwhelmed in hand-to-hand fighting.

'Men fired into each other's faces,' said Lieutenant John Lee of the 28th Virginia. 'There were bayonet thrusts, cutting with sabers, hand-to-hand contests, oaths, curses, yells, and hurrahs.'

Private Randolph Shotwell of the 8th Virginia said: 'To retreat was nearly as dangerous as to advance, and scores of men threw themselves behind some piles of stone in front of the works, and held up their hands in token of surrender.'

'The bullets seemed to come from front and both flanks,' said Lieutenant George W. Finley of the 56th Virginia, 'and I saw we could not hold the fence any longer.' As the Union line approached, he told his men to cease fire and surrender. 'The sharp, quick huzza of the Federals told of our defeat and their triumph,' he said.

As Union reinforcements arrived, Lieutenant James Crocker, adjutant of the 9th Virginia, said:

The final moment has come when there must be instant flight, instant surrender, or instant death. Each alternative is shared. Less than a thousand escape of all that noble division which in the morning numbered 4,700; all the rest either killed, wounded or captured. All is over. As far as possible for mortals they approached the accomplishment of the impossible. Their great feat of arms has closed. The charge of Pickett's Division has been proudly, gallantly and right royally delivered.

HELLISH FIRE

Even as the Confederates surrendered, the killing continued. Captain Guilan V. Weir's Battery C of the 5th US Light Artillery had been ordered up from the reserve to fire on the Confederates as the Union soldiers forced them back.

'Numbers of the enemy came up in front of, and through the battery, to give themselves up,' he said, 'throwing themselves on the ground, as my guns in their front were fired.'

One Rebel soldier came up to him and asked: 'Where can I go to get out of this hellish fire?' Weir pointed to the rear and said: 'Go down there.' Then he added: 'I wish I could go with you.'

ENTIRELY REPULSED?

On the ridge, General Meade and his son came across Haskell. Recognizing the Lieutenant, General Meade said: 'How is it going?' Haskell said that he believed the attack had been repulsed.

'What? Is the assault entirely repulsed?' said General Meade incredulous. He looked out over the field, confirming what Haskell had told him was true, and said simply: 'Thank God.'

Meade was not a man to show his emotions. He said he caught himself as he was about to doff his hat and cheer. Instead he merely waved his hand and said: 'Hurrah!'

His son, though, threw off his hat and cheered loudly three times. However, the general was not sure that there would not be another attack. Informed that General Caldwell was now in charge, Meade told Haskell to tell him to reform the line. The men were to be kept in their places.

'If the enemy does attack, charge him in the flank and sweep him from the field, do you understand,' said Meade. A message was flashed from the far right: 'We have repulsed them on every part of the line.'

Meade shook hands with officers from the First and Eleventh Corps. Then Major Mitchell arrived with a message from Winfield S. Hancock saying he had been injured in the counterattack.

'Say to General Hancock that I regret exceedingly that he is wounded and that I thank him for the country and for myself for the service he has rendered today,' said Meade.

GETTYSBURG CYCLORAMA

Union General Winfield Scott Hancock crossing a farm road on a black horse heading in the direction of the Confederate breakthrough at 'The Angle'. In the distant background white puffs of smoke show the position of Union artillery on Little Round Top.

CHAPTER 12

THE NOTHINGNESS OF FAME

UNNECESSARY LOSS

Below, Colonel Joseph C. Mayo, now commanding Kemper's Brigade, tried to rally his men for another assault. But most of them were already on their way back to Seminary Ridge. A private standing next to him said: 'Oh, Colonel, why don't they support us?'

Anderson was about to commit Wright's and Posey's Brigades, when Longstreet stopped him. Any further action would result in 'unnecessary loss … the assault had failed.'

But Anderson had already committed Wilcox's Brigade who, with Lane's Brigade, were marching on McGilvery's guns. An Alabamian said that 'a storm of shot and shell was poured upon us.' Lieutenant James Wentworth of the 5th Florida said: 'It was the hottest work I ever saw. My men were falling all around me with brains blown out, arms off and wounded in every description. I used every exertion in my power to cheer the men on.' Then a shell burst above them and Wentworth was knocked out.

Haskell brought up more guns from Alexander's reserve and poured on the agony. Wilcox had still made no contact with the Virginian's right.

'After some little delay, not getting any artillery to fire upon the enemy's infantry that were on my left flank,' said Wilcox, 'and seeing none of the troops that I was ordered to support, and knowing that my small force could do nothing save to make a useless sacrifice of themselves, I ordered them back.'

Lang found his men scattered among the bushes and rocks. It was impossible to make his voice heard above the noise of the artillery and small arms, so he could not organize any movement to check the advance of the enemy. With infantry on both flanks and artillery to the front, he ordered a retreat.

'I am afraid that many men, while firing from behind rocks and trees, did not hear the order, and remained there until captured,' he said.

CONTINUOUS CHEERING

News that the attack had failed was conveyed to General Rodes who was ready to support the left wing. Soon after, Longstreet heard 'loud and continuous' cheering from the Union lines. Arthur Fremantle said he saw some thirty officers riding along the ridge opposite. Although a party that size invited artillery fire, the guns remained silent.

On the battlefield, many Rebels simply surrendered. Lieutenant Colonel C.H. Morgan on Hancock's staff said: 'Thousands of them sought safety by … holding up their handkerchiefs or a piece of white paper in token of surrender.'

However, one defiant Confederate was shot dead for refusing to lower his gun when surrounded by the men of the 13th Vermont.

Sergeant James A. Wright of the 1st Minnesota said: 'As soon as the smoke lifted sufficiently to permit us to see, all that could be seen of the mighty force that had been driven so furiously against us was scattered and running to the rear – that is, all that were able to run. The bodies of many unfortunate victims marked the course of the assault.'

It was only when he heard cheering that Sergeant Wright felt the pain welling up. 'My neck and face were bleeding,' he said. 'I then found that the left shoulder, breast and sleeve of my blouse were

> **The dead in every direction lay … scattered as far as the eyes could reach.**

ornamented with shreds of lead and splinters of wood, and several of the latter were driven into the side of my face and neck.'

STOP FIRING, YOU FOOLS

Still some men reloaded and shot at anything gray. According to Lieutenant William Harmon, General Alexander Hays tried to prevent any further useless slaughter:

> *General Hays rode along the line swearing like a pirate, as the best of men sometimes will in battle. He was trailing a Confederate flag in the dust behind his horse and was shouting, 'Stop firing, you fools; don't you know enough to stop firing; it's over – Stop! Stop! Stop!'*

Companies went out to collect prisoners and view the carnage. Captain Winfield Scott from the 126th New York said: 'There were literally acres of dead lying in front of our line. I counted sixteen bodies in one rod square [thirty square yards], and the dead in every direction lay upon the fields in heaps and scattered as far as the eye could reach.'

AN OLD AND VALUED FRIEND

Captain Henry Bingham, a member of Hancock's staff, saw a number of Union privates carrying one wounded Confederate. He was an important prisoner who they said was General James Longstreet.

'I dismounted my horse and inquired of the prisoner his name,' said Bingham. 'He replied, "General Armistead of the Confederate Army."

Confederate dead gathered for burial at the south-western edge of the Rose Woods, July 5, 1863.

Observing that his suffering was very great I said to him, "General, I am Captain Bingham of General Hancock's staff, and if you have anything valuable in your possession which you desire taken care of, I will take care of it for you."'

Armistead then said that General Hancock was 'an old and valued friend' and asked Bingham to convey a message. 'Tell General Hancock for me that I have done him and done you all an injury which I shall regret or repent ... the longest day I live.'

Armistead then gave Bingham his spurs, watch chain, seal and pocketbook. Bingham then told the men to take him to the rear to one of the hospitals. The mortally wounded general died in captivity.

DISMOUNTED SKIRMISHING

To the east of Gettysburg there were a series of indecisive cavalry charges and counter-charges, until the 3rd Pennsylvania Cavalry reduced the Rebels to dismounted skirmishing and a number of artillery engagements. Still Jeb Stuart left the field that night claiming that he had secured Ewell's left.

To the south, Brigadier General Judson Kilpatrick Third Division of the Cavalry Corps were in action. A detachment of the 1st Brigade, commanded by Brigadier General Elon J. Farnsworth drove the Confederate pickets from Bushman's Hill, allowing Battery E of the 4th US Light Artillery to set up there, while the 1st Vermont Cavalry under Colonel Addison W. Preston pushed along the dirt track that led to Bushman's Farm.

Meanwhile the 1st Division's Reserve Brigade under Brigadier General Wesley Merritt probed along Emmitsburg Road. This drew a response from the Confederate cavalry there, as well as Anderson's Georgia infantry and three batteries. They threatened to overrun one of the batteries, but a Georgia regiment arrived in time to save it. Dismounted, they were held in check by a superior Confederate force.

KIL-CAVALRY

Kilpatrick then sent the 1st West Virginia under Colonel Nathaniel R. Richmond to make a mounted attack on the Confederates to the west of Big Round Top. But no one had noticed the rail fence there. When cavalrymen dismounted to try and knock down the fence, the 1st Texas fired on them. A second mounted attack by the 5th New York and 18th Pennsylvania also failed.

But Kilpatrick, who was nicknamed 'Kil-cavalry', was not a man to give up. Next he selected the 1st Vermont to have a go. Farnsworth, its brigade commander, spoke to Major John W. Bennett who had been on the skirmish line there that morning, then went to see for himself.

'Major, I do not see the slightest chance of a successful charge,' he said.

When told the situation did not look promising. General Kilpatrick said: 'Well, somebody can charge.' Farnsworth's lips turned white, and he replied: 'If anybody can charge, we can, sir.'

Before they set off, Farnsworth said to one of his officers: 'Kil is going to have a cavalry charge. It is too awful to think of ...' Nevertheless he led it.

STREWN WITH BOULDERS

Two battalions of the 1st Vermont Cavalry detachment charged nearly a mile into the enemy lines, receiving the fire of five regiments of infantry and two batteries. At first, they brushed aside the skirmish line of the 1st Texas. But the picket line from Hood's Division was posted up the slope of Big Round Top and could fire down on them.

Confederate General Evander Law, who had halted Merritt on the Emmitsburg Road, pulled back to take charge. He threw the 4th Alabama across the track the cavalry were using. They were too late to catch Farnsworth who was with Major William Wells' battalion, but they did catch the second battalion under Captain Henry Parsons.

The lead battalion crossed Plum Run, turned away from Devil's Den where the ground was strewn with boulders, then crossed Rose Run, heading for Bushman's Farm. When they reached the crest overlooking the farm, they spotted the batteries that had stopped Merritt's column. They all turned southward. Then Law and the 9th Georgia appeared among them.

Elements of the 4th Alabama started firing at their rear. The Union cavalrymen turned south, galloped back through the 1st Texas skirmish line, past Bushman's Hill, back to their starting point. Along the way, Farnsworth was knocked off his horse by a shell. He took a horse from a junior and led Wells' battalion back toward Big Round Top in the hope of joining up with Parsons.

Wells and Parsons escaped with their lives; Wells

was awarded the Medal of Honor. Farnsworth was killed, though the circumstances of his death remain unclear.

Kilpatrick had done little to secure the left of the Union line. As soon as the danger on Cemetery Ridge had passed, Meade rode out to the left to issue orders for pickets and skirmishers to be sent out. By the time they reported back, it was so late in the evening that he abandoned his plans to make an assault there.

A SAD DAY

Lee attempted to rally his men, telling them that it would all come right in the end. Fremantle noted that he 'did not show signs of the slightest disappointment, care, or annoyance.'

When he addressed a few words to the British observer, all he said was: 'This has been a sad day for us, Colonel – a sad day; but we can't expect always to gain victories.'

While James Longstreet sent his staff to the rear to rally his troops, he went to the artillery, to impress on them the necessity of holding ground if they were attacked. On the line of cannon, he bumped into Pickett who was sobbing. 'General, I am ruined,' he said. 'My division is gone; it is destroyed.'

Later Pickett met Lee, who told him to regroup his division. 'General Lee, I have no division now,' said Pickett. 'Armistead is down, Garnett is down, and Kemper is mortally wounded.'

'Come, General Pickett,' said Lee. 'This has been my fight and upon my shoulders rests the blame. The men and officers of your command have written the name of Virginia as high today as it has ever been written.'

Hill ordered his men to reform on Seminary Ridge. Among them was Davis. Asked where his brigade was, Davis 'pointed his sword up to the skies, but did not say a word, and stood there for a moment knocking pebbles out of the path with the point of his sword. He could not talk, and neither could I,' said Private David Holt of the 16th Mississippi.

TELEGRAPH NEWS

While Lee was planning his withdrawal from Gettysburg, Meade sent a note to General Halleck in Washington, saying: 'The loss upon our side has been considerable ... After the repelling of the assault, indications leading to the belief that the enemy

might be withdrawing, an armed reconnaissance was pushed forward from the left, and the enemy found to be there in force.'

The Secretary of the Navy, Gideon Welles had gone to bed when a courier arrived from the War Department telling him that news was arriving from a correspondent at Hanover station, giving his name as a reference. He hurried over to the telegraph office where President Lincoln was waiting.

The messages from Hanover station were coming from Homer Byington, a freelance reporter for the *New York Tribune* who Welles knew. The telegram said: 'A great and bloody battle was fought, and our army has the best of it, but the end is not yet.'

There was good news in Richmond too. John Beauchamp Jones's son Curtis had been in a skirmish with Union soldiers.

'What the enemy suffered is not known, but he fell back, and ran toward the White House,' Jones confided to his diary. 'And this induced a general belief that the enemy had retired, finally, being perhaps ordered to Washington, where they may be much needed.'

IN THE STOCKADE

Some two thousand Confederate prisoners were held in a temporary stockade near Rock Creek. The Army of the Potomac's Provost Marshal Marsena Patrick addressed them:

Prisoners, you are here now in my charge; quite a large number of you. I guarantee to you the kindest treatment the nature of the case will permit, so long as you conduct yourselves in a becoming manner. If, however, there should be any attempt, on your part, to escape me, woe be unto you. My splendid cavalry is at hand, armed and ready for action, and in numbers almost equal to your own, and in case of any disturbance among you, they shall be ordered to charge you, cutting and slashing, right and left, indiscriminately.

Seeing Major John C. Timberlake at the front, Patrick stopped to talk to him. 'A few more men, major, and you would have won your independence right here,' he said. Timberlake responded: 'We have lost it right here.'

A Harvest of Death

"Slowly, over the misty fields of Gettysburg – as all reluctant to expose their ghostly horrors to the light – came the sunless morn, after the retreat by Lee's broken army. Through the shadowy vapors, it was, indeed, a 'harvest of death' that was presented; hundreds and thousands of torn Union and rebel soldiers – although many of the former were already interred – strewed the now-quiet fighting ground soaked by the rain, which for two days had drenched the country with its fitful showers.

The rebels in the photograph are without shoes. These were always removed from the feet of the dead on account of the pressing needs of the survivors. The pockets turned inside out also show that appropriation did not cease with the coverings of the feet. Around is scattered the litter of the battlefield – accoutrements, ammunition, rags, cups and canteens, crackers, haversacks etc and torn letters that may tell the name of the owner although the majority will surely be buried unknown by strangers, and in a strange land.

Such a picture conveys a useful moral – it shows the blank horror and reality of war, in opposition to its pageantry. Here are the dreadful details! Let them aid in preventing such another calamity falling upon the nation."

Photographed by Alexander Gardner, July 1863. From *Gardner's Photographic Sketch Book of the War*, 1865 – 66.

AS HE DIED TO MAKE MEN HOLY, LET US DIE TO MAKE MEN FREE.

PART 4

THE FOURTH DAY AND THE HEREAFTER

CHAPTER 13

WINDOWS OF HEAVEN

'All day on the 4th did we await the expected attack,' said Captain W. Blackford, Jeb Stuart's engineering officer. 'But another and greater danger now threatened in the rains. We were nearly forty miles from the Potomac whose fords were deep and wide at their best.'

He feared that, if the level of the river rose, the Army of Northern Virginia would not be able to return safely to Southern soil. Most Confederates could not understand why Meade did not finish them off.

'We all expected this to be the heaviest day of fighting of the battle, notwithstanding the terrible work that has already been done,' one Virginian artilleryman wrote in his diary, 'but in this we were, I must say pleasingly, disappointed.'

General Longstreet's aide Major G. Moxley Sorrell had an explanation:

> Notwithstanding our great losses of the second and third, we were permitted to hold the field on the fourth by Meade's inactivity. His army was very strong, had not suffered as had ours, and an enterprising general might seemingly have had us on the run in short order. But no! He had taken a taste of our mettle that day before and wanted no more of it.

OUR POOR WOUNDED

Brigadier General John D. Imboden's cavalry brigade had been guarding the army's supply train at Chambersburg. He was told to report to Lee's headquarters. When the general saw him at around 1:00 am, he told Imboden: 'As many of our poor wounded as possible must be taken home. I have sent for you because your men are fresh, to guard the trains back to Virginia. The duty will be arduous, responsible, and dangerous, for I am afraid you will be harassed by the enemy's cavalry. I can spare you as much artillery as you require, but no other troops, as I shall need all I have to return safely by a different route from yours.'

After discussing the route he was to take, Lee gave him a sealed package for President Jefferson Davis. If he was captured, he was to destroy it.

Imboden's train would carry an estimated five thousand wounded men who were fit to travel but could not walk, as well as the animals collected by Ewell's foragers. It would occupy around twenty miles of road and take a northerly route to the Potomac via the Cashtown Gap, Marion, and Greencastle – a distance of around forty-five miles. Cut off from the rest of the army, it would be given a strong escort. Its advance guard would be the nine hundred men of the 18th Virginia Cavalry under General Imboden's brother, Colonel George W. Imboden, with the six twelve-pounder Napoleons of Captain John H. McClanahan's Staunton Horse Artillery Battery. Interspersed along the column would be squadrons of the 62nd Mounted Infantry under Colonel George H. Smith and six Napoleons and two twelve-pounder howitzers from Major Benjamin F. Eshleman's Battalion.

Imboden was also allocated another two Napoleons, six ordnance rifles, and two ten-pounder Parrotts under Major Charles Richardson. At the rear would be a battery of three Blakely rifles under Captain William B. Hurt, along with a rearguard consisting of two cavalry brigades from Stuart's Division.

The train took all day to assemble west of Gettysburg on the Chambersburg Pike and set off at 5:00 pm.

We must return to Virginia.

ROBERT E. LEE

BLAKELY RIFLE

The Blakely rifle was a rifled muzzle-loading cannon designed by British army officer Captain Theophilus Alexander Blakely. It was not used by the British Army because it had a similar Armstrong gun, designed by Sir William George Armstrong, who became superintendent of the Royal Arsenal at Woolwich. Instead, Blakely rifles made under license in Britain were exported, notably to the Confederate states during the Civil War.

They came in numerous bores – 2.5-inch (six-pounder), 2.9-inch, 3.5-inch (twelve-pounder), 3.75-inch (sixteen-pounder), 4-inch (eighteen-pounder), 4.5-inch (twenty-pounder), 6.4-inch (hundred-pounder), 7-inch (120-pounder), 7.5-inch (150-pounder), 8-inch (200-pounder), 9-inch (250-pounder), and 11-inch and 12.75-inch that fired 450-pounder shells or 650-pound solid shot. Various bores came in numerous versions. There were at least nine types of the 3.5-inch twelve-pounder. Different types of rifling were used – flat-sided bores, or bores with grooves cut in them that engaged flanges or studs on the shell which were made in copper or brass.

The twelve-pounder used at Gettysburg was made of iron and steel, with a barrel weighing eight-hundred pounds. A charge of 1.5 pounds gave it a range of two thousand yards. However, it had a dangerously powerful recoil that often damaged its carriage. Longstreet's artillery chief Colonel Alexander said: 'The only advantage to be claimed for this gun is its lightness, but this was found to involve the very serious evil that no field-carriage could be made to withstand its recoil. It was continually splitting the trails or racking to pieces its carriages, though made of unusual strength and weight.'

One famous Blakely rifle was 'The Widow Blakely', a 7.5-inch rifle used by the Confederates in the defense of Vicksburg. On May 22, 1863, a shell exploded in the gun's barrel while it was bombarding a Union gunboat. The explosion took part of the end of the muzzle off, so the Confederates cut the 124-inch barrel back to a hundred inches and continued to use it as a mortar until Vicksburg fell.

Blakely Rifles and ammunition in the arsenal yard, Charleston, South Carolina.

HOWITZER

The howitzer was a smoothbore cannon with a short brass barrel. The Model 1841 twelve-pounder used at Gettysburg had a range of 1,100 yards with a one-pound charge. The low muzzle velocity and relatively short range meant that it was used as high elevations to attack targets behind cover. This also made the howitzer vulnerable to longer-range artillery. Consequently, they were usually deployed in mixed batteries, with one or two howitzers in a four-gun battery.

The Model 1841 could fire all ammunition except for solid shot and was the most effective piece at under four-hundred yards. Colonel Alexander said: 'On several occasions during 1863 and 1864 where mortar-fire was desirable in the field, the twelve and twenty-four pounder howitzers were used for the purpose very successfully, by sinking the trails in trenches to give the elevation, while the axles were run up on inclined skids a few inches to lift the wheels from the ground and lessen the strain of the recoil. The skids would not be necessary where the desired range is not great.'

The howitzer was also light, at just eight-hundred pounds, so it could be advanced easily with the infantry. Colonel Alexander had earmarked two howitzer batteries to do this during Pickett's Charge, but due to a mix up this did not happen.

At Gettysburg, Lee had twenty-nine twelve-pounders and four twenty-four-pounders — twelve percent of his artillery; Meade had just two twelve-pounders.

A 12-pounder Howitzer captured by Butterfield's Brigade near Hanover Court House, May 27, 1862.

MOVING OUT

The night of July 4, residents heard the sounds of wagons moving out of town to the west. Some went to tell the Union sentinels. Parties of Union soldiers searched the houses and found Confederate soldiers who they took prisoner. Civilians ventured out onto the streets. Hearing a commotion, General Schimmelfennig, crawled out of his hiding place and made his way toward the patrols.

By 7:00 am General Meade was writing to Halleck that the enemy had removed their pickets. An hour later, Colonel Wlodzimierz Krzyzanowski led the 26th Wisconsin and 119th New York on a reconnaissance past the south-western outskirts of Gettysburg, towards Seminary Ridge.

General Slocum led a brigade-sized force out to the east. They turned and marched into the town on the Hanover Road. At Middle Street and Washington, sixteen-year-old Julia Jacobs cried out, warning them of Rebel snipers. They put bullets through her door. Union troops threw a barricade across Middle Street, then saw off the threat with an exchange of fire.

The 4th Pennsylvania Cavalry followed York Pike into town, capturing a number of Rebels on the way. The US Sharpshooters probed west from Little Round Top, while US Regulars supported by a brigade from the Sixth Corps pushed down Emmitsburg Road, finding the Confederates about a mile behind their previous position. A Virginia battery in the Peach Orchard opened up, forcing the Union soldiers to go to ground.

Meade wrote to Halleck at midday, informing of the situation and explaining that he would not be going on the offensive. 'I shall require some time to get up supplies, ammunition, etc., rest the army, worn out by long marches and three days' hard fighting,' he said.

BURYING THE DEAD

There were other more pressing tasks. 'No fighting today, but we are burying the dead,' Private Leon of Daniel's Brigade wrote in his diary on July 4. 'They have been lying on the field in the sun since the first day's fight; it being dusty and hot, the dead smell terribly.' He went on to note 'the funny part of it is, the Yankees have all turned black.'

A detail from each company was formed into a squad. Armed with spades and shovels, they searched the field for the dead. When they found a body, they dug a shallow pit.

'There is no systematic work, time being precious, and the dead are buried where they fell,' said one of Kershaw's Brigade.

Thomas Galway of the 8th Ohio said: 'Each regiment selects a suitable place for its dead and puts a headboard on each individual grave. The unrecognized dead are left to the last, to be buried in long trenches.'

Fifty yards from the breastworks on Culp's Hill, an officer from the 147th Pennsylvania said: 'I saw a deep ditch or long excavated series of graves dug and a number of dead Union soldiers lying ready for interment.'

DISCARDED WEAPONS

The battlefield was strewn with discarded weapons that had to be collected. The men of the 15th New Jersey seized the opportunity to collect the new, more reliable Springfield rifles, to replace the older Enfields they had been issued with. Bayonet-tipped muskets abandoned by the Confederates were stuck, point down, in the ground until 'there were acres of muskets standing as thick as trees in a nursery.'

The Union also had to conduct an inventory of the Confederate flags they had taken. There was also the question of what to do with prisoners of war. Lee sent out a party under a flag of truce in the afternoon to suggest an exchange of prisoners. But Meade would rather have Lee burdened by Union prisoners than reinforced by able-bodied Confederates and declined the offer.

THE WINDOWS OF HEAVEN

The light rain in the morning gave way to heavy thunderstorms in the afternoon. Soon the creeks and runs were flooded and aid stations had to be moved to higher ground.

'The very windows of heaven seemed to have opened,' said Imboden. 'The rain fell in blinding sheets; the meadows were soon overflowed, and fences gave way before the raging streams. During the storm, wagons, ambulances and artillery carriages by the hundreds – nay thousands – were assembling in the fields from Gettysburg to Cashtown … Canvas was no protection against its fury, and the wounded men, lying upon the naked boards of the wagons, were drenched. Horses and mules were blinded and maddened by the wind and water, and became almost unmanageable. The deafening roar of the mingled sounds of heaven and earth all around us made it almost impossible to communicate orders, and equally difficult to execute them.'

Those Confederate wounded not well enough to be on their way to Cashtown had been removed from the makeshift field hospitals in the town and taken to the already overstretched infirmaries to the west of the town. That evening a chaplain of the 42nd Mississippi visited one of these:

I found myself in the midst of three or four hundred men of the brigade in which I served, who were too severely wounded to be transported to Virginia ... I then turned to the tenderest and saddest ministry of my life, as under open skies, on the bare ground, or a mere pile of straw, these gallant men lay heroically suffering or unconsciously moaning their lives away.

Foreign observer Fitzgerald Ross said he was shocked at the sight of 'fine young fellows, many of them probably crippled for life ... Many were to be left behind, too severely wounded to bear removal.'

Unfinished Confederate graves near the center of the Gettysburg battlefield.

CHAPTER 14

LOST AND GONE FOREVER

The Army of the Potomac were better equipped to deal with casualties. The medical director Dr Jonathan Letterman had developed systems to deal with the thousands of wounded that resulted from Civil War battles. But the medical supplies were kept miles to the rear between Union Mills and Westminster with the baggage trains on Meade's orders, lest they be captured.

'Lost supplies can be replenished,' Letterman protested, 'but lives lost are gone forever.'

Along with the medical supplies were tents to give the wounded shelter. With close to 21,000 wounded Union and Confederate soldiers left behind at Gettysburg, men lay outside the aid stations, exposed to the appalling weather.

Describing the scene, General Schurz said:

A heavy rain set in during the day ... and large numbers had to remain unprotected in the open, there being no room left under roof. I saw long rows of men lying under the eaves of buildings, the water pouring down on their bodies in streams. Most of the operating tables were placed in the open where the light was best, some of them partially protected against the rain by tarpaulins or blankets stretched upon poles. There stood the surgeons, their sleeves rolled up to the elbows, their bare arms as well as their linen aprons smeared with blood, their knives not seldom held between their teeth, while they were helping a patient on or off the table, or had their hands otherwise occupied; around them pools of blood and amputated arms or legs in heaps, sometimes more than man-high ... As a wounded man was lifted on the table, often shrieking with pain as the

It was a field of blood on which the demon of destruction reveled.

attendants handled him, the surgeon snatched his knife from between his teeth ... wiped it rapidly once or twice across his blood-stained apron, and the cutting began. The operation accomplished, the surgeon would look around with a deep sigh, and then – 'NEXT!'

'It was a field of blood on which the demon of destruction reveled,' said Letterman. When Meade moved on in pursuit of Lee, he wanted to take the Army surgeons with him. 'What! Take away surgeons here where a hundred are wanted?' Letterman protested.

INDEPENDENCE DAY

There were celebrations for Independence Day at Gettysburg.

'Was ever the Nation's Birthday celebrated in such a way before?' said New Englander Elisha Hunt Rhodes. 'This morning the 2nd Rhode Island was sent out to the front and found that during the night General Lee and his Rebel Army had fallen back ... At twelve midday, a National Salute with shotted guns was fired from several of our batteries, and the shells passed over our heads toward the Rebel lines.'

Another soldier wrote home to his mother in New York: 'While you were celebrating, we were busy burying the dead.'

A member of the Union Eleventh Corps captured on July 1 said: 'Rain and with hungry bellies, I shall long remember this Independence Day.' And a member of the 151st Pennsylvania, also a prisoner, grumbled: 'Glorious old fourth, but cannot enjoy it much in my present position – no rations, no clothes but what is on my back, and old half of a blanket.'

Dr Jonathan Letterman

Born in 1824 Major Jonathan Letterman was an American surgeon credited as being the originator of the modern methods for treatment of armies on the battlefield. Dr Letterman is known today as the 'Father of Battlefield Medicine'. His system enabled thousands of wounded men to be recovered and treated during the American Civil War. As Medical Director of the Army of the Potomac, his organizational skills and patient management were unequaled. The task of treating countless wounded in and around Gettysburg was left up to his undermanned staff who worked diligently to save Union and Confederate soldiers alike. Many convalesced at 'Camp Letterman', the general field hospital east of Gettysburg, before being transferred to permanent hospitals in the North.

Dr Jonathan Letterman (seated left), medical director of the Army of the Potomac and staff.

Victory!

A bulletin board outside a newspaper office on Pennsylvania Avenue, in Washington, DC, announced a 'Glorious Victory for the Union Army' and the President issued a sober proclamation on Independence Day:

JULY 4, 1863, 10:30 A.M.
ANNOUNCEMENT OF NEWS FROM GETTYSBURG
The President announces to the country that news from the Army of the Potomac, up to 10 p.m. of the 3rd is such as to cover that Army with the highest honor, to promise a great success to the cause of the Union, and to claim the condolence of all for the many gallant fallen. And that for this, he especially desires that on this day, **HE WHOSE WILL, NOT OURS, SHOULD EVER BE DONE**, be everywhere remembered and reverenced with profoundest gratitude
ABRAHAM LINCOLN

He also noted: 'Rebs retreating as fast as possible, through drenching rain. Long train of wagons, containing wounded rebels, household furniture, in fact anything they could carry off, chairs, bed quilts, covers, lids, mowing machines, scythes, and their horses decorated with sleigh bells.'

But some captured men were not downhearted. A Wisconsin soldier recalled the men 'celebrated the nation's birthday by singing patriotic songs and making ourselves jolly generally.' Another said they were 'wondering what news we would likely hear, when one of our officers, disregarding all possible consequences, gave vent to his feelings and in honor of the day began a patriotic song. We others took courage and all joined in the chorus.' When the Confederate guards did not intervene, he wondered: 'Could it mean that they were beaten on July 3rd.'

A New Jersey soldier thought so, saying: 'We have whipped the Rebels and we are bound to annihilate them ... Today is Independence Day, God grant it may be the restoration of the Union.'

The Confederates were not so sanguine. An Alabama officer said: 'I remembered that it was the 4th of July, and that the villains would think more than ever of their wretched Independence Day.'

Some Rebels did not even think they had been beaten. At 1:00 pm, Colonel Arthur Fremantle, the British observer, came across a cottage full of Confederate soldiers, 'none of whom had the slightest idea of the contemplated retreat, and all were talking of Washington and Baltimore with the greatest confidence.'

He moved on to Longstreet's camp which had moved three miles down the Fairfield Road. There 'I heard reports coming in from the different generals that the enemy was retiring, and had been doing so all day.'

However, he noted that the Confederates were moving off with 'wagons, horses, mules, and cattle captured in Pennsylvania.' That evening he got a ride on the doctors' covered buggy. During his discussions at Longstreet's headquarters, it became clear to Fremantle why the Confederates had lost. 'It is impossible to avoid seeing that the cause of this check to the Confederates lies in the utter contempt felt for the enemy by all ranks,' he said.

Robert E. Lee himself admitted this failing. 'I thought my men were invincible,' he said.

DRIVE OUT THE INVADERS

Meade issued General Order No. 68 congratulating the Army on its victory at Gettysburg, but added: 'Our task is not yet accomplished, and the commanding general looks to the army for greater efforts to drive from our soil every vestige of the presence of the invader.'

When President Lincoln read this, he famously exclaimed: 'Drive the invaders from our soil! My God! Is that all? ... Will our generals never get that idea out of their heads? The whole country is our soil!'

Other dispatches from the Army he also found disquieting. 'These things all appear to me to be connected with a purpose to cover Baltimore and Washington, and to get the enemy across the river again without a further collision,' said Lincoln, 'and they do not appear connected with a purpose to prevent his crossing and to destroy him.'

At a cabinet meeting, Gideon Welles noted: 'The President said this morning with a countenance indicating sadness and despondency, that Meade still lingered at Gettysburg, when he should have been at Hagerstown or near the Potomac to cut off the

HEADQUARTERS, ARMY OF THE POTOMAC,
JULY 4, 1863

General Orders, No. 68.

The Commanding General, on behalf of the country, thanks the Army of the Potomac for the glorious result of the recent operations.

An enemy superior in numbers and flushed with the pride of a successful invasion, attempted to overcome and destroy this Army. Utterly baffled and defeated, he has now withdrawn from the contest. The privations and fatigue the Army has endured, and the heroic courage and gallantry it has displayed will be matters of history to be remembered.

Our task is not yet accomplished, and the Commanding General looks to the Army for greater efforts to drive from our soil every vestige of the presence of the invader.

It is right and proper that we should, on all suitable occasions, return our grateful thanks to the Almighty Disposer of events, that in the goodness of his Providence He has thought fit to give victory to the cause of the just.

By command of Major General Meade.

Official S. Williams

Asst. Adjt. Gen.

Sutler's Tent, Army of the Potomac headquarters. A sutler or victualer sold provisions from the back of a wagon or a temporary tent, traveling with the army when it went into battle.

HEADQUARTERS, ARMY OF NORTHERN VIRGINIA

General Orders, No.74
July 4, 1863
The army will vacate its position this evening. General A.P. Hill's corps will commence the movement, withdrawing from its position after dark, and proceed on the Fairfield road to the pass in the mountains, which it will occupy, selecting the strongest ground for defense toward the east; General Longstreet's corps will follow, and General Ewell's corps bring up the rear. General Longstreet's corps will be charged with the escort of the prisoners, and will habitually occupy the center of the line of march. General Ewell's and General Hill's corps will alternately take the front and rear of the march.
R.E. LEE
General

retreating army of Lee ... He feared the old idea of driving the rebels out of Pennsylvania and Maryland, instead of capturing them, was still prevalent among the officers.'

WHAT TO DO?

Indeed, with the battle won, Meade had no clear idea of what to do. The Fairfield Gap in South Mountain was on the direct route from Gettysburg to Hagerstown and the Potomac. It was within easy reach of a mixed force of infantry and cavalry – one or two brigades, or even a division, of Major General John Sedgwick's fresh Sixth Corps. Before the end of the day on July 4, such a strike force could be on its way south to Emmitsburg, then move westerly toward the gap.

If Lee was forced to fight there, the rest of the Army of the Potomac could attack him from the rear. Or if that move forced Lee to divert to the Cashtown Gap, Meade would have a better chance of cutting him off from the Potomac. The problem was, to pull this off, Meade would have to make a move before Lee did and Meade, by nature, was a cautious man.

He held a council of war where he reminded his generals that they were still under orders to protect Washington and Baltimore. There was no clear consensus whether they should stay at Gettysburg or withdraw, though it was clear that no one wanted to give up the field of victory. If they did stay, should they attack Lee? This proposition received a unanimous no.

Major General Sedgwick and his staff on the steps of the headquarters of the 6th Army Corps.

However, it was agreed that, if Lee withdrew, they should only send the cavalry in direct pursuit. The infantry would march south and west in an attempt to cut Lee off from the Potomac. Yet again, Meade was happy to leave the decisions to Lee – in the hope that, as he had during the battle, he would make the wrong ones.

HUGE TRAIN

Meade was right. Lee was heading for the Fairfield/Monterey Pass. A huge train under Major John Harman was sent off that way. It was twice the length of Imboden's and comprised the Army Reserve quartermaster and subsistence trains, along with the trains of Ewell's three divisions, plus the thousands of cattle, sheep, and hogs they had collected.

Lee had issued orders for the train to move on July 3 and it was assembled that night, departing around 3:00 am on the 4th. It was escorted by the three-hundred troopers of the 1st Maryland Cavalry Battalion under Major Harry W. Gilmor and a battery of four three-inch ordnance rifles under Captain William A. Tanner. These two units formed the advance guard, while the rear guard was provided by what was left of the Army of Northern Virginia.

In the middle of the column were 3,500 Union prisoners, given to the care of Longstreet. In practice, guard duty devolved to what was left of Pickett's Division as they were now in no state to fight. It was a slight that Pickett would not forget.

When the column reached the Monterey Pass, Hill's Division was to take up positions to defend it while the rest of the army moved through. Longstreet and Ewell would camp there until Hill had withdrawn from the pass. Then they would set off again, heading for Hagerstown and the Potomac crossings.

CAVALRY DUTIES

Jeb Stuart's Division were assigned the regular cavalry duty when an army is on the move. They were to scout ahead and to the flank, and escort and protect the column of marching men. They would also provide an advance guard and a rear guard, opening routes and guarding passes, crossings, and bottlenecks, often dismounted.

Lee's orders said:

General Stuart will designate a cavalry command, not exceeding two squadrons, to precede and follow the army in its line of march, the commander of the advance reporting to the commander of the leading corps, the commander of the rear to the commander of the rear corps. He will direct one or two brigades, as he may think proper, to proceed to Cashtown this afternoon, and hold that place until the rear of the army has passed Fairfield, and occupy the gorge in the mountains; after crossing which, to proceed in the direction of Greencastle, guarding the right and rear of the army on its march to Hagerstown and Williamsport. General Stuart, with the rest of the cavalry, will this evening take the route to Emmitsburg, and proceed thence toward Cavetown and Boonsborough, guarding the left and rear of the army.

These orders were issued on July 3, but Stuart did not receive them until July 4 when, after Ewell had fallen back, he had gone to Lee's headquarters to find out what was happening.

ACTED QUICKLY

Stuart then acted quickly. He sent brigades under Brigadier General Fitzhugh Lee – Robert E. Lee's nephew – and Colonel Lawrence S. Baker to Cashtown to guard the trains of Longstreet and Hill, and cover the right flank of the army during the retreat.

Brigades under Brigadier General William E. 'Grumble' Jones and Lieutenant Colonel Beverly H. Robertson were to escort batteries under Captain Marcellus N. Moorman and Captain Roger P. Chew that were already near Fairfield to Jack's Mountain. With five ordnance rifles, two twelve-pounder howitzers, and one Napoleon they were to hold the two roads to the Monterey Pass.

Stuart himself would ride with the brigades under Colonel Milton Ferguson and Colonel John R. Chambliss to Emmitsburg, then to cross the South Mountain by the Raven's Rock Pass to cover the left of the army.

The cavalry would hold the Cashtown Pass for Imboden's train and the Monterey Pass for Harman's train and the main body of the army. The Raven's Rock Pass would be held in case Union cavalry tried to use it to cut off the Confederate withdrawal.

A.P. Hill.

Ewell.

Fitzhugh Lee

R.E. Lee

Beauregard

Longstreet.

The Rebel Army of Virginia.

CHAPTER 15

On the morning of July 5, Meade issued orders for the army to march south to Middletown. By noon he had changed his mind and canceled them.

That afternoon, there were several clashes. Stuart crossed the Raven's Rock Pass and routed Kilpatrick. The Sixth Division caught up with Lee's rear guard. The head of Imboden's train reached Williamsport, but 130 wagons were seized by Union cavalry seven miles north at Cunningham's Crossroads.

The Army of Northern Virginia camped for the night between the Fairfield Gap and Monterey Pass. Sedgwick reported that they appeared to be making a stand there.

Early the following morning, Lee's army resumed the march. There was another clash between Stuart and Kilpatrick at Hagerstown. Ferrying the wagons across the swollen river at Williamsport was painfully slow, so Lee sent Alexander out to reconnoiter other defensible crossings.

That afternoon Meade finally became convinced that Lee was retreating and reissued orders for the army to march on Middletown. Later, Buford's Division attacked Imboden at Williamsport in what became known as the 'Wagoner's Fight.' Arming every possible man, Imboden managed to hold Buford off until Fitzhugh Lee's Brigade arrived, in an action that saved four thousand wagons and thousands of animals.

HOLD UP AT WILLIAMSPORT

The next day, the streets of Williamsport were jammed with up to five thousand wagons and more than twenty thousand horses and mules. Over a thousand animals were lost in the fast flowing waters of the river. Meade was making good time, despite the heavy rain, and Lee realized that he was not going to get his army across before Meade arrived, so sent out his staff to reconnoiter a defense line facing east from Hagerstown to Falling Waters.

By then a Confederate ordnance train had arrived at Williamsport, on the south side of the river, and the ferry began bringing the ammunition over on each return journey. Meanwhile Stuart clashed with Buford and Kilpatrick who were now screening Meade, who halted at Boonsboro to secure supplies for his men and animals.

THE DOWNSVILLE LINE

As always, Meade was cautious. He advanced slowly to Funkstown where Stuart, supported by Longstreet, held him at bay. Lee then occupied a nine-mile defensive line along Salisbury Ridge from Hagerstown to the village of Downsville near the Potomac. The Downsville Line was on high ground behind Marsh Creek which was swollen with rain and Meade, very sensibly, declined to attack it.

This gave Major Harman time to rebuild the pontoon bridge. Seven of the original pontoons had been salvaged. The rest had to be made of materials to hand. Barns, wharves, and warehouses down the nearby Chesapeake & Ohio Canal were taken down. Tools were requisitioned and fifteen pontoons were fashioned and caulked, then floated down the river to complete an eight-hundred-foot bridge in just sixty-eight hours.

By then the level of the river began to fall and the Confederates began wading across. The wagons jamming Williamsport now began moving down to Falling Waters to cross the river there under cover of fog.

> The streets of Williamsport were jammed with five thousand wagons and twenty thousand horses.

COUNCIL OF WAR

Meade called another council of war. His corps commanders voted unanimously for not attacking. Later, Meade got a telegram from Halleck saying: 'You are strong enough to attack and defeat the enemy before he can effect a crossing. Act on your judgment and make your generals execute your orders. Call no council of war. It is proverbial that councils of war never fight.'

On the night of July 13/14, the last of the Confederates pulled out leaving behind camp fires – lit with some difficulty in the renewed rain – to make the Union army think they were still there. Meade sent out reconnaissance parties the next day, but the enemy had escaped. Meade was sharply criticized, though he retained command of the Army of the Potomac until the end of the war which lasted two more years.

Order of the Day

On July 11, Robert E. Lee issued an Order of the Day that was to be read out to every regiment on the Downsville Line. It said: 'You have penetrated the country of our enemies, and recalled to the defense of their own soil those who were engaged in the invasion of ours. Once more you are called upon to meet the enemy from whom you won, on so many fields, names that will never die. Let every soldier remember that on his courage and fidelity depend all that makes life worth having, the freedom of his country, the honor of his people, and the security of his home. Soldiers, your old enemy is before you. Win from him honor worthy of our right cause, worthy of your comrades dead on so many illustrious fields.

Meade's Map of Hagerstown, Funkstown, Williamsport, and Falling Waters, Maryland (1863).

THE FINAL ACT

The Confederate Army was now safely back across the Potomac. Meade waited three days to follow. He was in no hurry. After a six-week siege the stronghold of Vicksburg had fallen on July 4, giving the Union control of the Mississippi and cutting off the Confederate states to the west of the river from those to the east.

The victor of Vicksburg, Major General Ulysses S. Grant was promoted to Lieutenant General and made commander-in-chief of all the Union armies the following March. Grant then harried Lee's army in the Wilderness Campaign from May to June 1864. General William Sherman took Atlanta on September 3, 1864, then continued his march to the sea. On April 9, 1865, Lee surrendered to Grant at Appomattox Court House.

Six days later Lincoln was assassinated. However, the decision made on the field at Gettysburg was not to be reversed. The Union was preserved and slavery was abolished by the Thirteenth Amendment to the Constitution, ratified on December 6, 1865. While the slaves freed by Union troops when they occupied the Confederate states and their descendants suffered many setbacks, the struggle towards full emancipation continued. Meanwhile the old Confederate states still glory in their Rebel tradition.

VICKSBURG

Both the Union and Confederate sides in the American Civil War considered the fortified city of Vicksburg, Mississippi, held the key to victory or defeat. It lay on the east side of the river halfway between Memphis, Tennessee to the north and New Orleans, Louisiana to the south. These two cities had fallen to the Union in the spring of 1862, along with Fort Henry and Fort Donelson, leaving Vicksburg the Confederate's only stronghold on the river. If it fell, the entire Mississippi would be in Union hands, cutting the Confederacy in two.

However, Vicksburg was in a perfect defensive position. It was built on high bluffs along the river, with its northern flank protected by swampy bayous. Confederate batteries along the bluff could fire down on Union shipping on the river. Even an attack by Union ironclads in May – June 1862 was beaten off. From mid-October 1862, Major General Ulysses S. Grant, then commander of the Army of Tennessee, made several costly attempts to take Vicksburg.

The ships needed to ferry the troops across the river would have to come from the Union fleet north of Vicksburg which was under the command of Admiral David D. Porter. They would have to run past the powerful Vicksburg guns. Once the Union forces were on the east bank, they would face two Confederate forces, one around Jackson, Mississippi, under General Joseph E. Johnston and the garrison at Vicksburg commanded by General John C. Pemberton.

Grant reorganized his force into four corps under Generals John A. McClernand, William T. Sherman, James B. McPherson and Stephen A. Hurlbut, though Hurlbut's corps was transferred to New Orleans before the offensive began. At the same time, a small force under General Nathaniel P. Banks began maneuvering along the Red River in Louisiana.

On the night of April 16, Porter successfully ran the Vicksburg batteries with twelve vessels, losing just one to Confederate fire. Then on the night of April 22, he ran a large supply flotilla past Vicksburg.

RUNNING THE VICKSBURG GUNS

Grant decided that, to take the city, he needed to attack it from the south and east. He would march his men down the west bank of the Mississippi, cross over the river and attack the city from the rear. However, Confederate gun batteries at Port Hudson, Louisiana to the south, prevented Union shipping coming up the river from Baton Rouge and New Orleans.

RIPPING UP THE TRACKS

On April 30, Porter ferried McClernand's and McPherson's men across the river. Grant then sent word north for Sherman to follow. The next day the Union forces engaged the Confederates ten miles inland at Port Gibson, Mississippi. Although Pemberton had over forty thousand men to defend the Vicksburg area, they were scattered across the region, Few were concentrated at Port Gibson, which fell easily.

Grant then moved north-east. Sherman joined him on May 8. On May 12, they took Raymond, Mississippi, cutting off Pemberton's forces from Johnston's. Two days later they took Jackson itself, neutralizing Johnston. Grant ordered Sherman to destroy Jackson's railroad facilities and heavy industry while he turned west, beating Pemberton in a major action at Champion Hill on May 16.

The following day, the Confederates fought a delaying action at the Big Black River Bridge. After they crossed, they destroyed the bridge behind them. Union troops simply built a new bridge and, by May 18, Grant's three corps were nearing Vicksburg's outer defenses from the east and north-east.

SIEGE AND SURRENDER

Sherman moved around to the north to take the heights overlooking the Yazoo River. With these hills in their possession, the Union forces could bring in reinforcements and supplies from the north. Grant then attacked Vicksburg with Porter giving artillery support from the river. The first assault failed. A second, all-out assault began at 10:00 am on May 22. Although Grant's men broke through at first, the Confederates quickly restored their original line of defense.

The Union suffered 3,199 casualties, while Pemberton lost less than five hundred men. This was enough to convince Grant that the miles of Confederate defensive works around the east of the city was too strong to be overcome by assault. So he ordered his engineers to besiege the city.

During the protracted siege, Pemberton's thirty-thousand-man garrison was reduced by disease and starvation, while the city's civilian residents were forced to seek shelter in caves and bomb shelters in the surrounding hills. Vicksburg suffered daily bombardments by Porter's gunboats and Grant's artillery, but eventually shortage of ammunition and hunger compelled Pemberton to ask for surrender terms on July 3. Grant offered none. The following day, Pemberton surrendered unconditionally. However, Grant magnanimously paroled the bulk of the garrison. He would face many of these men again six weeks later at the Second Battle of Chattanooga.

With the fall of Vicksburg and the Union victory at Gettysburg the previous day, the South was finished as a fighting force.

Battery Sherman, one of the Union Forts defending Vicksburg after the siege, c. 1864.

CHAPTER 16

ALL MEN ARE CREATED EQUAL

On November 19, 1863, President Abraham Lincoln arrived in Gettysburg for the dedication of the National Cemetery where bodies from the battlefield had been reinterred. More than 12,000 people crowded into the town on that day, and neither accommodation nor transportation was adequate. They had not come to hear anyone make a speech. They were relatives of the men killed in the battle and they wanted to see where their men were buried or at least where they had died. From all over the country they had come and, as the President surmised, they would little note nor long remember any fine speeches that might be made.

During the ceremony, Edward Everett, a well known orator who ran against Lincoln in the 1860 presidential election, was to give what was headlined as the 'Gettysburg address.' It lasted two hours and now is long forgotten. Following him,

> **Government of the people, by the people, for the people.**

Lincoln's dedication was just 267 words long. The following day, Everett wrote to Lincoln, saying: 'I wish that I could flatter myself that I had come as near to the central idea of the occasion in two hours as you did in two minutes.'

The speech has a prominent place in the history and popular culture of the United States, but its exact wording and location are disputed. The five known manuscripts of the Gettysburg Address differ in a number of details and also differ from contemporary newspaper reprints of the speech. Modern scholarship locates the speakers' platform 40 yards (or more) away in the Evergreen Cemetery rather than at the Soldiers' National Monument.

Of the five versions, the Bliss version, written well after the speech as a favor for a friend, is viewed by many as the standard text. Its text differs, however, from the written versions prepared by Lincoln before and after his speech. But it is the only copy that Lincoln signed and dated 'Address delivered at the dedication of the cemetery at Gettysburg, November 19, 1863.'

LINCOLN'S LANGUAGE

Adam Gopnik, an analyst of Lincoln's language, wrote in *The New Yorker* in 2007 – 'Lincoln's rhetoric is deliberately Biblical. Lincoln had mastered the sound of the King James Bible so completely that he could recast abstract issues of constitutional law in Biblical terms.'

Hence his opening sentence 'Four score and seven years ago our fathers brought forth on this continent, a new nation, conceived in Liberty, and dedicated to the proposition that all men are created equal' is intentionally dramatic and ringing with the religious portent of a Biblical sermon.

Several theories have been advanced by Lincoln scholars to explain the provenance of Lincoln's famous phrase 'government of the people, by the people, for the people.' The most probable origin of the phrase comes from William Herndon, Lincoln's law partner, who wrote in the 1888 work *Abraham Lincoln: The True Story of A Great Life,* that he had brought to Lincoln some of the sermons of abolitionist minister Theodore Parker (1810 – 60) of Massachusetts. One of these was a lecture on *The Effect of Slavery on the American People* – 'Lincoln … read and returned it. He liked especially the following expression, which he marked with a pencil, and which he in substance afterwards used in his Gettysburg Address: "Democracy is direct self-government, over all the people, for all the people, by all the people." '

THE GETTYSBURG ADDRESS

Four score and seven years ago our fathers brought forth on this continent, a new nation, conceived in Liberty, and dedicated to the proposition that all men are created equal.

Now we are engaged in a great civil war, testing whether that nation, or any nation so conceived and so dedicated, can long endure. We are met on a great battle-field of that war. We have come to dedicate a portion of that field, as a final resting place for those who here gave their lives that that nation might live. It is altogether fitting and proper that we should do this.

But, in a larger sense, we cannot dedicate — we cannot consecrate — we cannot hallow — this ground. The brave men, living and dead, who struggled here, have consecrated it, far above our poor power to add or detract. The world will little note, nor long remember what we say here, but it can never forget what they did here. It is for us the living, rather, to be dedicated here to the unfinished work which they who fought here have thus far so nobly advanced. It is rather for us to be here dedicated to the great task remaining before us — that from these honored dead we take increased devotion to that cause for which they gave the last full measure of devotion — that we here highly resolve that these dead shall not have died in vain — that this nation, under God, shall have a new birth of freedom — and that government of the people, by the people, for the people, shall not perish from the earth.

Abraham Lincoln delivering the Gettysburg Address.

CASUALTIES AT GETTYSBURG

UNITED STATES		CONFEDERATE STATES
3,155	KILLED	4,708
14,531	WOUNDED	12,693
5,369	CAPTURED OR MISSING	5,830
23,055	TOTAL	23,231

GRAND TOTAL	46,286

CONGRESSIONAL MEDAL OF HONOR

There were no military awards or medals at the beginning of the Civil War. It was seen as a European tradition that had no place in the New World. However, Congress instituted a decoration for valor for the navy in 1861 and for the army the following year.

On March 3, 1863, Congress extended eligibility to officers. As the criteria were somewhat loosely worded, some 1,200 medals were awarded for gallantry during the Civil War. Congress tightened the rules in 1916 and appointed a board of five retired generals to review previous awards. Some 911 awards, mainly from the Civil War, did not meet the new standards and were struck from the list. Sixty-one Union officers and soldiers were awarded the Medal of Honor for the actions during the Battle of Gettysburg.

CONFEDERATE MEDAL OF HONOR

On October 13, 1862, the Congress of the Confederate States passed 'An Act to authorize the grant of medals and badges of distinction as a reward for courage and good conduct on the field of battle.'

There is no record of any such medal being awarded. In 1900, the United Daughters of the Confederacy began awarding the Southern Cross of Honor to veterans. However more than a century after the end of the war, the Sons of Confederate Veterans began drawing up a Confederate Roll of Honor. The first medal was awarded in 1977. There are fifty-three names on the Confederate Roll of Honor, including those of a nurse, a chaplain, and the commandant of a Confederate prison. Five were awarded for acts of gallantry at Gettysburg.

THE LAST CIVIL WAR VETERANS

Starting in the 1920s, 30s, and 40s, Civil War soldiers began passing away in rapid numbers, nearly three a day. The glorious reunions of proud veterans at Gettysburg and the cities of the South were coming to an end; there were too few healthy enough to attend. The Grand Army of the Republic closed its last local chapter. The Rebel yell fell silent. The campfires went dark. Echoing down the years were Gen. Robert E. Lee's last words: 'Strike the tent'.

By the start of the 1950s, about 65 of the blue and gray veterans were left; by 1955, just a half dozen. As their numbers dwindled they became artifacts of a shuttered era, curiosities of an ancient time, sepia-toned figures still inhabiting a modern world from their rocking chairs and oxygen tents. They had gone to war with rifles and sabers and in horse-mounted patrols. They had lived off hardtack and beans. Now they seemed lost in a new American century that had endured two devastating world wars fought with armored tank divisions, deadly mustard gas, and atomic bombs that fell from the sky.

Bruce Catton, chronicler of the Civil War, wrote of his hometown heroes: 'For the most part they had never been 50 miles away from the farm or the dusty village streets; yet once, ages ago, they had been everywhere and had seen everything ... All that was real had taken place when they were young; everything after that had simply been a process of waiting for death ... As they departed, we began to lose more than we knew we were losing.'

[The Last Civil War Veterans is an excerpt from *Last of the Blue and Gray* by Richard A. Serrano.]

50th Reunion of Veterans at Gettysburg, 1913.

"He is coming like the glory of the morning on the wave,
He is Wisdom to the mighty, He is Succour to the brave,
So the world shall be His footstool, and the soul of Time His slave,
Our God is marching on."

From *The Battle Hymn of The Republic* by Julia Ward Howe (1861)

FURTHER READING

Adkin, Mark, *The Gettysburg Companion* (London: Aurum, 2008)

Bicheno, Hugh, *Gettysburg* (London: Cassell, 2001)

Boritt, Gabor, *The Gettysburg Gospel: The Lincoln Speech That Nobody Knows.* (New York: Simon & Schuster, 2005)

Catton, Bruce, *Never Call Retreat – The American Civil War Trilogy.* (New York: Doubleday & Co., 1965)

Catton, Bruce, *Gettysburg: The Final Fury* (Garden City, New York: Doubleday & Co., 1974)

Editors of Time-Life Books, *Gettysburg: Voices of the Civil War* (Richmond, Virginia: Time-Life Books, 1995)

Doubleday, Abner, *Reminiscences of Forts Sumter and Moultrie* (New York, Harper & Brothers, 1876)

Doubleday, Abner, *Chancellorsville and Gettysburg* (Charles Scribner's Sons, 1882)

Gopnik, Adam, *Angels and Ages: Lincoln's language and its legacy.* (*The New Yorker* May 28, 2007)

Haskell, Frank A., *The Battle of Gettysburg: A Soldier's First-Hand Account* (Mineola, New York: Dover Publications, 2003)

Hassler, Warren W., *The First Day at Gettysburg* (Tuscaloosa, Alabama: University of Alabama, 1970)

Herndon, William H. & Welk, Jesse W. *Abraham Lincoln: The True Story of A Great Life* (New York: D. Appleton and Company, 1892. Vol II., p 65.)

Huntington, Tom, *Guide to Gettysburg Battlefield Monuments* (Mechanicsburg, Pennsylvania: Stackpole Books, 2013)

Luvaas, Jay, et al, *Guide to the Battle of Gettysburg* (Lawrence, Kansas: University Press of Kansas, 2012)

Martin, David G., *Gettysburg, July 1* (Cambridge, Massachusetts: Da Capo Press, 2003)

Oates, William C., *The War Between the Union and the Confederacy* (Dayton, Ohio: Press of Morningside, 1974)

Pfanz, Harry W., *Gettysburg: The Second Day* (Chapel Hill, North Carolina: University of North Carolina Press, 1987)

Reardon, Carol, and Vossler, Tom, *A Field Guide to Gettysburg* (Chapel Hill, North Carolina: University of North Carolina Press, 2013)

Sears, Stephen W., *Gettysburg* (Boston: Houghton Mifflin, 2003)

Serrano, Richard A., *Last of the Blue and Gray* (Smithsonian Books, 2013)

Trudeau, Noah A., *Gettysburg: A Testing of Courage* (New York: Perennial, 2003)

Tucker, Phillip T., *Barksdale's Charge: The True High Tide of the Confederacy at Gettysburg* (Havertown, Pennsylvania: Casemate, 2013)

www.nps.gov/gett/index.htm – Gettysburg National Military Park (US National Park Service) US Department of the Interior.

THE GETTYSBURG ADDRESS

Abraham Lincoln at Gettysburg National Cemetery where he gave his famous address to a big crowd of citizens and soldiers. Photographed about noon by Matthew Brady, just after Lincoln arrived by train and some three hours before the speech was delivered. To Lincoln's right is his bodyguard, Ward Hill Lamon.

Lamon was a physically imposing man, and often took it upon himself to guard the president, but he was famously absent the night Lincoln was assassinated.

INDEX

PICTURE CREDITS

Internal: Archive photographs courtesy of Library of Congress Prints and Photographs Division /
13 © Archive Farms. Inc / Alamy / 14 © Archive Pics / Alamy / 33 © Everett Collection Historical / Alamy / 46
© Images-USA / Alamy / 52 © Matthew Cuda / Alamy / 65 © North Wind Picture Archives / Alamy / 77 ©
INTERFOTO / Alamy / Cover: Gettysburg Cyclorama / Cannon © Mary H. Swift / Alamy